INVERCLYDE LIBRARIES

Ye Olde Good Inn Guide

A Tudor Traveller's Guide to the Nation's Finest Taverns

Mr James Moore
& Mr Paul Nero

The History Press

First published 2013

The History Press
The Mill, Brimscombe Port
Stroud, Gloucestershire, GL5 2QG
www.thehistorypress.co.uk

British Library Cataloguing in Publication Data.
A catalogue record for this book is available from the British Library.

ISBN 978 0 7524 8061 9

Typesetting and origination by The History Press
Printed in Great Britain

CONTENTS

ACKNOWLEDGEMENTS

Many people did a lot of 'hands on' research to help us put together this Tudor bible to drinking. So we'd like to thank the efforts of Felicity Hebditch in particular, as well as Philippa Moore, Geoffrey Moore, Dr Tom Moore, Dr Claire Nesbitt, Daniel Simister, Jim Addison, Pamela Smith, Jan Hebditch, Richard Hebditch, Peter Spurgeon, Sarah Sarkhel, William Poole, Fiona Poole, Sam Moore, Tamsin Moore, Alex Moore, Laurie Moore, Juliet Stuart, Tricia Hurle, Philip Martin, Amit Ummat, Melissa Watson, Charlie Dalton at Smart Garden Offices.

Disclaimer

In 1599 the truth was a slippery customer. We have endeavoured to make sure that each of the establishments we feature be correctly named and that the events ascribed to them are truthful. We do humbly apologise for any inaccuracies and will be sure to amend them in any future edition of *Ye Olde Good Inn Guide*. Any similarity to innkeepers, owners and goings on in times which come after this date, must be considered purely coincidental and unintentional.

A VERY MERRIE GUIDE ...

They have long been both the scourge and the backbone of Merrie England and in this year of our Lord 1599, 'tis reckoned that there are some 20,000 alehouses, inns and taverns spread across our great nation. Indeed, a growing number of drinking places of all sorts abound. In the city of Canterbury alone the number hath doubled in a mere handful of years while in the town of Taunton, in the county of Somerset, they have risen by a third.

But how does the wary traveller know which of these establishments to seek out and which to avoid like the plague itself? Which of our ancient inns will offer the most comfort? And how can thee tell a bawdy brewhouse of ill repute from a cosy ale-lover's paradise? This trusty guide be the first of its kind, a handbook of the best watering holes in the country. 'Tis destined as an aid to those who ply the great highways and byways of the land so that they may enjoy the pleasures of our great drinking establishments while remaining secure of both their purse ... and their stomach. Covering each county in the land and all the most important towns and cities, we feature the best and oldest establishments, reveal their notable features and tell thee how they can be found. We also give guidance on the differing kinds of hostelry thee will encounter, who thee shall meet and where to find the celebrities of our time. We tell what thee will be able to eat and drink, what forms of entertainment might be provided and even what words and phrases to use.

Our service, it must be observed, comes none too soon. There are now some 4 million souls upon our island and, by our present calculations, one licensed drinking place for every 200 or so of the population. As the number of us English hath increased so hath concern for the laziness and disorder believed to be bred in the baser drinking dens, viewed by many as hotbeds of potential rebellion. The respected Justice William Lambarde of Kent was not far wrong when he recently described alehouses as 'nurseries of naughtiness'.

Kings and governments have been trying to regulate drinking for many centuries. The alehouse began with the Romans and their wayside tabernae. By Saxon times they had become so popular that by the year 965 King Edgar ordered that they be limited to only one per village and even set out to standardise drinking horns. In 1215 that great document, Magna Carta, set out to establish a standard measure for 'wine, ale and corn'. Then, in 1267, came the first attempt to set the price of drink in the Assize of Bread and Ale. Ale-conners, still used today, were also appointed by local court leets to assess the quality of the beer and the measures in which 'twas served. Indeed, William Shakespeare's father, John, was appointed ale-conner in Stratford in the 1550s. The common method for testing the brews may amuse, but 'tis said to be rather effective. Before passing judgement the ale-conner dons a pair of leather breeches, pours some of the beer on a bench or stool and promptly sits in it for some minutes. If their bottoms do not stick to the wood, then the liquor be deemed passable. If the brew be deemed unfit the brewer responsible was likely to be made to drink his own concoction until he be overcome or may simply have it poured over his head.

In Edward III's time (1327–1377) measures were brought in to stop innkeepers charging too much for their food, ending the great and outrageous cost 'kept up in all the realm by innkeepers and other retailers of victuals to the great detriment of the people travelling through the realm'. Subsequently, King Henry VIII gave powers for the closing of alehouses if they interfered with local men's archery practice, though he well understood the importance of beer to his soldiers, taking great breweries on wheels when on campaign with his army abroad. In 1544, whilst on such manoeuvres in Picardy, one of Henry's military commanders noted that his soldiers had no beer 'these last ten days' which be 'strange for English men to do, with so little grudging'.

'Twas not until the year 1552, in the reign of King Edward VI, that alehouses had to be licensed by local justices of the peace. This act was passed 'as intolerable hurts and troubles to the common wealth of this realm doth daily grow and increase through such abuses and disorders as are had and used in common alehouses and other houses called tippling-houses'. Though we must note that, to this day, thee do not need a said licence to set up a beer stall at a fair and that those upmarket places, known as inns, do not require such a licence at all, though there are attempts to regulate their numbers. Ensuing measures have given local authorities the power to close or fine any house which steps out of line, and have banned the playing of illegal games like dice and cards and have endeavoured to impose specific drinking hours upon tipplers.

While exceedingly common, drunkenness be also punishable, sometimes by the imbiber being made to parade through the streets wearing a hollow beer barrel known as the 'drunkards cloak', sometimes by being put in the stocks or pillory. Thee do not have to be rendered unconscious to feel the full force of the law; be warned that thee can be brought up on a charge for merely wetting thy bed through over indulgence or simply sleeping off the effect of booze somewhere thee shouldn't. In Manchester, a growing town, persons found drunk shall be 'punished all nighte in the donngeon and moreover paie presently whene they be released to the constables to be geven to the pore'.

One very sensible edict, recently introduced, instructs that those who make the beer should not also be the ones who make the barrels in which 'tis kept, in a bid to curb dishonesty in the sphere of weights and measures.

Having told all this 'tis fair to say that, in general, efforts to curb and regulate drinking through this, the sixteenth century after our Lord's birth, have largely failed. Beer be now simply too good and the alehouses, taverns and inns of the land too useful as places of relaxation, commerce, debate and profit to be crushed. There be fierce competition between them and very sizeable fortunes to be made and lost. In fact, during the present dynasty, London brewers have been under obligation to keep on making beer, even if the raw commodities are too costly, as they have oft been of late because of bad harvests. Their business be considered so important to peace and economic life that if they 'shall at any time sodenly forbere and absteyne from bruynge, wherby the King's subject should bee destitute or unprovided of drynke' their property can be requisitioned by Her Majesty.

Given the hardships of the time, the situation described by the writer Philip Stubbes as recently as 1583 in his book, *Anatomie of Abuses*, be unlikely to alter any time soon. He tells us that:

Every county, city, town, and village and other place hath abundance of ale houses, taverns, inns which are so fraught with malt worms [drunkards] night and day that thee would wonder to see them. Thee shall have them sitting at the wine and good ale all day long, yea, all night too, peradventure a whole week together, so long as any money be left; swilling, gulling and carousing from one to another, till never a one can speak a ready word.

1

YE ALEHOUSE, TAVERN OR INN?

An old drinking ballad ...

Who that drynketh well, mych be he the gladder;
Who that drynketh to moch, more be he the madder;
When he goth to his bed, his slepe be the sadder.
At morowe, when he waketh, his brayne be the bradder;
Whan he loketh in his purse, his sorowe be the sadder.

On thy travels around the kingdom thee will find that drinking places break down into three basic sorts – the alehouse, tavern and inn. Which of these thee patronise will largely reflect thy standing in the present social order. In 1577 the government conducted the first ever survey of hostelries, asking local magistrates 'to inquire what number of inns, taverns and alehouses are in every shire'. This remarkable investigation was primarily undertaken in order to levy a tax which would be used to pay for repairs to Dover harbour, with the intention that each licensee would pay 2 shillings and fourpence. The tax, when finally introduced in 1580, was, we learn, short-lived and difficult to collect. However, while Dover harbour may still be in some state of dilapidation, the survey gives us a wonderful window into the drinking habits of our age. When the reports came in from all over England they suggested that there were upwards of 19,000 establishments in the country. More than eight out of ten were alehouses, one out of ten were inns and no more than 340 were classed as taverns across the whole of England.

The alehouse

On the lowest social rung of our drinking hierarchy be the humble alehouse, kept mostly by poor folk. Once 'twas the alewife, oft a widow, who had fallen on hard times, who was likely to be in charge, brewing her own ale on the premises. Today, in the age of Elizabeth, many more men are in charge of the nation's hostelries, partly because of the economic difficulties of late. Finding employment isn't easy, yet making ale and beer be reasonably straightforward and open to almost any person. As Henry Chettle observed as recently as 1592, 'I came up to London, and fall to be some tapster, hostler, or chamberlaine in an inn. Well, I get mee a wife; with her a little money; when we are married, seeke a house we must; no other occupation have I but to be an ale-draper.'

The alehouse keeper, or tippler, may be the salt of the earth but can also be the swine of the land, for while some are good, honest folk, many will be in league with highway robbers and receive stolen goods. Others will be happy to trade with thee, taking something in kind for the ale they serve. If thee are known to the alehouse keeper he may allow thee to put thy drinks on the slate. Equally, take care to examine thy change for clipped or counterfeit coins.

The ancient sign of an alehouse was a bush on the end of a pole – the ale-stake. This tradition be kept up, though wooden signs are now coming in. These are most oft simple carvings or pictures, without any words, for how many customers can read? In the north of the country a wooden hand on a pole may be the sign that drink can be had.

Inside, the entire property be likely to consist of fewer than five rooms, usually including a parlour for drinking and most probably a fireplace at which to warm thyself. Furniture be for the most part simple: a couple of benches, a few stools, a trestle table, perhaps a pew from a dissolved monastery. Chairs are status symbols and much cherished; any occupant (probably a regular) will most likely use his knife before surrendering it. Windows are unlikely to have glass, more likely wooden shutters, so watch thy purse as hooking them away on a line be common, a practice known as angling. Thee are likely to be served through a hatch or direct to thy table rather than at any sort of bar. Though small, alehouses are oft bustling places which can be selling a weighty 35 gallons of beer every week.

Alehouses have little proper accommodation, though taking in travellers and itinerant workers be encouraged by local authorities who wish to curb the burgeoning number of vagabonds who tramp the streets.

Be advised that thee should not be proud about where thee sleep if thee are allowed to stay. Thee might well end up bedding down with a stranger. Indeed, in 1584 one tippler, Evan ap Rice, was reprimanded for 'lodging strange men in his bed with him and his wife'. More likely thee will be sleeping on a table, bench or on the rush-strewn floor along with the dog – oft a fearsome beast to keep away thieves. There may be a common privy, running into an even more common ditch. Some tipplers may keep tidy houses but others are very shabby indeed. One alehouse keeper in Cheshire was recently found to be running a house with so many gaps in the walls that 'twas possible to see the inhabitants a-bed through the walls.

As we have seen, the alehouse ought, by law, to be licensed. But nearly half a century on perhaps half are not and many spring up, then close down again as fast. Indeed, many may not be alehouses alone; there be a strong tradition of the blacksmith serving customers a brew while their horses are shod.

The tavern

After the alehouse we come to the tavern, a rare and more upmarket establishment. Since 1533 alehouses have been banned from selling wine, while taverns may serve both wine and ale and offer food. As the writer Robert Copland told us, 'Wine was not made for every haskard, but beer and ale for every dastard.' 'Tis the sort of place thee are likely to find William Shakespeare's rumbustious character Sir John Falstaff, from his recent celebrated play *Henry IV*. Thee might find a painted bunch of wooden grapes or vine leaves to indicate that the place be a tavern rather than an alehouse. But beware; just because the clientele may be wealthier, the tavern can still be a tawdry, battered old place. One in London was recently told to shut up a window as it looked into a gentleman's 'fairest room'.

The selling of wine hath been treated with some suspicion by the upper echelons, who no doubt know how good it be. Edward VI restricted the sale of wine and the number of taverns hath also been strictly limited these past years. In general, only two taverns per town are allowed, apart from in a very few places. In 1553 London was allowed forty, York nine and Bristol six, with Norwich, Chester, Hull, Exeter, Gloucester, Canterbury, Cambridge and Newcastle four each, but a smattering more have been permitted since 1570.

While ale or beer be a daily drink, wine be certainly considered something special and the price be quite strictly controlled. The grapes for wine are rarely grown in England in these times, so wines must be imported, making it an expensive commodity. Those who drink at taverns are oft connoisseurs of its quality. As the scholar Sir Thomas Elyot observed, 'neither ale or biere is to be compared to wyne'. Taverns frequently have partitions so drinkers can enjoy some privacy but accommodation be scarce – these are places for meeting and showing off.

The inn

At the top end of our drinking scale be the inn. Many were once pilgrims' hostels – also known as hospices – owned by great monasteries, for the Church was once the biggest brewer in the land. Many churches still make their own ale, but, since their Dissolution in King Henry VIII's time, most of the aforementioned lodging places have been transformed into secular places for travellers to stay, providing food and drink as well as income for a whole new class of business-minded men who have become rich on the proceeds. The number of inns hath also increased in line with the growth of the merchant class, especially the boom in the wool and cloth trade which requires merchants to travel great distances to markets and to make deals.

Inns can oft be very large indeed, accommodating scores of persons and with stabling for their steeds. Built of stone or sturdy timber, perhaps even with a tiled roof, the inn be, in many small towns, the most important building after the local church and manor house. In architectural style there are generally two sorts: the courtyard inn, perhaps with a gabled front that faces directly on to the street and hath an archway through to the courtyard with galleries on the flanks and stairs leading to the bedchambers; alternatively there may be a large building at the front housing all the accommodation and a yard at the back with stables.

Inside, the decor be much more lavish than in the alehouse or tavern. Thee may find fine glass windows with latticed lead, panelled rooms, great inglenook fireplaces where a whole throng of men may warm themselves, even lavish paintings and murals on the plaster walls and chambers with individual playful names such as the Sun, Moon, Rose or Dolphin. Throughout there may be oak furniture, with perhaps a four-poster bed to lie in and certainly a trunk in which to put thy clothes and belongings. As thee will guess, most inns cater for the most well-to-do travellers, with one observer, William Harrison, noting, in his *Description of England*, first published in 1577 as part of *Holinshed's Chronicles*, that a person who stayed in one 'may use an inn as his own house'. He tells us that the rooms are well furnished with 'bedding and tapestry … for beside the linen used at the tables which be commonly washed daily … each comer be sure to lie in clean sheets'. Levinus Lemnius, a doctor from the Low Countries who visited our fair isle recently, remarked on 'the nosegays finely intermingled with sundry sorts of fragrant flowers in the bedchambers and the privy rooms [which] entirely delighted my senses.'

Beds at inns are indeed likely to be quite comfortable, perhaps even coming with their own damask or linen curtains. In 1578 the authorities in York even ordered that each inn should have at least six comely and honest beds. However, even in the best establishment there be still a risk of being molested by fleas or bedbugs. There be most likely a 'pysse pot' but certainly no bath. Thee may be offered a pail of water to wash in but are more likely to be expected to follow the usual practice of cleaning thyself with linen. Bringing thy own tooth-cleaning device be essential. Reading *Ye Olde Good Inn Guide* late into the night will be difficult as candles, oft shoddily made, will offer the only light.

There may be a central hall for communal eating, or food may be brought to thy room. A meal will cost between 4*d* and 6*d*, while lodging thy horse might cost as much as 12*d*. Thee will get a key for thy chamber and if thee lose anything Harrison tells us that 'the host be bound by a general custom to restore the damage'. Thee may even be able to retire to a garden full of herbs or indulge in games played on a lawn. Some inns are now divided into separate chambers and rooms, which denote the social background of the patron. Thee will oft find the inn catering to large parties of men sat at long tables with servants attending to their needs.

The grandest inns will have lavish signs. They are usually a carving or painting, perhaps of a boar's head, swan, star, crown or bull. The queen's head be a common sign, though she be said to be displeased with some of the likenesses she hath witnessed on her travels through the realm, condemning 'unskilful and common painters'. Yet some inns have garnered royal patronage. Down the centuries kings and queens have been prepared to stay in them, particularly Queen Elizabeth on some of her stately 'progresses' around the kingdom.

Running an inn can be a profitable business and they are oft owned by local lords and men of a better sort. Canterbury innkeepers, for example, are drawn from the top of the local elite. Inns are not only used for accommodation but as meeting places for the whole local community. They are oft used as the venue for courts while trade be, in many parts, moving away from the open market place to the inn.

All inns will have a yard with stabling and oft host packhorse trains transporting goods around the kingdom. In charge of this be the ostler, who will look after thy horse and make sure thy bags are taken to thy chamber. He may not be an honest type, so be careful how much thee tell him about thy belongings and travel plans. Dogs, especially Talbot hunting dogs, are oft a feature, and a hazard, in the yards. This breed hath even given its name to some inns around the land. Be assured that, if need be, thee should be able to hire carts or a new horse and even buy pasture for animals.

Thy travels

In general, travel be either on foot, horse, or waggon, usually pulled by oxen. A goodly second-hand horse will cost thee £1 to £2 to purchase. Thee will be glad to hear that saddles have lately become more comfortable. Very occasionally will thee see a coach, ferrying the well-to-do, though they are uncomfortable as they have no springs. These wealthy types may also be carried on the shoulders of their servants in a 'litter'. Thee are certainly destined to arrive muddy, perhaps worse, as even town streets are full of potholes and strewn with faeces, as well as the blood from butchers' stalls and general muck of all manner. Also note that thee should be wary of robbers who lurk near inns at night, hoping to rob the rich; open cellar hatches have done for many a traveller in the largely unlit night-time streets.

Some highways, such as the Great North Road, are well made up and there are a few stone bridges and paved streets in London and the bigger towns. But the country roads are rough, especially in winter, despite new laws stating that men of each parish should spend several days a year working at bettering them. On a steed thee might cover up to 40 miles in a day, though royal messengers can travel up to 100 miles a day using relays of horses kept at certain, specified, inns. Since the time of Henry VIII innkeepers have been given a penny a mile for the horses used for this. On foot there be little chance of making much more than 15 miles a day, though this should be enough to get thee betwixt lodging places.

The countryside be mostly large open fields, with some enclosed. There will be much wasteland too, but not as much woodland as thee might expect as these are being thinned, thanks to the demand of shipbuilding and other trades. If thee need directions thee may have to rely on locals, not always the most trustworthy folk. And, frankly, 'tis worth treating their estimations of distance with a pinch of salt since the statute mile was only introduced in 1593 and its exact measure be almost entirely unknown to the general populace.

Behold! Saxton's Unique Atlas of England and Wales

Available since 1570, this great atlas by the celebrated cartographer Christopher Saxton for the first time lays out maps of every county in one volume. It shows each of the most important towns and cities of our realm and also the rivers, hills and boundaries which the traveller will encounter. An invaluable aid to those who wish to explore this great nation and which any wise reader will want to own for himself.

❀

2

WHOM SHALL THEE MEET?

Eight kinds of drunkard

The first be ape-drunk, and he leaps and sings and hollows, and danceth for the heavens; the second be lion-drunk, and he flings the pots about the house, calls his hostess whore, breaks the glass windows with his dagger, and be apt to quarrel with any man that speaks to him; the third be swine-drunk, heavy, lumpish and sleepy, and cries for a little more drink and a few more clothes; the fourth be sheep-drunk, wise in his own conceit, when he cannot bring forth a right word; the fifth be maudlin-drunk, when a fellow will weep for kindness in the midst of his ale, and kiss thee, saying By God, captain, I love thee; go thy ways, thou dost not think so oft of me as I do of thee; I would (if it pleased God) I could not love thee so well as I do, and then he puts his finger in his eye, and cries; the sixth be martin-drunk, when a man be drunk, and drinks himself sober ere he stir; the seventh be goat-drunk, when in his drunkenness he hath no mind but on lechery; the eighth be fox-drunk, when he be crafty-drunk, as many of the Dutchmen be, that will never bargain but when they are drunk.

(Thomas Nashe, poet)

Slumming it at the alehouse

A place both of strangers and regulars, the local alehouse be a melting pot of trades and people from all walks of life. Here thee will find labourers, drovers, tinkers, carriers, bakers, hawkers, shipwrights, itinerant weavers, butchers, colliers, shepherds, foreigners, perhaps men at arms or even the local clergyman. In these times there are many beggars tramping the highways and alehouses are also places where such people go to seek work. While rare, 'tis not unknown for a gentleman to enjoy the charms of an alehouse too. The Dover magistrate John Godwin, for instance, be a well-known fan of local tippling houses.

Women may frequent alehouses, but usually only with their husbands or a group of other ladies. They are a particularly popular place for unwedded couples to cavort on fair days and thee may encounter groups enjoying impromptu, illicit marriages, post-church wedding feasts or those who have repaired to the alehouse after a funeral to drink to the memory of the departed. Alehouses can also sometimes play host to unmarried couples, seeking a place where they can enjoy an illicit encounter away from their spouses.

At this point we should advise that alehouses are also the haunt of many a woman who be no better than she ought. Thomas Platter, a visitor to our country from Switzerland, wrote recently that he found 'great swarms' of prostitutes at London's alehouses. Some are employed not only to service thy sexual needs but to draw thee into gambling games where thee may be beguiled of thy purse.

The reviving nature of drink also makes our alehouses convivial places in which drinking each other's health and, of course, the queen's, be commonplace. Indeed, there are many drinking customs. Some drinking pots have hoops marked upon them which can be used for drinking games, of which there are many sorts. There also be puzzle jugs where thee must put all thy fingers on the right holes, or the beer shall pour out.

Blaggards abound at alehouses too. One report from Netherbury in Dorset tells that in a row of cottages: 'in which poore people dwell ... they take the liberty to themselves to keep unlicensed alehouses and have divers disorderly meetings where manie stolen goods are consumed to the great griefe and losse of their honest neighbours.' Note too, in a time when everyone carries a knife it's important to be wary of getting into fights, which can flare up at any time. This be not helped by the fact that there are many youths; the average age of people in our nation be just 22 years.

Living it up at the tavern or inn

As we have mentioned, moneyed folk are rarely to be found at an alehouse, sticking to the tavern and the inn. Here thee will find royal messengers, servants of the government, constables taking wrongdoers to trial, merchants hawking their wares and perhaps a physician travelling to see a patient. In London thee will meet many lawyers. There may be rich farmers too, taking their produce to the big markets in the towns. There also be every chance that thee may rub shoulders with some people of celebrity too. The playwright William Shakespeare be a lover of taverns and inns – even setting the opening of his recent comedy, *The Taming of the Shrew*, at an hostelry upon a heath. Among other famous people of our age, who are known to partake of their charms, are the likes of writer Ben Jonson and the great explorer Sir Walter Raleigh.

As well as providing inspiration for creative works and places where new colonies and adventures are planned, inns are more oft venues where trade business deals are hammered out. Beware what thee say, however; they are also the haunt of spies both of foreign and domestic governments. Also be advised that thy horse can be requisitioned at a moment's notice by a royal official. And while the pilgrims may have gone, since Henry VIII's Dissolution of the some 600 monasteries and religious houses, senior clergy will be found in the inn though it may be better to avoid the topic of religion; a slip of the tongue can still get thee executed.

If thee are staying in one of the finer inns thee may also, if thee are very lucky indeed, have the opportunity to meet the aristocracy and even royalty. King Henry be known to have used inns, not only on his travels, but for some of his romantic liaisons and Queen Elizabeth be well known for her stately progresses around the kingdom, having visited twenty-five counties to date. She hath slept in some 240 different places during her reign and while she oft stays with local dignitaries, many inns number among her lodging places too. With more than 500 people to feed in her retinue, we imagine local innkeepers are overjoyed to hear of her imminent arrival though also fearful they will not be found up to scratch.

A ruff crowd?

If unsure whether thee will fit in at a particular drinking establishment look at how the customers are dressed. Working folk in the alehouse will typically be clothed in a linen shirt, woollen doublet, loose-fitting tunic or perhaps a leather jerkin with a woollen hat atop their head and either woollen trousers or hose on their legs. Some shall have shoes or boots; others will be shod in wooden clogs. Better off men may also wear breeches above their stockings, a doublet of fine material over their shirt, a felt hat with a feather and perhaps a gown or cape if they be very important. Flashy codpieces, favoured in earlier decades of the century, are now rarely seen. Beards, however, are in trend, as are earrings. Beware that there are laws to stop unworthy types wearing certain garment and cloth. Even if thee are a middling sort, only a lord or lord's progeny may wear velvet.

For women a linen smock or shift and woollen gown be most common, with posher ladies wearing elaborate hooped skirts called farthingales. Note that if a woman be showing a good deal of cleavage, not uncommon even for the queen, she be likely to be unmarried. Ruffs, for well-to-do folk of both sexes, are seen around the neck, mostly made of linen, but of lace among the very wealthy. Size doth matter – the bigger the ruff, the more important thy drinking or lodging partner be, though if yours be not so big thee can always allow thyself a smirk at the weight of the other's cleaning bill.

Beware the buboes

At any establishment thee may be shocked at the sight of unfortunate folk who have been the victim of agricultural or archery accidents, which are both common. More troubling are those who are carrying deadly disease. Wherever thee imbibe beware those who perspire too readily. They may have the dreaded sweating sickness, a disease said to take life swiftly. In 1517 it killed half of Oxford's population. It goes without saying that thee should avoid those who appear to be harbouring buboes in their armpits and swellings elsewhere about their body. The plague be still a regular visitor to these shores and may break out in any given town, at any time.

3

WHAT SHALL THEE EAT AND DRINK?

A little bread shall do me stead,
Much bread I not desire.
No frost nor snow, no wind, I trow,
Can hurt me if I would,
I am so wrapt, and thoroughly lapt
Of jolly good ale and old.
Back and side go bare, go bare,
Both foot and hand go cold;
But, belly, God send thee good ale enough,
Whether it be new or old.

(William Stevenson)

Prithee, will it be ale or beer sire?

'Ale for an Englishman be a natural drink', the writer Andrew Boorde exclaimed in the 1540s. Indeed, it hath long been a daily drink for every inhabitant of this land, consumed with every meal. Ale be the general substitute for water, considered a dangerous commodity which be perhaps drawn from a local well at an alehouse or a pump at an inn. Water be considered a better drink for horses than for people. Indeed, Boorde warns us that 'tis 'not holesome sole by it selfe'.

Made from fermented malted barley and water, ale be sweetish or spicy, thick and fulsome and must be drunk quickly, perhaps as speedily as a few days, for it does not travel well. Happily, in the last hundred years, there hath been a revolution in our drinking habits, thanks to the introduction of hops from the Low Countries, now grown across the southern counties of the kingdom. This new form of bitter-tasting ale be known as beer, from the Old English '*beor*'. Though at first unpopular, and famously banned by King Henry VIII as an evil, 'tis now the fashionable drink of choice. The key difference with ale be that for beer hops are added and boiled with the wort, that magical liquid made from malt. Beer hath the benefit that brews can be kept for longer, thanks to the acids and tannins. Indeed, this hath made it popular with seafaring types because it can last for many weeks. A navy ship must carry some 56 tonnes of beer on an average voyage to keep its crew well oiled.

Barley be the usual grain used for beer, though in some areas where 'tis not available rye and oats be used. The quality of ales and beer can vary greatly. Nottinghamshire 'tis famed for good ales, but Cornish ale does not have such a fine reputation. Andrew Boorde may have been a little harsh when he said that: 'It wyll make thee to kacke, also to spew, it be like wash that pigs have wrestled in,' but the lack of good malt in this region may be the culprit.

Heady brews

Beer be oft stronger than ale, which, in recent years, hath caused much worry to the authorities and Puritan folk, especially in the towns, where idleness and troublemaking are oft ascribed to these new brews. In fact, there be now a trend for very strong beers, oft called March or October beers – so named because these months have the best temperatures for good brewing. Some beers come with names that suggest their potency, such as double double, mad dog, dagger ale, huf cap and pharaoh – and they come with a goodly price tag too. Perhaps the strength of these brews account for the fact that people are known to pawn their belongings just to get a draught.

Small beer, made using the malt for a second time, be a weaker, cheaper beer much appreciated by the masses. It be damned by

Prince Hal in William Shakespeare's play *Henry IV Part II* as a 'poor creature' while the rebel Jack Cade in *Henry VI, Part II* vows to make 'it felony to drink small beer'.

In his *Macbeth*, Mister Shakespeare does appear to damn double beer too – which be made by pouring the first brew back through the grain. Watch carefully next time thee frequent a playhouse or admire the travelling players in an inn courtyard. Shakespeare favours ale and sack.

The strength of beer be certainly of concern to today's royalty. In 1560 Good Queen Bess complained that 'a kynde of very strong bere calling the same doble doble beer which they do commonly utter and sell at very grate and excessive pryce'. She ordered that it be banned. We fear this edict hath not been greatly observed, though in 1588, fourteen personages were brought before the mayor in St Albans and reprimanded for strong brews, selling them 'against all good law and order'.

Royal brews

King Henry VIII enjoyed a pot of ale and had his own brewhouse at Eltham Palace in Kent. Queen Elizabeth sups 'common' beer, favouring that which be aged one month. In 1593 alone her court washed down 600,000 gallons of the refreshing liquid. But, as we have already mentioned, she frowns upon anything too potent and 'tis said to get very grumpy indeed if her beer be served too strong. Whilst visiting Grafton, Oxfordshire, on her way to Kenilworth Castle, she encountered beer, an observer noted, 'so strong as there was no man able to drink it … it did put her far out of temper'. Mary, Queen of the Scots, liked her ale too, served with beef, for breakfast.

Of costs and quantities

While costs vary the price of a draught remains relatively cheap, yet 'tis rising thanks to poor harvests. Expect to pay upward of halfpenny for a quart of ale, which be two pints. Beer be usually more expensive. The average daily wage for a labourer be about 2 shillings a week, for a skilled worker it can be 12*d* a day.

Three or four pints are commonly taken during a session in the alehouse, unless the drinkers are engaged in one of the legendary drinking bouts that have recently become popular. In Coventry we learn that the average consumption be some seventeen pints of ale per week. But 'tis not uncommon for a whole gallon of ale or small beer to be the common daily consumption; 'tis certainly the typical allowance for a servant in a large household and beer forms part of the pay packet of many workers in the land.

There be presently, nowhere in the realm, a Queen's levy upon ale or beer.

Where thy beer be made

Though beer be transported on waggons to the big cities, most brews thee will come across, especially those in the alehouse, are likely to be made on site or in a nearby brewhouse. However, the advent of beer hath seen brewing become more commercial as it needs more equipment, for the longer heating process. The alewife may now buy her beer and sell it at a premium rather than brew it herself.

Bigger brewing concerns are certainly becoming more common thanks to wily merchants, especially in southern counties. London hath more than twenty large brewers and many smaller ones, the chronicler John Stow tells us that Southwark hath twenty-six. Norwich hath five ale brewers and nine beer brewers. Many brewers have formed trade associations. Indeed, since 1550 the Brewer's Company of London hath united both ale and beer brewers, which remain distinctly separate, within its ranks.

Much lamented these past years, especially by the poor, are the church ales once brewed by each parish, for they raised much money for alms as well as for the repair of the nation's churches. Thee may still find them here and there but 'tis felt that ale and the Good Book should see a parting of the ways. Yet the Church complains that the demise of church ale hath left them short of money. One bishop of the land quoth: 'Some ministers have complained unto me, that they are afraid they shall have no Parish Clerks for want of maintenance for them.'

Thy drinking vessel

In the alehouse beer be likely to be served in jugs from a barrel and thence to an earthenware or wooden pot, which may or may not have a handle. Sometimes it will be hooped to show how much be inside and will typically hold a pint or two. At some establishments drink may be poured from a leather black jack sealed with pitch or thee may even be given, as a novelty, a horn to quaff from. At the better sort of inn thee may be served thy drink in a wooden or pewter tankard, perhaps with a lid to keep out foreign bodies. While at the alehouse thee may even take away thy ale in a bucket to consume in the comfort of thy own home. Whatever the vessel, there be many an argument about short measure. Seek out a quart-pot stamped with an official seal. Beware though that thee may even find thyself partaking in communal drinking supping from one great pot. Of late, even bottled beer be becoming known. Feeling queasy? Ask for an egg yolk to be served in thy beer, a well-known remedy.

Take comfort in a Campion's:
The beer of Queen Bess

Tis time to purchase a barrel of Campion's and toast the queen. For Henry Campion's London brewerie be much admired by Her Majestye and made her official supplier. Ditch thee the strange brews made by the foreigner brewers who come lately to this city like Jacob Wittewrongle of Grantham Lane, who, we do attest add obnoxious weeds of all sort to their liquors. Seek out the best at our brewhouse in Hay's Wharf Lane, where, to gentlemen, a sample of the goods will be provideth.

❀

A drop of wine?

Though English wines have been tried they are not known for their quality – as the chancellor to Henry II observed they had to be drunk with 'closed eyes and tense jaws'. So, wine be generally imported, and therefore more expensive than beer; it may cost thee dearly, especially away from the capital city. In Norwich in 1587, for instance, a gallon of claret cost a weighty 2s 4d.

The price of the best wines also reflect that, being placed in casks which let the air in, they are difficult to keep, especially given their long journeys from the vineyards in Germany and France and sometimes even further afield in the Mediterranean.

But both red and white wine are available and, sometimes to disguise wine that be going off, it may also be served warm, sugared or spiced with cloves or nutmeg. Spiced wine be oft called hippocras. Sweet wines are thought better than others. Malmsey, a sweet wine, comes from as far away as Crete. Bastard, from Burgundy, be thought of as an excellent red wine. Sack be fortified wine. There are some eighty kinds of wine available and the trade in them be run, in London at least, by the vintners company.

Be careful how much thee take. We recall Sir Thomas Elyot's warning in *The Castle of Health* that 'deep red and sweet wines cause melancholia and are hurtfull to the eyes'. William Turner's tome, *A New Boke of the Natures and Properties of all Wines that are Commonlye used here in England*, may now be forty years old, but he hath advice for those with a tendency to gallstones saying that 'red wines breed the stone more than whyte Rhennish and whyte French wines doe'.

Just as there be the ale-conner, whose duty it be to test the beer, the quality of wine be also closely monitored as are each of the casks to make sure they contain the correct quantity before leaving port for the rest of our land. Who knows, if thee be very lucky, thy wine might even be served in a glass.

On what other drinks may thee sup?

As well as ale, beer and wine thee may, particularly in the west of the kingdom, be served cider or perry. And in some rare establishments, particularly one in Barking, near London and several in Salisbury, thee may want to try a kind of rough '*aqua vitae*' spirit, oft made from the dregs of ale. In Scotland a similar type of liquid, made from malted grain and known as usquebaugh, be so popular that attempts have been introduced to control the trade. A new strong drink called gin be also becoming known, introduced from the Low Countries. Most of these spirits are used for medicinal purposes.

And so to eat

As we all know, wine and beer increase the appetite, so what shall thee eat? What be not always realised, by humble folk, be that beer be actually an important source of energy for the ordinary Englishman in itself. And in the alehouse other food be scant and meagre; there are sometimes buns doused in ale or perhaps a savoury or sweet pie, but little else. In taverns and inns, however, the food can be sumptuous.

Bread be staple fare. In the north the climate be considered too cold for wheat and rye tends to be used in the bread instead. In the counties of Hertfordshire, Buckinghamshire and Middlesex a cherry tart might be provided; in the Somerset levels a duck may grace the table. In Gloucestershire, Cheshire and Leicestershire the cheese be considered very good. The famous farmer's lunch of bread, cheese and an onion be not unknown in a better alehouse.

Once again, Andrew Boorde in his *Dyetary of Health* tells us that beef be a common food and 'it doth make an Englyssheman strong'. It will oft come salted. Thick soups made with oats and herbs as well as peas or beans are a staple too. Boorde says that 'Potage be not so much used in al crystendom as it be used in England'.

At an inn thee might typically be offered a mutton pie or perhaps a dish of pork and souse or the leg of a chicken followed by an apple pie. But some of the food can sound quite exotic, especially in the inns of London where oysters, anchovies, roast capon, pigeon, venison, black pudding, conger eel and even strawberries may be available. Turkeys, from the Eastern counties, are a new delicacy and potatoes are a mere wonder. Sugar be a very new item but much used and admired in inns by the gentlefolk – though the price be fearful. As recently as the 1570s, it could be had for fourpence the pound, but then it jumped quickly to half a crown, so currants and raisins are oft turned to for sweetness. Good tidings came when Sir Francis Drake captured much sweetmeat and conserves, returning so much sugar cane on his ship the *Golden Hind* that the teeth of English diplomats rot much. Thus our reputation in foreign parts be one of poor dentistry.

In some places thee may find that fish be the only dish on offer on a Friday due to a law revived by Queen Elizabeth, though 'tis not always observed. Don't expect to eat the tomatoes. Indeed, salads are, in the most part, frowned upon, for as one writer tells us they 'will make thy stomach sick'. Milk be off the menu too. 'Tis a drink of the poor and children, though sometimes of use as a good stomach liner before a drinking bout.

In an inn thy food be likely served on wooden platters with pudding oft served on the flip side, though pewter platters are also coming in. Who knows, thee may even get a spoon? In a good inn thee might possibly eat with a fork, a relatively new notion much associated with Italians, though considered effeminate in some parts of England. If thee really want to be sure of cutlery it be as well to follow the custom of bringing thy own. Certainly always carry a knife at the very least and a toothpick, some beautiful ones in ivory are available. Whatever thee eat at the inn or tavern a wooden salt cellar be invariably found. If thy manners are lacking don't worry too greatly, eating with thy fingers be still common.

In some taverns thee may bring thy own food; in others there be a sort of 'all thee can eat' deal for a set price or perhaps warm food for thee to take with thee on thy journey. Beware, thee may find that there be little food in the late evening as most people prefer to eat heavily at noon – this meal being called dinner – and perhaps take an early supper at six of the clock. Breakfast, where 'tis given, be bread, butter and sage and beer or even wine.

4

HOW SHALL THEE BE ENTERTAINED?

A contemporary drinking song

Toss the pot, toss the pot, let us be merry, And drink till our cheeks be as red as a cherry: We take no thought, we have no care, For still we spend and never spare: Till of our money our purse be bare, We ever toss the pot.

There be much more than drink to keep thee amused in the alehouse, tavern or inn be it in the form of gaming, gambling, wenching or even high culture. Be warned, however, that each of these pleasures comes with its own set of risks.

The singing of ditties

Music and singing are common diversions, with many a bawdy alehouse song heard. There are bands of strolling minstrels setting up in hostelries too and morris dancers are sometimes seen. Thee may see fiddlers, but the playing of bagpipes be more normal across the kingdom. Stephen Gosson, in 1587, wrote in his *Short Apologie of the Schoole of Abuse* that, 'London be so full of unprofitable pipers that a man can no sooner enter a tavern than two or three cast of them hang at his heels to give him a dance ere he depart'.

To see one of Mister Shakespeare's plays

Thee may be lucky enough to encounter one of the groups of thespians who perform the latest plays at the inn yard. With their courtyards, surrounded by galleries, many inns make natural theatres. Indeed, thee may find thyself sharing lodgings with minstrels and troubadours. Before his sad death two years ago, Mister James Burbage brought much profit to the innkeepers from touring shows. Burbage's splendid London Theatre was the first one built for the purpose and constructed much to the plan of a traditional inn.

The players or 'actors' are formed into companies, such as the Lord Chamberlain's Men, which be Shakespeare's company, patronised by noblemen and closely monitored by the authorities. Thee will find many of the latest works performed, penned by the likes of Christopher Marlowe, the author of the popular play *Tamburlaine*, whose mysterious death in 1593 hath robbed the theatre of many laughs. Or perhaps thee will be able to catch a work by William Shakespeare himself? His *Henry IV* was an undoubted triumph and he hath many more works planned for the coming century. Indeed, so popular have these plays become in the 1590s that London and Southwark now have a number of purpose built theatres, some using the dismantled timbers of Mr Burbage's, which closed in 1597, to cater for a population hungry to observe the latest work. Expect to pay a penny a ticket, more if thee wish to sit.

The taking in of tobacco

Smoking tobacco be a new pastime much admired. In London alone there are some 7,000 tobacco shops and in alehouses thee may even be able to smoke from a communal pipe. William Harrison tells us that 'these days of takin-in of the Indian herb called tobacco ... be greatly taken up and used in England' for the treatment of disease and for its mellowing effect. A quarter of an ounce will cost a sizeable 10*d* in a tavern. Many local authorities frown up the 'weed' as 'tis thought to be a source of fires. Ben Jonson, in his new play *Every Man in his Humour*, includes the line:'Ods me, I marvel what pleasure or felicity they have in taking their roguish tobacco. It is good for nothing but to choke a man, and fill him full of smoke and embers.'

The playing of games

Despite regulations aimed at curbing them, playing games for money be commonplace as we know from the case, just last year, of John Collyn, the alehouse keeper from Barling in Essex, reported as allowing dice-playing, cards, tables (a form of backgammon), shove-groat, and skittles. Pitch penny be much played – tossing a coin from some fixed distance into a hole carved in a bench. Henry VIII himself was a keen shove-ha'penny player, once losing £9 in a game – the fate of the winner be not known.

On all games money be wagered and gambling be surely more of a bane in England than drink itself. Dice are to be found everywhere and thee would do well to examine them carefully before playing. Consider purchasing Gilbert Walker's *A Manifest Detection of the Most Vyle and Detestable Use of Dice Play*. He hath discovered fourteen methods in which dice are tampered with. 'Gords', for example, are hollowed out on one side, while 'fullams' are secretly loaded with lead.

Card games are popular too. It would be wise to learn the rules of Primero, which be known across Europe, and a favourite of both Henry VIII and Elizabeth. 'Tis a form of poker played for money where bluffing thy opponent be the key. Piquet, a trick-taking game for two, be another that thee may be invited to play. There be also loggats, a game where sticks are thrown as close as possible to a stake in the ground, something called milking cromock; another known as guile-bones; and another called fox mine host. Marbles, draughts and chess can all be found, as well as casting the barre, a kind of shot putting. In almost every case betting on the outcome be expected, so keep thy purse with thee at all times.

Whether playing cards or dice, watch out for cheats; there are many ruses around. Some men will pretend to be poor at games, encouraging thee into higher wagers, then suddenly show their skills. Other cheaters will employ women to beguile thee. Gilbert Walker warns us as much when he says 'Take this for a maxim that all the bawds in the country be of the chetor familiar acquaintance.' If thee want to understand the tricks of fingerers and cheaters of all sorts then read the *Fraternitye of Vacabondes* by John Awdeley of 1561. Indeed, the tome hath given us the very first written account of the word 'rogue.'

Huge sums will also be wagered at cock-fighting, bear-baiting or bull-baiting. All these are to be seen at inn yards or in purpose-built arenas, which most large towns boast. A prize bird at a cock fight can be worth as much as £5. In some places thee may be invited by thy fellow guests to see a wrestling match, especially in Cornwall and Devon.

Beware sporting pastimes – especially football

If thee are well-to-do thee may be entitled to play sports only deemed fit for the upper echelons, such as tennis and bowls – a favourite, of course, of our heroic Sir Francis Drake, who be said to have finished his game at Plymouth Hoe before whipping the Spanish at sea in 1588. But the masses oft ignore the directives against these 'posher' games. An alehouse in Somerset be even said to keep a set of bowls. Crude forms of tennis can be seen in the streets outside hostelries, with one writer saying that 'tis played for a crown even on work days. Thee may well be invited to take part in a game of nine-pins or quoits before the inn, or watch quintain, a form of mock jousting, while thee sup on the alehouse bench in the sun. Many hostelries harbour their own skittle alleys too.

In the North Riding we hear of an alehouse keeper who keeps his own football. This game was banned in 1540 but be still much played by teams of those who gather in alehouses. The ball be traditionally made from a pig's bladder, but more lately leather, and played across a great distance, involving an almighty scrum for the ball as each team tries to get the sphere to the other team's home. These are more brawls for a ball than anything elegant. One writer tells us that football be played by two teams of men with 'beastly fury and extreme violence'. Another describes football as 'more of a fight than a game' which can and does, we are assured, frequently end in death.

Drinking contests

If all this does not divert thee then perhaps thee may be of strong enough liver to engage in a drinking bout. Matches are even held between alehouses of different towns. Our esteemed William Shakespeare be apparently a member of a Stratford drinking club which once took on a team at the Falcon in the Warwickshire town of Bidford-on-Avon. Apocryphal, or no, the tale hath it that Mr Shakespeare was, the next morning, found asleep under a crab apple tree. As the rhyme goes, when he was woken the next morning by his friends, they encouraged him to partake of a rematch. But the bard be said to have uttered: 'No, I have drunk with Piping Pebworth, Dancing Marston, Haunted Hillboro', Hungry Grafton, Dodging Exhall, Papist Wixford, Beggarly Broom and Drunken Bidford.'

Fairs and celebrations

Whitsun still be the natural time to locate the Church ale in those parishes that still produce a brew. Check for Whitsun-ales or May-ales by attending church as be thy obligation. For a large sum to be realised for the parish through the sale of ale, notices may be read at ten, a dozen or a score pulpits where the flock be implored to come and tipple and raise funds. When the day approaches to open the ale, cuckoo kings be chosen and princes too. Church bells will ring merrily and bagpipes sound to pipe delegations from nearby villages. Enjoy the ale at the long tables, but take heed of recent chroniclers who warn: 'he that can get the soonest to it, and spend the most at it, for he that sitteth the closest to it, and spendes the most at it, he be counted the godliest man of all the rest because it be spent uppon his Church forsooth.'

Feeling bawdy?

There be one pleasure that will be available for a price at many of the lower establishments – the services of a comely wench. 'Tis fair to say that prices differ vastly, though a quick session in the sack should set thee back no more than 6d a time. 'Tis a brave alehouse keeper that offers such a service, for the fine can be as much as 20s.

Indulging can be equally perilous. Indeed, the physician Andrew Boorde, who we have heard from in the previous chapter, was imprisoned and died, shortly after being found cavorting with three loose women in Winchester.

5

WHAT SHALL THEE SAY?

Herewith a useful guide to some of the language thee are likely to encounter at the alehouse:

Ale-conner official appointed to monitor the quality of brews
Ale-knight hardy drinker
Ale-stake pole projecting from an alehouse
Angler thief who uses a hook on a line through an open window
Bait to stop at an inn to feed the horses
Baratour a brawler
Bard a poet
Barley hood fit of temper brought on by boozing
Bastard a sweet Spanish wine
Belamour lover
Bellibone a beautiful woman
Belly-cheer feasting
Ben bouse a good drink
Bawcock a fine fellow
Bawd lewd woman
Bizzle get drunk
Black jack a leather drinking vessel, sealed with pitch
Blow boll a regular tippler
Bob to cheat
Bodkin a dagger
Boggard a privy
Boll to quaff the bowl, to drink ale
Bombard large leathern vessel to carry drink
Boon companion drinking pal

Bordello brothel
Brandewijn brandy
Bubber wine drinker
Carouse drink each other's health
Carpet knight knight of the boudoir rather than the battlefield
Clapperdudgeon a sham beggar
Clenchpoop a clown
Cod's-head an idiot
Conie catcher a cheat
Cozener trickster
Cupshotten drunk
Cut-purse thief
Dell a wench
Dizzard a fool
Double beer strong beer
Doxy a thief's mistress
Duckies a woman's breasts
Dutch widow a prostitute
Fap drunk
Featherbed mattress
Flapdragon a combustible put in liquor, to be swallowed whilst
    flaming
Foist to cheat in dice
Footpads robbers
Fopdoodle a thick person
Fullam loaded dice
Gorebelly a fat person
Groat fourpence coin
Gull drink
Harlot unfaithful woman
Hochepot a soup or stew
Hostelry or hostry inn
House of easement privy
In his cups drunk
Jakes a privy
Jarkman a forger
Jernie to swear

Knokylbonyarde a contemptible fellow
Lag to steal
Lion drunk seriously sodden
Lirrypoope silly individual
Mead sweet fermented drink made with honey, known as
    metheglin in Wales
Mountebanks a cheater
Nappy heady or strong
Nip a bung to steal a purse
Nog a strong beer from East Anglia
Nob to cheat
On the nail immediate payment
Palfrey good riding horse
Palliard a rascal
Penny father skinflint
Pillory public punishment device, like the stocks
Pot a drinking vessel
Pot house alehouse
Pot valiant drunk
Poset ale milk poured into ale and spiced
Prigger horse thief
Quass to drink in excess
Punk a prostitute
Rampallian scoundrel
Rogue highway thief
Roister noisy reveller
Rouse large glass for drinking someone's health
Shake the elbow to gamble
Snudge miser
Stew brothel
Swive fornicate
Tippler alehouse keeper
Tippling house alehouse, also known as a tup-house or boozing
    ken
Tip-merrie drunk
Trencher a plate made of stale bread
Sack a dry wine from Spain

Sirrah sneering form of address
Small beer weaker beer
Stews brothels
Sweating sickness a deadly disease of the time
Upsee-freeze drunk
Wassail a drinking bout
Wench female servant
Worsted stocking common type
Vagabond vagrant

Warning: Idle words can cost thy life

England be a free country and proud of it. But we do caution against letting the beer doeth too much talking. Since 1581 innkeepers and tipplers are required to report instances of the use of seditious words. First offenders are liable to a fine of £200. Those unable to pay this equivalent of about 400 years' wages will be put in the pillory and perhaps lose both their ears.

Conspirators with their ears cut off will not be told twice. Death by hanging be generally prescribed for second offences. Sedition may also be considered high treason, in which case hanging, drawing and quartering shall be applied.

Please note that what constitutes a seditious word be at the discretion of the local magistrate, men not known for either consistency or mercy, especially when in drink. Sedition could include – but be not limited to – speculating when Her Majesty may die, when the government will change, or that the uprisings in Ireland may last into next year.

❀

6

YE COUNTY BY COUNTY GUIDE

❀ LONDON & MIDDLESEX

'Would I were in an alehouse in London. I would give all my fame for a pot of ale, and safety.' This be an exclusive snippet from a new play by William Shakespeare, on the life of *Henry V*. Today there would certainly be many places to choose from. The nation's greatest city now numbers 200,000 people and 'tis home to more than 100 inns and at least 1,000 alehouses to cater for its seething masses.

First we will focus on the hostelries of London and Middlesex, north of the Thames, while those to the immediate south of the city beyond the river – and among the fleshpots of Southwark – are properly considered in the county of Surrey, later in this guide.

The city of London itself be growing fast, and thee will find a multitude of merchants engaged in every conceivable trade here, as well as a throng of new immigrants. The city be enclosed by a wall with the River Fleet marking its boundary in the west and Aldgate in the east. London be built mainly of timber with the most important buildings constructed of stone, the greatest structure of all being St Paul's Cathedral, though it hath not had its spire since 'twas struck by lightning in 1561. Other important buildings include the royal residences of Baynard's Castle and Bridewell Palace as well St Bartholomew's Hospital and the Royal Exchange, a great place to do business, opened by the queen herself in 1571. This building hath a licence to sell alcohol but if thee want a cheaper, speedy draught, thee may wish to seek out John Price, who cheekily sells pick-me-ups from a hidey hole beneath it. At the east end of the city, of course, be the Tower of London, where for a princely sum, thee can even arrange to visit the dungeons.

The Thames be the principal highway of the city and the banks of the river swarm with sails, especially around the main docks of Queenshithe and Billingsgate. There be only one crossing point over the river – London Bridge. The bridge itself be some 800ft long, with twenty great stone piers. 'Tis lined with some 200 shops and even a chapel. The gates at each end are closed at night and above the southern end great spikes carry the heads of traitors, dipped in tar. Wherries also carry people across river. Some boats, for sport, even try to 'shoot the bridge', taking to the dangerous rapids caused by the bridge's footings.

The city's best inns are located on the main thoroughfares, especially those leading north, south, east and west out of the city. Around six of the finest inns in the capital have been used as theatres in the last few decades, including the Bull in Bishopsgate, though these performances have sometimes upset the authorities, as they are considered to cause unrest and crime. In fact, the government have tried to ban the players within the city walls, even setting up their own sponsored companies. In recent years there hath been the construction of new theatres built specifically for the purpose, first to the north of the city, such as the Curtain in 1577 and now the Globe and the Rose on Bankside to the south, all of which retain much of the look of the galleried inn courtyards they are seeking to supersede. Queen Elizabeth herself be a fan of the theatre. The newly built Globe hath just seen William Shakespeare's *Julius Caesar* performed for the first time.

Alehouses abound across London, especially in the back alleys and across the water in the 'liberties' of Southwark. Here, in the poorer areas, every one in six houses be a drinking den. Across the city magistrates are concerned about the multitude of alehouses and victualling houses which are increasing daily.

There are many entertainments to be had in the city before retiring to a watering hole. At Tyburn, to the west of the city, many gather to watch public hangings – up to thirty people a day can be dispatched upon the three-sided gallows. There be wrestling at Bartholomew Fair and, since 1576, licensed gaming houses as well as special arenas for animal baiting as at Paris Gardens along Bankside and cockfighting, like the one in Shoe Lane where huge sums are wagered.

The export of cloth hath become one of the city's major trades and commerce be thriving, with guilds and livery companies making good use of the inns. One of the most important groups, the weavers, hold their meetings in taverns.

Outside the city's walls lies the county of Middlesex which hath some important inns of its own and wondrous sights. The Strand, lined with the houses of the rich, links the city of London to the palaces of Whitehall and Westminster as well as the great abbey of old, where many former kings of England are buried. Further afield, to the west, be the palace of Hampton Court, so famously associated with Cardinal Wolsey and Henry VIII.

If thee fear that the size and clatter of London be too much for thee, take heart from the words of the contemporary commentator John Stow. In his great *Survey of London* he tells us that 'tis 'the fairest, largest, richest and best inhabited city in the world'.

CHEAPSIDE

THE MERMAID
'To witness a literary wit combat'
If thee want to see some of the greatest literary figures of our age then this is fast becoming the place to be. Here thee may find thyself rubbing shoulders with the likes of the playwright Christopher Marlowe, also rumoured to be a spy, the young poet John Donne, the great traveller and writer Thomas Coryat and the orator Richard Martin.

We learn that thee might be wise to call in on a Friday when thee may be lucky enough to witness one of the so called 'wit-combats' between the celebrated dramatist and poet Ben Jonson and that country lad turned playwright William Shakespeare. In these humorous debates they try to outdo each other for rhetoric, cleverness and wondrous wordplay.

The Mermaid be a refuge for troublemakers too. In 1591 an eccentric pair called Edmund Coppinger and Henry Arthington preached nearby that one William Hacket, a deranged man from Northamptonshire later executed for his heresies, was the Messiah reborn. After their ravings caused a riot, they were forced to take shelter in the tavern.

Sited betwixt the crowded stalls of Cheapside itself and with easy access to the river, The Mermaid also serves excellent seafood suppers. The oysters go down particularly well with a goblet of double beer. Ask the tavern keeper William Johnson to recommend the latest, best brew.

Latterly: Believed to have been on the corner of Bread Street until destroyed in the Great Fire of London 1666.

BISHOPSGATE

THE BULL
'All the Queen's Men'
Located within the walls of the city on the road to the west, this great inn lies behind a row of shops and be sought out through a long covered passageway. There are three courtyards within the complex that makes up the inn, with one measuring some 70ft by 20ft. However, 'tis the smallest, measuring 45ft by 35ft, where something magical happens. Here plays are oft performed, both in summer and in winter, making The Bull one of the many inns where the growing enthusiasm for the theatre hath flourished. In one of his books, written in 1578, the writer John Florio observed that the question be oft asked: 'Where shall we goe? To a playe at the Bull ...?'

And indeed The Bull hath now become one of the inns where The Queen's Men perform, a group of players patronised by Queen Elizabeth herself and set up to be sure that no performances become unfavourable to her monarchy. Richard Tarlton, the funniest man of our times and Bess' own jester, oft played here before passing on in 1588. Tarlton be thought the only man who could improve Her Majesty's bad moods and the writer Thomas Nashe noted that audiences began 'exceedingly to laugh when he first peept out his head'. Yet The Bull be known as a haunt of thieves, turning laughter to tears for many of its customers when, after the performance, they realise that their purse be missing.

Latterly: Demolished in the nineteenth century.

The cutpurse thwarted ...

The dramatist Robert Greene in one of his cony-catching pamphlets observed ...

A good-fellow that was newly entered into the nipping craft, and had not as yet attained to any acquaintance with ye chief and cunning masters of that trade, in the Christmas holidays last came to see a play at The Bull within Bishopsgate, there to take his benefit as time and place would permit him. Not long had he stayed in the press but he had gotten a young man's purse out of his pocket, which when he had, he stepped into the stable to take out the money and to convey away the purse. But looking on his commodity, he found nothing therein but white counters, a thimble and a broken threepence ...

❁

THE WHITE HART
'If thee should miss the curfew'

The inn be described thus in 1583: 'An inn in the parish of St Botolph without Bisshoppesgate between the cemetery of the parish church of St Botolph south, the gate or entry of the late house of the Blessed Mary of Bethlehem north and from the high street east to the garden of Bethlehem and the ditch of la More.'

First built in 1480, the inn was once part of the priory and hospital later known as Bedlam, founded in 1246 by Robert Fitzmary. Today the inn serves the roads leading to the north and eastern counties and makes a good stopping point if a traveller hath missed the curfew sounded by the bells of the churches in the city at 9 p.m., whence the gates to the city are closed until sunrise the following morning. If thee are new to London thee might want to rest here before emerging into the chaos of the streets the next morning.

Latterly: The White Hart, 121 Bishopsgate, London, EC2M 3TH, www.nicholsonspubs.co.uk.

EASTCHEAP

BOAR'S HEAD TAVERN

This be one of several Boar's Heads in London, causing much confusion to the traveller ... and writer! Another, in Whitechapel, serves as an inn-yard theatre. While yet another, over the water in Southwark, be run by a real Sir John Fastolf, which makes the puzzle even greater, for the Boar's Head in Eastcheap – to which this entry alludes – hath been chosen by the playwright William Shakespeare as a setting for his play *Henry IV*, which features that loveable fictional rogue, Sir John Falstaff.

The Boar's Head of which we speak be set by the London Stone – that ancient relic thought by some to be a Roman milestone. In 1537 the Boar's Head was run by Joanna and William Broke, who were succeeded in 1588, by Thomas Wright, who was knighted and said to be 'a very discreet and honest gentleman'.

'Twas in this large tavern's convivial atmosphere, famous for its carving of a great boar's head at its front, that Mr Shakespeare placed his revellers, Prince Hal, the future king and Falstaff, that hedonist who lived for drink and carousing: 'Why, there it is – come, sing me a bawdy song; make me merry.' The tavern be a well-chosen venue as it outclasses its neighbours, the Chicken and the Three Kings for good cheer and be said, by some, to be the greatest tavern in London.

Latterly: Demolished in 1831 to build the approach for the new London Bridge.

Queen Bess' tavern grub

According to legend, when Queen Elizabeth was released from the Tower of London in 1554, after her imprisonment by Queen Mary, she went straight from her confinement to the King's Head in Fenchurch Street for a dinner of boiled pork and pease-pudding.

FLEET STREET

THE DEVIL'S TAVERN
'Of ribald company'
Of the many hostelries around Fleet Street, this place be infamous, not least for its comical sign which shows St Dunstan – the saint of the parish in which he sits – pulling the nose of Lucifer with a pair of pincers. The sign hath caused much merriment but hath also caused disgust among more po-faced types. Indeed, the authorities have lately discussed having it torn down, but for now it remains to taunt the humourless.

Inside this well-worn establishment are to be found playwrights – among them that wit Ben Jonson – and other creative types who many have dubbed devils themselves. As a drinking den The Devil's antiquity be certain for 'tis mentioned as already being old in an 1563 play called *Jacke Jugeler*, in which the character Jack, to another's nquiry of where they are to dwell, replies: 'At the Devyll if thee lust, I cannot tell!'
Latterly: Demolished in 1787. Now Child's Private Bank, 1 Fleet Street, London, EC4Y 1BD.

Check thy tippler's licence

As thee pick thy place to imbibe beware that many of the places thee frequent may be playing fast and loose with the rules. In 1562 some sixteen tavern-keepers in the parish of St Dunstan's were under investigation for 'holdying typlers within the parishe for that they sell and utter their drinke by stone crewetts and potts nott seiled and wantnge measure'. In 1576 one William Powell was presented before the courts 'for keepinge victuallinge without a licence in a sellar at Temple Barre, under the house of Symon Cannon, and for receivinge of idle persons into the same sellar to eate and drinke'.

GRACECHURCH STREET

THE CROSS KEYS
'See the dancing horse'

'Tis not just plays that one can witness at London's theatre inns, of which The Cross Keys be one of the most famous. One of the strangest diversions of recent years be Marocco, the dancing horse. 'Tis kept by one William Bankes, a Staffordshire man, who hath, in his time, been a resident at The Cross Keys and be famous for showing off his famously talented steed at the local inn yards. Named after the trend for Moroccan leather saddles, this nag be a remarkable beast, able to perform all sorts of tricks for the crowds. Clad in silver horseshoes, his feats are one of the great sights of the times. 'Tis said he be able to stand on two legs, pick out harlots from the audience, bow to the queen, piss on command and even count. The poet John Bastard tells us: 'Bankes hath a horse of wondrous qualitie, For he can fight, and pisse, and daunce, and lie, And finde thy purse, and tell what coyne ye haue.'

The Cross Keys stands adjacent to The Bell, the fourth inn used as a playhouse. Its recent owner Thomas Smythe, was one of the wealthiest men in the parish.

Latterly: Now demolished. Standing near the site be The Crosse Keys, 9 Gracechurch Street, City of London, EC3V 0DR, tel: 020 7623 4824, www.jdwetherspoon.co.uk.

THE MITRE
'A glimpse of the queen?'

Next to the London palace of the Bishops of Ely, who have had a residence here since 1290, be a curious place to whet one's whistle, for 'tis not technically in London but part of Cambridgeshire. 'Twas built in 1546 by one Bishop Goodrich as a watering hole for the servants at the palace which boasts sumptuous gardens, orchards, vineyards and be famed for its strawberry fields. These delicacies are so renowned that they are even mentioned in William Shakespeare's exciting play, *Richard III*.

If thee manage to talk thy way into this holy drinking den 'tis possible thee may get a glimpse of Her Majesty the Queen for she demanded a portion of the grounds for Sir Christopher Hatton – her late favourite statesman – and she be still seen hereabouts. *Latterly: Ye Olde Mitre, 1 Ely Court, Hatton Garden, London, EC1N 6TD, tel: 020 7405 4751, www.yeoldemitreholborn.co.uk*

ISLINGTON

QUEEN'S HEAD
'Sir Walter Raleigh's own inn?'

In 1588 the explorer and royal favourite Sir Walter Raleigh was granted a special patent 'to make licences for keeping of taverns and retailing of wines throughout England', and 'tis actually rumoured that Sir Walter owns this grand inn. It boasts three lofty storeys which project over the street below and be constructed with much ornate oak and carved timbers. It hath wood panelling inside with stuccoed ceilings and a grand stone fireplace, perfect for the esteemed knight, famous for making tobacco popular in England, to sit beside with his beloved pipe. What be certain be that Islington be a haunt of Sir Walter and indeed Queen Elizabeth herself. For the village, which be north of the city, be known as a playground of the rich and famous. Other names associated with the place are the recently late Lord High Treasurer, Burghley and 'tis reputedly a summer residence of the Earl of Essex, that other favourite of Her Majesty. If so, she must surely have been a visitor herself. The inn must, at least, owe its name to Bess.

Latterly: The original was demolished in 1829. The Old Queen's Head lays claim to its heritage, 44 Essex Road, London, N1 8LN, tel: 020 7354 9993, www.theoldqueenshead.com.

LUDGATE

BELL SAVAGE
'Of revolts and revels'
This famous inn, now boasting some forty rooms and with stabling for a hundred horses, hath a puzzling name and many theories have been put about to explain its origin.

It hath stood next to the walls of the city at Ludgate – that western entrance to the city – since at least 1420 and may have received its moniker from the name of the first innkeeper here, a William Savage. But others say that there was a lady who ran the place called Isabella Savage or that 'twas named after a famous French beauty. Others say that it hath, in its time, sported a sign with a savage-looking man standing upon a bell.

Whatever the truth, in 1453, John French gave his mother Joan the 'inn, with its appurtenances, called Savage's Inn, otherwise called the Bell on the Hoop' ('the hoop' being a garland of ivy).

In the middle of this century it made its mark in history when 'twas a backdrop to that dastardly plot known as Wyatt's Rebellion. In 1554 Sir Thomas Wyatt rose up with 4,000 others against the proposed marriage of Queen Mary to Philip of Spain. The mob soon occupied the city of Rochester and then marched upon London, but his forces were repelled at the city gates and his supporters fled. 'Tis said that he rested him awhile upon a stall against the Bell Savage gate before surrendering himself. Wyatt was subsequently executed at Tower Hill.

From the 1570s the Bell hath been a stage for more drama – this time for the people's entertainment, for it hath doubled as a playhouse. During performances, one side of the yard be curtained off and a stage erected on trestle tables. As many as 500 people cram into the place, packing both the courtyard and the two tiers of galleries, to see the latest works. They pay differing amounts, depending on the comfort that they can afford – 'one penny at the gate, another at the entrie of the Scaffolde, and the thirde for a quiet standing'.

Some of the finest works of our age have been performed here and we hear that Mr William Shakespeare's new play, *Love's Labour's Lost*, be to get an airing at the inn soon.

One observer hath said of the inn's dramas that 'thee shall finde neuer a woorde without wit, neuer a line without pith, neuer a letter placed in vaine'. Indeed, so powerful was one performance of Christopher Marlowe's play *Doctor Faustus*, that the Devil was said to have been truly conjured up, as in the work itself and several of the audience members driven insane.

The greatest clown of our age, Richard Tarlton, oft came down from his own tavern near St Paul's to raise a smile with his comic ditties and doggerel verse. The Bell be also known for its thrilling public displays of fencing and bear baiting.

Latterly: Demolished in 1873 to make way for a railway viaduct. Limeburner Lane be now on the spot.

VINTRY

THREE CRANES
'Where wine arrives … and be quickly dispatched'
Where better to quaff a good vintage than where thee can be sure of its source? This be the case at the Three Cranes, named after the three great wooden structures that stand here by the banks of the Thames. 'Tis at this place where wines from as far afield as Bordeaux are brought ashore from the ships using these great machines. Though the wharf be the centre of the city's wine trade, and be frequently visited by city officials, the

Cranes be ramshackle place where men are known to hide from their creditors 'drunk with fear'. Ben Jonson believes that while the good food be enticement, its main attraction lies in the fact that 'tis a haunt of literary pretenders, saying: 'A pox o' these pretenders to wit ... not a corn of true salt, not a grain of right mustard amongst them all.'

Latterly: Demolished. It used to stand where Upper Thames Street meets Southwark Bridge.

WAPPING

THE PELICAN
'Necking ales near the noose!'
That erudite traveller John Stow describes this shambling riverside village as a 'continual street, or a filthy strait passage, with alleys of small tenements or cottages ... inhabited by sailors' victuallers'. Among this stink, squalor and den of seafarers be The Pelican, a seedy place dating from 1520, where thee are destined to mix with a motley crew of smugglers, mast makers, sailors, pirates or men at arms. 'Tis a clientele that hath seen the alehouse dubbed locally as the Devil's place.

There be a certain frisson from being in such a dangerous but exotic neighbourhood where sights and sounds as well as smells – like the waft of that wondrous weed tobacco – assault the senses. Along with the bare-knuckle fights and cock fighting, there be a further ghoulish extra attraction here, for The Pelican be near the spot on the river where the capital's pirates and ne'r-do-wells have been hung these last hundred years. Tradition hath it that their bodies are left dangling at low water mark until three tides have washed over them. Be warned that thee may even find thyself sharing a bench with these villains; condemned pirates are allowed a final quart of ale in a nearby inn before their deaths.

An air of ill-luck certainly seems to linger around this area. 'Twas the place from which Sir Hugh Willoughby set sail in 1553, seeking a north-east passage to the Orient. He and his crew were later found frozen to death in the icy wastes of northern Russia.

Nearby Limehouse hath seen the launching of more successful adventures. From below The Grapes, a new hostelry dating from 1583, Sir Walter Raleigh set sail for the New World.

Latterly: The Prospect Of Whitby, 57 Wapping Wall, London, E1W 3SH, tel: 02036 034 385, www.taylor-walker.co.uk.

Other hostelries of note ...

FLEET STREET

COCK AND BOTTLE
A well-known haunt of printers – a burgeoning trade in this area – since 1549.

Latterly: Ye Old Cock Tavern, 22 Fleet Street, City of London, London, Greater London, EC4Y 1AA, tel: 020 7353 8570, www.taylor-walker.co.uk.

HOLBORN

THE WHITE HART
A small alehouse that be reputed to have been serving since 1216.

Latterly: The White Hart, 191 Drury Lane, Holborn, London, WC2B 5QD, tel: 020 7242 2317, www.mspubs.co.uk

THE SHIP INN
'Site of secret masses'

On the surface this drinking place, established in 1549, be seemingly simply a place to quench thy thirst. But it also be rumoured to be a place where those loyal to the Roman Church say mass, posting lookouts and escaping to the spacious cellars when there be the chance of being spotted at their nefarious practices.

Latterly: The Ship Tavern, 12 Gate Street, Holborn, London, WC2A 3HP, tel: 020 7405 1992, www.theshiptavern.co.uk.

PINNER

THE CROWN
Built in 1540 on the site of an older alehouse. There be a famous street fair here.
Latterly: The Queen's Head, 31 High Street, Pinner, HA5 5PJ, tel: 020 8868 4607.

The Crown, Pinner, Middlesex, later the Queen's Head. (© Mr James Moore and Mr Paul Nero)

ST MARTIN'S-LE-GRAND

BULL AND MOUTH
Great galleries run around three lengths of the yard at this inn, which dates to 1429 in the reign of Henry VI. Though its association be more with Henry VIII, for it takes its name from Boulogne Mouth, after the king took the French town by siege in 1544.
Latterly: Formerly at the corner of Bull and Mouth Street and Aldersgate Street. Demolished in 1829.

❊ BEDFORDSHIRE

Opinions are mixed on this county, which while business-like, hath not inspired our poets or other great writers to florid descriptions or overblown praise. Its main town be Bedford, on the River Ouse, a settlement of which William Camden, in his great survey, *Britannia*, said be a 'towne to be commended for the pleasant situation and anciently thereof [rather] than for beauty or largeness'. Established by the Saxon chief Beda, who made a ford here, 'tis now an important place in the lacemaking trade, much helped by the recent fashion for the intricate designs among the gentlefolk – though how they keep such fripperies clean we shall never understand.

Woburn Abbey be a good grand house to be seen. 'Twas taken from its religious order in the time of King Henry VIII and given over to the Dukes of Bedford.

This small county hath relatively poor pickings when it comes to good inns for the traveller, though in towns like Dunstable those hurrying to more weighty destinations are well catered for. Indeed, the beer be good, as the southern part of the county grows much barley for the making of liquor. This be not a region known for its unruliness. For, over the centuries, it hath been congratulated for supplying its quota of wool to the royal household in full and on time.

DUNSTABLE

WHITE HORSE
'So good King Henry shunned the prior'
With regular jousting tournaments over the centuries and sited on the old Watling Street, a Roman road still in use today by those travelling north-west from London, Dunstable be a thriving place which that great writer of these past decades, William Camden, described as 'populous and full of inns'.

There be one inn called the King's Head but 'tis, ironically, the White Horse that can claim royal patronage. Its fine stone archway allows horses and coaches through to the well-equipped stables, which in 1537, once saw Henry VIII dismount in search of a bed. The innkeeper here must have been very proud, for the king had snubbed the local prior who, in his dudgeon, even wrote to Thomas Cromwell, the king's chief minister, to complain that His Majesty would not stay 'in my poor house which I have made ready to receive him', begging him to change the monarch's mind.

Given that the same priory was where the king's marriage to Catherine of Aragon was annulled in 1533 and announced by Archbishop Cranmer, thee might forgive him for being put out, especially since the king once said that he wanted to make the town a cathedral city. Maybe 'twas a sign of things to come. The priory was dissolved in 1540. The White Horse, however, survived and was still there when Queen Elizabeth visited the town in 1572. She managed to miss the dose of plague which subsequently hit the town in 1582, causing devastation.

A renowned house like the White Horse be a good destination if thee value thy steed, for the competition among inns seems to have turned some who run them into blaggards. In 1596 an innkeeper called William Bennell was brought before the courts as an accomplice of two horse stealers. We have not discovered if he owned the Nag's Head, also a well-known Dunstable inn.
Latterly: Became The Anchor and now adjoins the White Horse, 13 High Street North, Town Centre, Dunstable, Bedfordshire, LU6 1HX, tel: 01582 664702.

BEDFORD

THE GEORGE
'Commodious and convenient'
Sited near the market, this may be a noisy place but 'tis solid, being built of stone in a gothic style with a tiled roof. It hath long been one of the chief inns of the town, possessing almost a licence to mint money. In 1476 when its owner Richard Illyngworth died

and passed it to his son Ralph he was wealthy enough to own four shops in the town too. The inn features a sculpture of St George and while its architecture lends a somewhat cold and clammy disposition to the place 'tis a much more satisfying structure than some of the dilapidated properties around the town.

Latterly: Closed in 1927. The remains can be seen at the rear of Debenhams in the High Street.

THE ROSE
'A good pedigree'

Thee can always tell that an inn be good if it hath existed a long time and can show who the innkeepers were throughout its long history. This be certainly the case with The Rose on Bedford's main street, where the family atmosphere and long dedication to service make it a cosy, if not grand, place to stay, should thee find thyself in the town both thirsty and without a lodging. In 1546 the owner was one John West who left it to his wife Joan. In 1572 she passed it on to her relations Robert and Elizabeth Moorer and so to their son Richard too. We praise the idea of handing the business of drinking down through the generations.

Latterly: The Rose, 45 High Street, Bedford, Bedfordshire, MK40 1RY, tel: 01234 353749, www.therosebedford.co.uk.

THE SWAN
'A stop on the way to school'

Another good stopping place be The Swan, on the banks of the River Ouse, near the town's only bridge. The Swan hath been here since 1507 and very popular with those coming from London to inspect the excellent school for which Bedford hath become renowned. While lacemaking be important hereabouts, the town be not known as one of our great centres of trade and suffered somewhat when a newer bridge at Great Barford was built. But the town hath received many plaudits for its educational excellence and Bedford School was granted letters patent by King Edward VI being aided by Sir William Harpur, a merchant born of Bedford, who, while rising to become Lord Mayor of London, never forgot his roots.

Latterly: The Swan Hotel, The Embankment, Bedford, MK40 1RW, tel: 01234 346565, www.bedfordswanhotel.co.uk.

Other hostelries of note ...

AMPTHILL

WHITE HART INN
The best of the many old inns in the ancient town which hath been here since the ninth century. Catherine of Aragon stayed in the town's castle after her estrangement from King Henry VIII.
Latterly: The White Hart Hotel, 125 Dunstable Street, Ampthill, Beds, MK45 2NG, tel: 01525 406683, www.whitehartampthill.com.

LEIGHTON BUZZARD

SWAN INN
Edward Carvell be the innkeeper here. Be wary if trading in livestock locally as the stealing of it be rife.
Latterly: The Swan Hotel, High Street, Leighton Buzzard, Beds, LU7 1EA, tel: 01525 380170, www.jdwetherspoon.co.uk.

❧ BERKSHIRE

Berkshire be a very old county whose name was first used around AD 860. 'Twas the site of fierce battles between Alfred the Great and the Danes and hath long been important because the Great West Road betwixt London and Bristol runs through its length. At this time the county extends all the way northwards to the River Thames, taking in the towns of Wantage and Abingdon.

In the east of the county be Windsor, made famous by its castle, a royal residence since the time of William the Conqueror and popular as a place to entertain foreign dignitaries with our recent monarchs.

Berkshire's largest town be Reading, booming thanks to its cloth and leather trade and now numbering some 5,000 inhabitants, despite losing its abbey. To the west of the county Newbury and Hungerford are important towns too. As of 1577 there were 63 inns, 17 taverns and 252 alehouses in the county, so thee should never lack places to rest.

HUNGERFORD

THE BEAR
'King Henry VIII's very own hostelry'
Meaning 'hanging wood ford' in Saxon, the town of Hungerford, which currently straddles the counties of Berkshire and Wiltshire, hath been known as 'the crossroads of England' for many centuries because of its strategic position connecting routes between Oxford, Salisbury, Bristol and London. Hence the popularity of The Bear, plumped proudly in Charnham Street which serves as the Great West Road. It began life as a hospice next to the Priory of St John and was used as such in 1464. Now an inn, it gets its name from former owners, the Earls of Warwick, who had a 'Bear and Ragged Staff' on their coat of arms. Henry VIII passed the manor of Chilton Foliat, of which The Bear was a part, to five of his six wives. Only Anne Boleyn failed to own this much-beloved hostelry.

This be a shining example of what an inn in our age ought to be, thanks to the honest upright folk who have managed its day-to-day running. In 1537 the innkeeper, Robert Braybon, gave evidence in a case of highway banditry. His testimony was key to the conviction of three highwaymen who had lodged at the inn after holding up a merchant near Windsor.

Today The Bear be kept by the unimpeachable John Underwood and still hosts royalty. We are led to believe that Queen Elizabeth's retinue stayed here in 1592 during one of Her Majesty's progresses through the western counties. We imagine they were kept in great comfort but sadly one of her coachmen, a Mr Slie, died whilst here of a malady. There are surely worse places to end thy days.

Latterly: The Bear Hotel, Hungerford, 41 Charnham Street, Hungerford, Berkshire, RG17 0EL, tel: 01488 682512, www.thebearhotelhungerford.co.uk.

HURLEY

THE OLD BELL
'Cosy and curious'
Nooks and crannies in which to enjoy a restful meal or drink abound in this creaky old inn founded as far back as 1135 as a guest house and hospice for the local Benedictine Priory of St Mary. Beneath its floors, or perhaps behind a fireplace, according to some rumours, 'tis said there be a tunnel once used

The Old Bell, Hurley, Berkshire, later the Olde Bell. (© Mr James Moore)

by the monks – though, in our experience these religious types have never been too shy about seeking out alcoholic refreshment in public view.

The name of the inn must be linked to a bell once used to summon the prior when people of importance arrived seeking lodgings. And what a glorious place to enjoy a night's sleep. The quaint overhanging upper storey, beautiful oriel windows, plasterwork and timber give the inn a well-worn air but one of great solidity.

These days the old priory hath given way to a new fine mansion known as Ladye Place, built by Sir Richard Lovelace who, it's said, used the booty he had accumulated while on voyages with Sir Francis Drake to construct a building which revels in the latest architectural extravagances and fancies.

Latterly: The Olde Bell, High Street, Hurley, SL6 5LX ,
tel: 01628 825881, www.theoldebell.co.uk.

READING

THE SUN INN
'A little creepy'

The Sun Inn be a jumble of a place in the town's Castle Street which includes a Norman archway in its structure, a sign of the building's great age. No one be quite sure when this place started serving beer or taking people to rest for the night but there be a vast subterranean hall and ample stabling for horses. Those who have stayed at the inn report hearing strange chanting noises from beneath the floors.

Visitors here may well encounter royal personages who oft pass through Reading. King Henry VIII, who had the local abbot hung, drawn and quartered in 1539, was a frequent caller and the current queen be known to have made the town a gift of mulberry trees to encourage silk weaving in the area.

Latterly: The Sun Inn, 6 Castle Street, City Centre, Reading,
RG1 7RD, tel: 0118 950 0867.

SONNING

THE BULL
'A medicinal beer'

Sonning used to be a very important place and the capital of a region called Sunningum in the seventh century. In Saxon times there was an old minster here and the Bishop of Salisbury had a palace. Pilgrims came to the old church to see relics relating to St Sarik, a mysterious saint who was linked to mental frailty; 'tis known that many of the worshippers came looking to cure madness. The Bull Inn was first set up to cater for these visitors, though whether they find that the well-respected ale helped ease or befuddle their troubled minds we cannot say.

Today the palace be in the ownership of Her Majesty the Queen, who be known to have visited. The name of the inn, in fact, comes from the proud bovine creatures on the coat of arms belonging to Sir Henry Neville, of the former palace.

Latterly: The Bull Inn, High Street, Sonning-on-Thames, Berkshire, RG4 6UP, tel: 0118 969 3901, www.fullershotels.com.

Iniquitous innkeepers

Maidenhead be a trim town which grew up around a bridge carrying the Great West Road over the River Thames. But in the last century it sadly received a reputation as a place where thee might be improperly overcharged for thy lodgings. As far back as 1459 William Mordall had an inn called The Bull and was found to take 'exorbitant gain'. In 1489 Alice Buckland was accused of the same misdemeanour and in this year we also find that John Francis was found to have 'charged an unlawful price for provisions'. We are assured that things are now much changed.

❀

WINDSOR

THE MERMAID

'Beware the plague … and the gallows'

With the increasing number of visitors to the castle, including aristocracy from both England and abroad, there are now some twenty-one inns, taverns and alehouses in the town, including The Goat, The Black Eagle, The Broad Arrow and the Hartshorn, to name but a few. Many of them are owned by the town corporation itself. One of these be The Mermaid, which, though it may be only a mere 25ft wide, hath an imposing position on the main street, facing Windsor Castle. 'Twas constructed in 1528, the same year in which the castle's St George's Chapel was getting its finishing touches. Standing across from the gates of the royal edifice, it must have witnessed many regal personages coming and going and makes a fine spot for people watching. If thee had been in the vicinity in 1563 it would be as well that thee hadn't hailed from London. In this year, when plague hit the city's streets, Queen Elizabeth removed herself and her court to Windsor. She then had a gallows erected at the town's market place to hang anyone who came from the capital with a whiff about them, in fear that they might be bringing the pestilence.

Latterly: The Castle Hotel, 18 High Street, Windsor, SL4 1LJ, tel: 01753 851577, www.mercure.com.

An Excerpt from Mister Shakespeare's
The Merry Wives of Windsor

Act II Scene II: A Room in the Garter Inn
Falstaff: 'I will not lend thee a penny.'
Pistol: 'Why, then, the world's mine oyster,
Which I with sword will open.'
Falstaff: 'Not a penny.'

THE KING'S HEAD
'Brews a muse for the bard?'
William Shakespeare be understood to have stayed in this alehouse, first built in 1525, when he was writing one of his exciting new plays, *The Merry Wives of Windsor*. 'Tis a drama based upon the love life of his most humorous character Sir John Falstaff, who first appeared in his *Henry IV* plays. Queen Elizabeth was said to have loved Falstaff so much that she requested a play which centred on him as the main character and, once penned, 'twas first performed to her personally qui. The Garter Inn, where many of the scenes in the play are set, be also here, nestled below the castle nearer to the river.
Latterly: Ye Olde King's Head, 7 Church Street, Windsor, SL4 1PE, tel: 01753 206701, www.yeoldekingshead.co.uk.

Other hostelries of note ...

FYFIELD

WHITE HART
Once a chantry giving relief to the poor, this place be now an interesting alehouse with a large hall.
Latterly: The White Hart, Main Road, Fyfield, Abingdon, Oxon, OX13 5LW, tel: 01865390585, www.whitehart-fyfield.com

COOKHAM

BEL AND DRAGON
People are believed to have been raising tankards here since 1417.
Latterly: The Bel & the Dragon, High Street, Cookham, Maidenhead, SL6 9SQ, tel: 01628 521263, www.belandthedragon.co.uk.

The King's Head, Windsor, Berkshire, later Ye Olde King's Head. (© Mr James Moore)

❀ BUCKINGHAMSHIRE

Buckinghamshire be a slender county that extends from lands near the River Thames in the south, to the Chiltern Hills and to the fertile northern country beyond. It sports some prosperous towns and villages which play host to some seventy-two inns and more than 300 alehouses.

Buckingham be at the centre for the new industry of brick making and, legend hath it, that Catherine of Aragon, Henry VIII's first wife, introduced the local women to lacemaking, now also an important trade for the town. However, 'tis Aylesbury which be of more interest, if only for its excellent hostelries. In his invaluable tome *History and Antiquities of England and Wales* John Leland tells us that this town on a hill be 'neatly well builded with Tymbre, and in it be a celebrated Market.' Indeed since 1529 it hath been the county town, made so by King Henry VIII, replacing Buckingham, perhaps to please the father of his second wife, Anne, who owned much land here. The county be rich in resources, especially its great beech trees, but if thee find thyself in Aylesbury market and can afford such luxuries, buy thyself one of the fine sheep fleeces, these are sure to warm the cockles and are said to be in demand as far away as Turkey.

AMERSHAM

KING'S ARMS

'A flurry of timbers'

The chronicler John Leland described Amersham as 'a very pleasant town, with a Friday market, and a single street of good timber buildings'. The fine sweep off the wide main street also contains a number of inns as the town be an important staging post on the road between London and Aylesbury, currently a day or two's journey from the great stink of the capital.

For the loftiest travellers the three-storeyed and gabled King's Arms – named in memory of Henry VIII – hath much to recommend it including a wonderful contemporary staircase and hall, with a huge courtyard at the rear to accommodate any amount of horses, carts and baggage.

Latterly: The Kings Arms Hotel, 30 High Street, Old Amersham, Buckinghamshire, HP7 ODJ, tel: 01494 725722, www.kings-arms-hotel.com.

The King's Arms, Amersham, Buckinghamshire. (© Mr James Moore)

THE CROWN

'Pleasing for its patriotic paintings'

One of the pleasant features of this inn be its artistic merit, which includes fine wood carvings and murals. One wall painting commemorates the visit of the queen to the town and the nearby manor of Shardeloes in 1592. Set above the fireplace, it features her coat of arms along with a supporting lion and dragon with the words 'God save the queen'. Others in the lodging rooms show cartouche shields in vivid blue green and yellow with dividing bands in red.

Do not let these gracious paintings lull thee into a false sense about the town itself being a sleepy spot. It hath long been a place of fierce debate and dissent when it comes to religious matters. Many of that reforming group the Lollards were put to death for their views hereabouts only a few decades ago.

Latterly: The Crown Hotel, 16 High Street, Amersham, HP7 0DH, tel: 01494 721541, www.thecrownamersham.com.

The Crown, Amersham, Buckinghamshire. (© Mr James Moore)

AYLESBURY

THE KING'S HEAD
'Where a king wooed his queen?'

Of the two taverns, two inns and twenty-five alehouses in the town The King's Head or 'Kyngeshede' be without doubt the best. Not only be it graced with breath-taking ancient architecture but also a breadth of history and intrigue which make it an ideal place to soak up the authentic atmosphere of 'Merrie England'.

The musty cellars of The King's Head appear to date as far back as the thirteenth century and it may well have got its name from Richard II. We do know for certain that the building in its present form was here in 1455, having then been built quite recently. In this year William Wandesford, a London wool merchant with royal connections, owned the inn and later the same century another merchant, Ralph Verney, was at the helm, expanding it.

Constructed of wattle and daub as well as great timbers, there also be a fine cobbled courtyard with ample stabling. The buildings themselves include a great hall supported by huge oak posts, which also features an exquisite stained-glass window. Each of its twenty lights sports a coat of arms or an intricate design. They include the arms of Henry VI (the king when fifteenth-century improvements were made) and his wife Margaret of Anjou. The couple may well have stayed here too. The upper lights show a series of angels holding shields, winged lions and swans, a creature long associated with Buckinghamshire as 'twas here that they were bred for the king's table.

The handsome features of the inn, and particularly the Solar Room above the great hall, certainly pleased a later monarch, King Henry VIII. He, rumour tells us, trusted the place enough to stay here as he courted the unfortunate Anne Boleyn. It turned out that the charms of Anne, whose father was Lord of the Manor in Aylesbury, could not be depended on in the same way as The King's Head as the queen's head was chopped off in 1536. Who knows whether her grizzly end hath any link to the ghouls now said to lurk at the inn which include a lady dressed in grey as well as floating pint pot.

Latterly: owned by The National Trust and run as The King's Head, Kings Head Passage, Aylesbury, tel: 01296 381501, www.farmersbar.co.uk.

The King's Head, Aylesbury, Buckinghamshire. (© Mr James Moore)

COLNBROOK

THE GEORGE
'Royal gaol for a night'

This bustling village be presently in the county of Buckinghamshire and a vital stopping point on the road from London to the west, situated 17 miles from the city itself and boasting some ten inns. It sits on a branch of the River Colne which trundles lazily through a small bridge while the busy traffic hurtles overhead.

King Henry VIII stayed in a local inn called the Catherine Wheel in 1516 but his daughter Queen Elizabeth spent a more worrisome night at the George in April 1555, for at this time, in the reign of Queen Mary, she was a prisoner, following Thomas Wyatt's uprising against Mary's proposed marriage to Philip of Spain. Kept in the lodge of a decaying manor in Woodstock in Oxfordshire for a year, she was then moved to Hampton Court via Colnbrook where many gathered to see her progress back to the royal court, once she had found favour again with Queen Mary.

The name of the George be reckoned to derive from a statue of St George that was once part of the porch at the parish church in the town of Dursley in Gloucestershire. Removed by a wily clothier, 'twas dropped from his waggon while passing through on a journey from his home to London.

In 1595 the owners of the George petitioned to have stalls selling meat and other goods, which had been set up in front of the inn to cater for travellers, removed as they were a nuisance.

Latterly: Ye Old George Inn, 146 High Street, Colnbrook, Berkshire, SL3 0LX, tel: 01753 682010.

THE OSTRICH
'Murder most fowl'

Colnbrook's most ancient inn be The Ostrich, one of a handful of drinking places in England with a good claim to be the nation's oldest. 'Twas known to have been here in 1106 and was then a hospice run by Aegelward of Sutton and given by one Miles

The Ostrich, Colnbrook, Buckinghamshire, later The Old Ostrich. (© Mr James Moore)

Crispin to the Abbey of Abingdon 'for the good travellers in this world and the salvation of their souls in the next'.

'Tis a theory that its present name, The Ostrich, be a corruption of hospice, rather than that the hostelry be named after an exotic bird. Other versions used over the years have been The Ospringe, Ostridge and Oastriche. Yet, in another reference, 'tis called The Crane. The present timber and plaster building, with its projecting upper storey, dates from 1500.

Because of its position on routes connecting Windsor and London Colnbrook hath seen much royal traffic over the centuries and was a popular place to change clothes and clean up before visiting the royal court.

Indeed as far back as 1215 King John be believed to have stopped at the inn on the way to Runnymede to sign the Magna Carta and in the fourteenth century Edward III met his son, the Black Prince, here after he returned from a military campaign in France. Luckily for these famous patrons they did not suffer the fate of Thomas Cole, a clothier from Reading. A recent book of 1597, by Thomas Deloney, links his murder to a chilling string of crimes by a former innkeeper at The Ostrich, John Jarman.

Jarman and his wife had constructed a cunning contraption to steal from their guests, a tipping bed that would fire them, head first, through a trapdoor and into a 'boyling caldron'. Cole, who used The Ostrich when on business trips to London, was, on his last visit, done away with using this dastardly device. When Cole's body was later found in the river an investigation was sparked and Jarman's crimes were discovered. 'Twas then that he confessed all, admitting that he and his wife had done away with some sixty persons in this bloody manner.

Latterly: The Ostrich Inn, High Street, Colnbrook, Near Slough, Berkshire, SL3 0JZ, tel: 01753 682628, www.theostrichcolnbrook.co.uk.

STONY STRATFORD

THE COCK
'Of cock and bull stories'

Set on Watling Street, where the old Roman thoroughfare crosses the River Ouse and now a main route to the city of Chester, there have been inns in Stony Stratford for centuries with the nearby forests being another draw for royal hunting parties. In fact, there are at least nine inns and eighteen alehouses here. The Rose and Crown on the main street, for example, was where, in 1483, the 12-year-old King Edward V stayed before being captured and taken to London to be imprisoned with his brother in the Tower. 'Twas the work of their uncle who subsequently became King Richard III after allegedly having them murdered.

Other inns in Stony include: the Grilkes inn, dating to 1317; the Cross Keys, dating to 1475; and the Horseshoe, dating to 1529. There also be an inn called the Bull, dating back to the fifteenth century. A bull-baiting ring be available for entertainment at the back of another inn, The Swan, which dates to 1526.

Yet another inn, The Cock, was built at the start of the century and in 1520 given for the maintenance and repair of the town's bridges. Occupying a prominent position on the High Street, some say that this be where the origin of the phrase 'cock and bull stories' for tall tales originated. Who can say whether this be true, but 'tis certainly worth taking what the local innkeepers tell thee with a pinch of salt. For, in 1596, two were found by the courts to be harbouring stolen goods.

Latterly: The Cock Hotel, 72–74 High Street, Stony Stratford, Milton Keynes, Buckinghamshire, MK11 1AH, tel: 01908 567733, www.oldenglishinns.co.uk.

Other hostelries of note ...

BIERTON

RED LION
A good alehouse to make for if thirst gets the better of thee on the road from Aylesbury to Leighton Buzzard.
Latterly: The Red Lion, 68 Aylesbury Road, Bierton, Aylesbury, Buckinghamshire, HP22 5BU, tel: 01296 432867, www.theredlionbierton.com.

FORTY GREEN

THE SHIP INN
Forty Green be famous for making floor tiles, many of which were used in Windsor Castle. Workers making these, and merchants trading them, are customers at the inn which hath existed since 1213 and there may well have been a Saxon alehouse on the spot.
Latterly: The Royal Standard of England, Forty Green, Beaconsfield, Buckinghamshire, HP9 1XT, tel: 01494 673382, www.rsoe.co.uk.

WENDOVER

THE GEORGE AND DRAGON
In 1577 Wendover be noted as having one tavern and eight inns. One of the latest, with every modern convenience, be The George and Dragon, dating to 1578.

Latterly: The George and Dragon, 4-6 Aylesbury Road, Wendover, HP22 6JQ, tel: 01296 586152, www.georgeanddragonwendover.com.

❧ CAMBRIDGESHIRE

The county be chiefly known for the university town of Cambridge. This seat of learning hath been famous for its colleges since the 1200s, but perhaps its finest sight be King's College chapel, completed in the reign of King Henry VIII. 'Twas at this college that Queen Elizabeth stayed upon her visit to the town of scholars in 1564, when the streets were lined with people cheering *Vivat Regina!* The streets themselves had been covered with sand to ease her passage and huge stocks of beer were brought in as well as sugar loaves, handed to Her Majesty's leading courtiers. A silver cup was presented to the queen who was also regaled with performances of the latest plays.

As elsewhere there are local terms for being the worse for wear. If a man be drunk in Cambridge he be said to have 'business on both sides of the street'.

Much of the country be fenland, which the writer William Camden says resembles an 'inland sea' in winter, and there be much fishing and collecting of thatch for roofs. The great cathedral at Ely must be seen by all admirers of architecture if they have the patience to make their way through the boggy landscape that surrounds that seat of holiness.

Outside Cambridge there are few inns and even alehouses are not as common with only 189 recently recorded in the whole county. We wonder at why this may be when the flatness of the land can induce boredom, though, as a seemingly godless place, the local popularity of puritanical beliefs may be the answer to this dearth of drinking dens. If thee do find one, the beer be good. Don't forget to taste the butter too; it melts deliciously on the tongue in these parts.

CAMBRIDGE

EAGLE AND CHILD
'Where Marlowe surely supped'
The Eagle and Child be an ancient inn that may once have been a pilgrim's hostel. One observer puts its date as far back as 1353, when beer was said to cost three gallons to the penny. Today the inn be owned by Corpus Christi College, which we think a handy way to make money out of the scholarly love for a tipple. On 26 March 1566 a new building to house the inn was erected with a forty-year lease at an annual rent of £3 6s 8d. There be a great gallery along the Eagle's first floor which allows plays to be acted out below. Some suggest that William Shakespeare hath performed here himself, but this may be mere hearsay. But we are more forcefully assured that the playwright Christopher Marlowe, who rose from the son of a humble shoemaker to be one of the land's finest dramatists and who won a scholarship to Corpus Christi in 1580, drank here. The beer no doubt fuelled his vivid imagination, for 'twas while at his rooms in the nearby seat of learning that he penned that fine work, *Tamburlaine the Great*.
Latterly: The Eagle, 8 Bene't Street, Cambridge, CB2 3QN, tel: 01223 505020.

WHITE HORSE
'A hotbed of dissent'
During the early part of this last century this was no ordinary wayside inn but a hotbed of religious dissent and theological musing. In 1517 Martin Luther nailed his ninety-five theses to the church door in Wittenburg, Germany and from the year 1521 some of the most famous of those who wanted to reform England's old Church in a similar vein met in this humble venue – known to exist before 1500 – to mull over the future of the Church while imbibing ale and wine. The inn became so infamous for this reformist chatter that 'twas dubbed Little Germany and those who led the theorising were known as 'Germans'. They included the future Archbishop of Canterbury, Thomas

Cranmer, and Hugh Latimer. The pair were later burned for their beliefs in the reign of Queen Mary. William Tyndale, famous for translating the Bible into English, also drank and debated here. He too would perish, burned at the stake in 1536, as were many more of the bold imbibers at the White Horse.

Note that before his ascent of the Church hierarchy, in 1515, Thomas Cranmer married Joan, the niece of the innkeeper at the nearby Dolphin Inn, which led to him being expelled as fellow of the university's Jesus College. When Joan died, in childbirth, in 1519, Cranmer was reinstated. Bad luck for both we feel.

Latterly: A blue plaque in Chetwynd Court King's College marks the spot where the inn once stood, at the Bridge Street end of All Saints' Passage.

A round up of Cambridge inns

Thanks to the men of learning and their students, Cambridge be teeming with inns. Whether the vast quantities of wine and ale consumed – oft in more than one location during an evening – ferment great thoughts be yet unknown to science but there are certainly many more grand places than already mentioned in which to conduct the experiment. These include the Antelope, Black Bull, Black Swan, Brazen George, Boar's Head, Cock, Falcon, Crane, Lion, Lilypot, Griffyn, Vine, Unicorn, Sun and Star.

❀

WHITTLESFORD BRIDGE

WHITE LION
'Of drovers and highwaymen'
This may seem a somewhat lonely spot now, but an ancient route, the Icknield Way, passed through here and it be still much used as a trading route for drovers taking sheep and cattle to market and for merchants making their way between the towns of Royston and Newmarket. In the latter, there are now horse races

to be seen. The innkeeper at the White Lion oft rents land to the drovers, though it would be amiss of us not to note that some who have kept the inn are rumoured to have been in league with the notorious highwaymen of Newmarket Heath. Thankfully the new ownership can be trusted.

The inn itself owes its existence to a bridge across the River Cam and was once part of the Hospital of St John, which catered for beleaguered travellers. The inn now prospers, providing beds for servants of the Crown and boasting great carved beams. Indeed, one keeper here left the huge sum of £150 to his sons in 1588. In these difficult times for Church men the hospital chapel hath fallen into great disrepair and be now, we understand, in use as a barn.

Latterly: The Red Lion, Station Road East, Whittlesford Bridge, Cambridge, CB22 4NL, tel: 01223 832047, www.redlionwhittlesfordbridge.com.

Other hostelries of note ...

FOWLMERE

THE CHEQUERS
A good resting place – in both senses. It hath long doubled as a place to stop with coffins being transported between London and Cambridge.

Latterly: The Chequers, Fowlmere, Hertfordshire, SG8 7SR, tel: 01763 208369, www.thechequersfowlmere.co.uk.

ELY

THE LAMB
Once known as the Holy Lambe, the inn was mentioned by Bishop Fordham in 1416 and provides a great spot for repose to those interested in the city's great cathedral or making their way to the port town of King's Lynn.

Latterly: The Lamb Hotel, 2 Lynn Road, Ely, Cambridgeshire, CB7 4EJ, tel: 01353 663574, www.thelamb-ely.com.

✾ CHESHIRE

This fair county, situated in the north-west of the realm, possesses people of good heart and bravery, for they stand ready to fight in the queen's name against the revolters of Ireland over the water.

The boom of babies in the 1580s hath made Chester grow to a population of some 7,000 and there be much trade in wine and leather, seemingly undented by many visitations of the plague. At Chester's fair, fine horses change hands, with customers coming from as far as Yorkshire, though mostly they cross the border from Wales. Catering be also well respected here and the inns and taverns provide good food, including a cheese, first made famous to the rest of the nation by one Thomas Muffet in the digestive remedies outlined in his work *Health's Improvement*. Beware flying dough in the streets, however; the city's bakers have of late protested that innkeepers do bake their own bread so ruining their trade.

The number of inns, alehouses and taverns in Cheshire hath grown much in the past decades and Chester alone hath a tidy forty-four inns, with its street known as The Row being a haven for drinkers, sporting, as it does, an inn, alehouse or tavern every few steps. In the county at large the distance between good inns remains far. This some may find surprising as the Company of Innkeepers, Victuallers and Cooks locally be thought ancient when the guild was incorporated in 1583. Only alehouses and tippling houses be plentiful, with more than 400 recorded in the villages.

The brewer in hell

Most famous across this county are the Mystery Plays of Chester based on biblical stories banned as Popery by Her Majesty Queen Elizabeth, though still performed surreptitiously nonetheless. In these works the brewer be much maligned; while Christ in his mercy redeemeth the sinners from hell, the brewer be sent to eternal damnation after he confesses:

> Some time I was a tavener,
> A gentle gossip and a tapster,
> Of wine and ale a trusty brewer,
> Which woe hath me bewrought,
> Of cans I kept no true measure,
> My cups I sold at my pleasure,
> Deceiving many a creature,
> Tho' my ale were nought.

Strange then, we observe, that in 1568, when there was a performance of the plays in the city, that the clergy at the cathedral paid for not just the stage but for the beer too.

❀

CHESTER

THE SWAN
'Beer maketh the boy'

Drink hath been available at a house here since the time of the monasteries, although whether this be from an inn or just a sideline of the monks of the estate of the Fraternity of St Anne on which The Swan now stands, be not known. After the Dissolution, the house became an inn but its religious links continued, for 'twas purchased in 1557 by the prebendary of Lincoln, John Deane, later a knight of the realm, who was also rector of St Bartholomew the Great in Smithfield, London. Mister Deane, a

good man, wished to build a free grammar school in Witton, near Northwich, in the county, to save souls and educate the minds of the local youths. He decided the best way to raise the money was to invest in an inn and make money from selling beer so that the young would then feel the benefit. Rents, profits and issues of the house are still paid to the school. Some folk are shocked that good little children are educated on the profits from the evil of drink, but others say that such charity shows how the bottle can truly be thy friend. The Swan be the priciest place on the Row, with a character to match; elegant, refined and full of people who drink much and say that they only partake to help the next generation.
Latterly: The Row be now Foregate Street, Chester.

THE SARACEN'S HEAD
'A dilapidated sight'

Opposite The Swan and purchased by Sir John Deane at the same time be The Saracen's Head, an inn that offers the same kind of fayre of The Swan, but of baser ingredients with prices to match. Though 'tis not of the quality of The Swan, The Saracen's Head be of some fame, its mark being the Warburton crest, a symbol from the Crusades.

The Mayor of Chester, John Hankey, was innkeeper here in the 1570s and he invested much in making it a place of welcome. As mayor, he did not have to heed much the ale laws, only under threat of arresting himself, and this makes The Saracen's Head more popular than the stuffy Swan. Having served as sheriff for more than fifteen years, constables were known to turn a blind eye to the misdemeanours conducted in the place and they themselves can oft be seen drinking here.

Of late the inn be in an ill state of repair. Indeed, one of its rooms, Coventry Chamber, recently fell down.
Latterly: Now 41–45 Foregate Street, Chester.

The prohibition of women of a certain age

An order of the Mayor of Chester in 1540 during the reign of Henry VIII read:

Whereas all the taverns and alehouses of this city be used to be kept by young women otherwise than be used by any other place of this realm. To eschew wantoness, brawls, frays and other inconveniences as thereby doth and may arise among youth and lightly disposed persons, as also damages to their masters, owners of the taverns and alehouses. Ordered: that after 9th June next, no tavern or alehouse be kept in the said city by any woman between fourteen and forty years of age, under pain of forty pounds forfeiture for him or her that keepeth any such servant.

Since 1581 the law hath gone further, forbidding all women, be they wife, widow or maid, to run a hostelry here.

CONGLETON

LION AND SWAN
'Erotic carvings and things that go bump'

A place of rest, good food, excellent drink and fine company for more than a hundred years, albeit that some of the company may already be dead.

Admire the impressive central fireplace, much adorned with intricate carvings, ornate decorations and unusual impressions, some demonic, others suggestive of the flesh. At night, the spirit of a young girl, naked as a new-born except for her clogs, tends the fire. She, 'tis believed, lived in the time of the Plantagenet kings, and took a potion to hasten the conception of a child, but it did nothing but choke her.

Though the inn be the place of a warm welcome, take care in the night to avoid the room at the topmost part of the building which turns cold when the spirit of a lady, or possibly a hound, bangs and scratches, making much commotion. Lodging at the Lion be not for those faint of heart, but for those with courage, the beer be good.

Latterly: The Lion and Swan, 1 Swan Bank, Congleton, Cheshire, CW12 1AL, tel: 01260 273115, www.lionandswan.co.uk.

NANTWICH

THE CROWNE
'Fiery brewers'

Boiling beer in order to achieve a goodly brew can be a dangerous business as one Nicholas Browne discovered in the December of 1583. The foolish fellow's brewing in the middle of the night started a fire in the high street of this proud market town. The ensuing blaze went on to destroy some 600 buildings. One of these was The Crowne, the finest of seven inns to be razed to the ground, much to the chagrin of the innkeeper Robert Crockett.

The good news for travellers upon the road between London and Chester be that the inn hath been reinstated to its former glory upon the same site which be notable as a former salt working, the substance on which Nantwich's fortunes were built of old. The new inn be of three storeys with a beautiful series of mullioned windows in oak and heavy carved corbels. The cost of rebuilding the inn hath been a hefty £313, 13s, 4d, most of it from the coffers of Crockett himself, who must surely have been keen to return the inn as quickly as possible to its prosperous business.

Our present queen did her part to contribute to the rebuilding of the town by donating timbers from the Royal Forest of Delamare.

Latterly: The Crown Hotel, High Street, Nantwich, Cheshire, CW5 5AS, www.crownhotelnantwich.com.

The Crown, Nantwich, Cheshire. (Courtesy of Phillip Martin at The Crown Hotel, Nantwich)

Other hostelries of note ...

CHESTER

THE PIED BULL INN

A hostelry since the Dissolution, when 'twas owned by Mr Richard Sneyd and known as Bull Mansion. The building hath a fine modern staircase. Many in Chester remember its glory days when Grimsditch, of the famed Cheshire family, was landlord in the 1570s. Adequate accommodation for horses and even coaches be provided, but the Bull be smaller, and less expensive, than the nearby Kings Head. If money be very stretched, the Red Lion tavern at the northern end of King Street, be cheaper still.
Latterly: The Pied Bull Inn, 57 Northgate Street, Chester, CH1 2HQ, tel: 01244 325829, www.piedbull.co.uk.

KNUTSFORD

THE WARREN DE TABLEY ARMS

Once a house for priests, this hath been an inn since the 1560s.
Latterly: The Bells of Peover, The Cobbles, Lower Peover, Knutsford, WA16 9PZ, tel: 01565 722269, thebellsofpeover.com.

❀ CORNWALL

'The ayre thereof be cleansed, as with bellowes, by the billowes, and flowing and ebbing of the Sea,' says Richard Carew in his soon-to-be published *Survey of Cornwall*. And the traveller would be wise to carry that writer's trusty tome if he trudges to this far flung part of the realm. Despite its airs, one should be wary of the Cornish people if thy be an outsider. They oft treat other English peoples as foreigners in their own land, even though this county be appointed a Duchy in 1337 by Edward III to provide for the

Raleigh much scorned in Cornish parts

Sir Walter Raleigh, a fine Devonian man of intuition, ability and intellect, be surely in no way deserving of the opprobrium poured upon him by those who dislike him in Cornwall. We leave it to those who know better whether his head should be severed from its body following the queen's former favourite's secret marriage that Her Majesty knew nothing about. For herself, the queen hath been so generous to this good knight conferring the title of Lord Lieutenant of Cornwall, though this hath peeved the Cornish, as evidenced by this ballad which we set down here for the purposes of the record only ...

> Ralegh doth time bestride,
> He sits twixt wind and tide,
> Yet uphill he cannot ride
> For all his bloody pride;
> He seeks taxes in the tin,
> He polls the poor to the skin,
> Yet he swears 'tis no sin,
> Lord for they pity.

❁

heir of the Crown and since then hath created most excellent Dukes of Cornwall.

As recently as 1549 the locals rose up violently against the introduction of the *Book of Common Prayer*. Innkeepers and their patrons oft speak in strange tongue, something betwixt Celtic and Breton. However, while he be treated with suspicion, the 'grockelith', as the visitor be known in this strange land, brings many groats into this far away county, more than 250 miles from London.

Our lamented King Henry VIII ordered castles to be constructed around this exposed peninsular. Those at Pendennis and St Mawes, on each side of the entrance to the Fal estuary, form part of the defences against the hated Catholic invaders, though any Frenchman, Spaniard or other follower of Rome then be at the mercy of the merciless Cornishmen, who are known to be excellent mariners, pirates and good wrestlers. Indeed, Cornish wrestlers have been sent to perform at court, although as Thomas Cromwell reported: 'their English be not perfect'.

Beds at the rare number of inns in this county have been in much demand from an invasion of workers from the German lands, brought to England specially to work in the tin mines, for they have clever trickery they call 'technological advances'.

Even Cornish people complain about the scant hospitality offered by the inns and taverns, with only a couple of score found across this vast county stretching from the Tamar to the tip of Land's End.

PENZANCE

THE DOLPHIN INN
'Where men were roused against the Armada'
After the last major outbreak of plague at this 'holy headland' town in 1578, near the tip of England, business was brisk for The Dolphin Inn. But after the infamous Spanish invasion of 1595, when wicked foreigners with evil Catholicism in their hearts reached the land their brothers of the Armada had much coveted, times have been harder. Yet while Penzance suffered much burning and attack by a force of 200 pikemen and musketmen, The Dolphin stood tall throughout, testimony that England will resist invasion.

Though some dismiss him as a base pirate, Sir John Hawkins, kind cousin of Sir Francis Drake, bedded here and commanded the Cornish fleet against the 1588 Armada, enjoying the good food and sea air that be a mark of his great Cornish inn. Here sailors were briefed before the failed Spanish invasion.

Today sailors and locals rub shoulders and enjoy a pipe, for the inn claims the very first tobacco pipe smoked by Sir Walter Raleigh.

Such be the esteem in which this inn be held that it hath been used as a local courtroom too.

Latterly: The Dolphin Tavern, Quay Street, Penzance, Cornwall, TR18 4BD, tel: 01736 364106, www.dolphintavern.co.uk.

Cornish stewed oysters

Cornwall be an excellent place for oyster-eating but be warned that in the shellfish lie dangers. Make sure thy innkeeper hath prepared them carefully for thy health be important. Here be an old recipe:

Straine the liqour from the oysters and wash them very clean and put them into a pipkin with the liqour: a pinte of wine to a quart of oysters; two or three onions, large mac, pepper, ginger and all these spices must be whole. Thy must add salt, vinegar, butter and sweet herbs and stew all these together. Some of the liquor must be taken out and put to it a quarter of butter, a lemmond mince and beaten up thick, setting it on fire, but not boiling. After the oysters hath dreined from the liquor, they should be dished and the sauce poured over and the dish garnished with ginger, lemmon, orange, barberries or grapes scaled.

❧

LOOE

JOLLY SAILOR
'Haunt of old soaks'
Local talk says that the alehouse here hath been around since 1516. Its name be surely due, at least in part, to the fact that seafarers may bring their vessel right up to the entrance, where mooring be plentiful, although the owners take no responsibility for those forced to abandon ship if caught on one of the hazardous rocks hereabout. Contraband be smuggled onto Looe Island and the innkeepers turn a blind eye to those in possession of stolen goods, although the authorities at the new Guildhall have been keeping a close watch, of late, on those who withhold taxes from Her Majesty. Undercover officers from the Customs drink here. Patrons who partake of one ale too many and are thus unable to

take sail of their vessel responsibly can access West and East Looe easily via the bridge over the river. It hath fourteen arches and hath been straddling the water here since 1411. Such a watery location makes the inn big on food from the sea. Try the turbot.
Latterly: Ye Olde Jolly Sailor Inn, Princes Square, West Looe, PL13 2EP, tel: 01503 263387, www.jollysailorlooe.co.uk.

Other hostelries of note ...

ST IVES

SLOOP INN
If they be a lover of fresh fish then the low oak-beams in the cosy rooms of this lovely harbour-side inn be worth seeking out. It excels in the cooking of pilchards.
Latterly: Sloop Inn, Back Lane, St Ives, TR26 1LP, tel: 01736 796584, www.sloop-inn.co.uk.

HELSTON

BLUE ANCHOR
Once a monk's rest house famous for its honey-based mead, this alehouse now brews the sweetest ales of its own.
Latterly: Blue Anchor, 50 Coinagehall Street, Helston, TR13 8EL, tel: 01326 562821, www.spingoales.com.

❀ CUMBERLAND

Hilly and remote, Cumberland be hostile, with the Scotsman close by, eager to invade and primed to attack. Only the inns be welcoming, and 'tis fearful that too few of them exist. Of big towns, there be but Carlisle, steeped in history, its castle its protector, its market a diversion, its people true English. Much hath they suffered of the plague which visited two years past. Yet the men and women of Carlisle be resilient, a characteristic borne out of their hostile location, and even in the face of the pestilence their numbers have risen; with 2,500 inhabitants, 'tis now a major city of the north. Admire here the Guildhall, bequeathed by Richard of Redeness, where the guilds of merchants, skinners, tanners, butchers, shoemakers, smiths, tailors and weavers conduct their administration. Carlisle's inns and taverns be sparse, but much frequented on horseracing days for which the city be renowned. A sport more popular than jousting, wagers be given and taken and much money changes hands if fancied beasts win the silver bell.

Though the Cumberland soil be fertile, life here be hard, much dependent on the sheep, which may be rustled by Reivers who live on the border, even though they may hang for their crimes. For those in the west, the fruits of the sea stave the hunger too. Industry be nascent in the mines, of salt, copper and silver and for this people be thankful and, subsequently, thirsty. Germans venture here to vex the native man of Cumberland with a condescending manner when advice they proffer about manufacturing and extraction. A mine called Goldscape on the Hindscarth hills sadly holds no gold, though many have looked. Only lead and silver hath it spewed and for this the Germans be responsible, under license of the Mines Royal Charter dated 1561. Keswick be a centre for the Germans to find board and lodging and for this the innkeepers are most grateful.

At Crosscanonby, minerals extracted from the sea are worked in the salt pans, saline success that hath led to much employment and means that meat survives longer and sailors may sail further.

KESWICK

THE GEORGE AND DRAGON
'Counting house for miners'
Known as the Bunch of Grapes and now The George and Dragon, this new venture hath doubled as a place to get a drink and for

those German miners of whom we spoke in our introduction to this county, to pay the dues on their silver to the queen's officers.

Something called graphite hath also been mined near here and be much discussed in the inn as a new source of wealth. Locals say 'tis very useful for marking sheep, others that it might in time be used to write on parchment, to which we, with our trusty quill pen, do scoff.

Latterly: The George Hotel, St John's Street, Keswick, Cumbria, CA12 5AZ, tel: 01768 72076, www.georgehotelkeswick.co.uk.

LOWESWATER

KIRKSTILE INN
'Shelter from the weather'
Shelter from the relentless rain at this fine inn where thee can enjoy thy days fishing in the nearby lakes of Loweswater or Crummockwater, or walking in the hill of Melbreak beyond. When the sun doth shine, admire the beauty of the area from the peaks. Constructed from sturdy Cumberland slate, the thick walls keep out the cold in winter and provide coolness in summer, conditioning the air so that all be well.

Latterly: Kirkstile Inn, Cockermouth, Loweswater, Cumbria, CA13 0RU, tel: 01900 85219, www. kirkstile.com.

❀ DERBYSHIRE

Come to Derbyshire 'well-cloathed' was the advice of renowned physician John Jones to those travelling to this county from balmier places. With high-peak country to the north, much of the region be put down to grazing sheep and there be now some coal working too. Curiously, despite its remoteness, Derbyshire be also home to a number of wealthy families and can boast some of the finest and grandest houses in England such as Chatsworth, Hardwick and Haddon Halls. Those that inhabit these piles do better than many unfortunates that live in the county where 'perished of colde on ye moore' be not an uncommon description of death to be found in the parish registers.

The main town be Derby, a town of a few thousand souls. Another attraction be the healing bath and well at Buxton, which Dr Jones tells us 'hath for many years past been frequented for the health of thousands'. No English monarch themselves hath visited Derbyshire these 100 years but the fame of Buxton be well known. In 1577 Queen Elizabeth advised her favourite, the Earl of Leicester, to take as much of its waters as he could, but just one twentieth of a pint of wine, to help ease his stomach problems.

'Tis a superstitious county where people believe, for instance, that Peak Cavern near Castleton be the gateway to hell. Many probably believe that the 726 alehouses, taverns and inns reported as existing in 1577 are better candidates for this title.

BUXTON

NEW HALL OR THE TALBOT
'Where Mary, the Scottish queen, took the waters'
The Romans made for the waters of Buxton to cure them of ill health and there hath been an inn here, catering for those with ailments for many years. It used to be called the Auld Hall but the present inn was improved with the sanction of Queen Elizabeth to house Mary, Queen of Scots. Although a prisoner, her gracious majesty didn't wish Mary to be in distress (until ordering her death of course) and so while being encased in a variety of houses in the region under the control of the Earl of Shrewsbury, she was allowed to visit the town in 1573 to ease her rheumatic pains.

She stayed at the restored inn, now renamed the New Hall or the Talbot and 'twas here that Mary scratched a poem of farewell to Buxton with a diamond ring on one of the bedroom window panes which read: 'Buxton, whose warm waters have made thy name famous, perchance I shall visit thee no more – Farewell.'

Given that Mary, even while hostage, needed many staff and thirty carts to transport her things from house to house during those years 'tis not improbable that the retinue took up the entire property. But other nobility hath called in, including the Earl of Leicester and Lord Burghley.

Latterly: The Old Hall Hotel, The Square, Buxton, Derbyshire, SK17 6BD, tel: 01298 22841, oldhallhotelbuxton.co.uk.

The palace built with ale

Four-times married Bess of Hardwick – a formidable woman – be said to be the second richest woman in England, beaten only by the queen herself. Her vast wealth be certainly proven in the construction, first of Chatsworth and then of Hardwick Hall, a magnificent mansion which features a grand winding staircase, soaring windows and be filled with the finest furniture and tapestries. During the building of the magnificent house ale was even boiled and mixed with the mortar in an attempt to stop it freezing during cold periods, without much success. Beer hath nevertheless been vital to the structure, as Bess built a special alehouse for her builders on site.

❀

DERBY

THE DOLPHIN
'Fishy goings on'

The first record of a hostelry in the town comes to us from the thirteenth century, when one 'William the Innkeeper' be recorded. Some believe he may have supplied the monks of Darley Abbey.

Today, The Dolphin, a fine half-timbered building dating from 1530, serves as the best inn in the town. It stands by the great church of All Saints, whose grand tower was built at the same time.

Near this spot, in 1556, a blind woman called Joan Waste was burned for heresy after refusing to renounce her Protestant faith. No doubt many who had witnessed the horror imbibed beneath the great beams of The Dolphin to still their nerves or celebrate, depending on their religious leanings.

The name of the inn may be linked to local fishmongers, as dolphins are seen as a friend to fishermen. Many believe something fishy be afoot within the inn's walls as the hostelry boasts a number of ghouls, including the ghost of a small girl who hath been seen sitting upon the stairs.

Latterly: Ye Olde Dolphin Inne, Queen Street, Derby, DE1 3DL, tel: 01332 267711.

Other hostelries of note ...

DRONFIELD

THE GREEN DRAGON
Once the meeting place for a religious guild celebrating the pureness of Jesus' mother, today this place whets the appetite of those who come seeking a fortune in the new black gold, with many a coal working nearby.

Latterly: The Green Dragon, Church Street, Dronfield, Derbyshire, S18 1QB, tel: 01246 415450.

HURDLOW

THE BULL
Beside an old Roman road from Derby to Buxton there be a comforting inn which was once a farmhouse but, to aid passing travellers and supply them with quenching ale, became an alehouse as far back as 1472. Its panelled rooms and stone flagged floor a welcome respite for those ploughing along the highway. There be also an interesting oak carving of a bull entangled in a thorn bush.

Latterly: The Bull I' Th' Thorn, Ashbourne Road, Hurdlow, Near Buxton, Derbyshire, SK17 9QQ, tel: 01298 83348, www.bulliththorn.com.

❊ DEVONSHIRE

As the only county in England to boast two coasts, one to the north, one to the south, Devonshire be a doubly dangerous place when it comes to fending off foreign invaders. But as our Spanish enemies have discovered to their peril, our gracious majesty's good knights Sir Francis Drake, born in the county's town of Tavistock, and Sir Walter Raleigh, coming from East Budleigh, hath made most excellent use of the seas in defeating the Spanish Armada of 1588 which threatened Merrie England with invasion. The loyalty of these good servants be commended, not least as they hail from a county that within living memory much resisted the instructions of our lamented King Henry VIII to burn the monasteries, our later Queen Mary to burn the priests and Edward VI to enforce the Protestant prayer book. Tankards be still secretly raised to the Devonshire brave who gave their lives in rising against the king in the 1549 Siege of Exeter, though there be danger in acquainting with those that do.

There be money to be made in Devonshire, from the building of ships and the blowing of tin, though this sadly be heavily taxed. Visitors will find that the coinage payable on tin causes debate in the taverns around the mining towns circling Dartmoor, an inhospitable wilderness to which only the foolhardy venture.

About 500 tons of wine were imported into Exeter's ports, which encompass Dartmouth and Barnstaple, last year. Plymouth hath been much expanding since Her Majesty came to the throne; today nearly 4,000 people live here and it achieved fame as the place where Drake calmly finished his game of bowls after hearing that the Spanish Armada had been sighted.

Exeter's population hath been static throughout, but it remains double the size of Plymouth and now boasts England's first canal. At 3ft wide, 16ft deep, the Exeter Ship Canal hath opened the city to world trade again, after the Countess of Devonshire blocked the River Exe for mills in the thirteenth century.

Drinkers are well serviced in Devonshire with 120 inns, 40 taverns and 400 alehouses across the county. Devon's cider be much commended and be oft a higher quality than the beer.

CHAGFORD

THREE CROWNS INN
'A place with mettle'
This newly opened inn hath quickly developed a deserved reputation for excellent ales and ciders and good honest food. The building, a fine example of Chagford's architectural individuality, dates, in part, back 300 years and until recently was the family seat of the Whyddons, prosperous people of these parts for many centuries.

Fondly remembered latterly be Sir John Whyddon's exacting work as a Justice of the King's Bench under the latter Henry Tudor and Edward Tudor, and the attention to detail he insisted upon when levying fines or ordering whippings. This inn displays mementoes of the Whyddon lineage and occupation. Admire a noose here or a pillory there as thee choose from a range of hearty savoury fare or puddings.

Whilst it possesses a number of fine bedrooms, some with views of the magnificent church not two steps away, most patrons are locals, quenching their thirsts after – and sometimes before and during – work at one of the many knocking and blowing mills serving the tin industry. 'Tis said that Chagford tin be a lesser metal than the other Devonshire towns. Drinkers at the Three Crowns though do emphasise that their tin be the best in the west. Shortcomings instead be due to extra work of extraction that mixes tin with impurities and is not related to the inattention caused by workers frequenting the Crowns. The opening of the inn and the decline of Chagford as a tin town is said to be entirely coincidental, for tin here be all but exhausted by the workers' efforts and they now turn their endeavours to spinning wool, which also causes much thirst.

Latterly: Three Crowns, High Street, Chagford, Devon, TQ13 8AJ, tel: 01647 433444, www.threecrowns-chagford.co.uk.

HARBERTON

CHURCH HOUSE INN
'God given ales'

As the name gives away, this inn be originally built to house masons working on Harberton's church and hath been welcoming guests for more than 200 years. Although nearby St Andrew's hath provided comfort to good Christian people since 1104, the present inn did not open until the fourteenth century.

After the workers, came the monks, taking advantage of the great hall for their communal meals and for sleep, the workshops and chapel. The Dissolution may have been bad for the monks, but for villagers in need of an ale, the coming of Henry's new church be a blessing. Built of stone and Devonshire cob, the main rooms consist of the great hall, where the monks ate and slept, and a chapel and a workshop. The stained glass in the inner windows be 200 years old or more and, though we not be ones to criticise the wise decisions of our majesty's gracious father, that it survives be a miracle. That then the clergyman, being unemployed, put the building to profitable use by brewing and selling church ale commends the Church House Inn to travellers. Dartmoor shepherds and tin workers occasionally drink here too. Pop into the accompanying church as it hath one of the finest stone pulpits in the country.

Latterly: Church House Inn, Harberton, Totnes, Devon, TQ9 7SF, tel: 01803 863707, www.churchhouseharberton.co.uk.

EXETER

BEAR INN
'Of good business and brews'

Finer than the New Inn on the High Street, the Bear Inn be a bear of a place, the biggest in the city bar its less salubrious rival. Its span be testimony to the work of the Tavistock abbots who insisted on spacious accommodation, no doubt jealous of their cathedral neighbours. Located at the new gates of Exeter Cathedral, this be no priest-ridden hovel. Many will remember its last innkeeper, Edward Brygeman, the warden of Exe Bridge and his attractive wife Jane, who ran the inn from 1538 for nigh on sixty years and who built a reputation for alcoholic excellence.

Though the Brygemans have now sadly gone to the great kegs in the sky, its mix of central location, excellent beer, accommodation and good cooking continue. The inn's proximity to the market makes it a place where much business be done and many hundreds of pounds changes hands on a Friday.

Built of Devonshire freestone and, like the cathedral, designed in the gothic style and decorated with fretwork panels, the inside be more homely than one may think from the grey exterior. In honour of the great bear-baiters of the county, Mister Brygeman commissioned a statue in the form of the countenance of a European brown bear, ferocious in demeanour, which sits in one corner, the snatched staff of a hapless baiter in its paws.

Latterly: The site of the Catholic Church of the Sacred Heart, South Street, Exeter.

THE SHIP
'A favourite of Drake'

'Next to my own shippe I do most love that old shippe in Exon, a tavern in Fyshe Street, as the people call it, or as the clergy will have it, St Martin's Lane … there yester'en I had some speech with a mariner fresh come hither from Plymouth. The power of Spain be already afloat, so in the morning, please God, I am for Plymouth and for another shippe than this.'

So wrote Sir Francis Drake in a letter about this small but comforting inn, though rumour hath it he once left for another reason, being ejected for taking too much liquor. Among those reckoned to be The Ship's other prestigious customers are the explorers Richard Grenville and Sir Humphrey Gilbert, famed for their expeditions in the new world. Admiral Sir John Hawkins, formerly controller of the Royal Navy, supped here while studying his charts and Sir Walter Raleigh was also believed to have drunk here in his youth.

Many still toast the much-missed Drake at this spot with a draught from their tankard. For he be now gone, perishing off the coast of Panama in 1596 and lies there at the bottom of the ocean, encased in lead.

Latterly: The Ship Inn, 1–3 Martins Lane, Exeter, EX1 1EY, tel: 01392 272040, www.gkpubs.co.uk.

SOUTH ZEAL

OXENHAM ARMS
'Ancient bones and battling privateers'
This noble building, with stone porch, mullions and stabling aplenty, welcomes travellers between Exeter and Okehampton. Since its acquisition by the Burgoyne family at the Dissolution it hath passed to the Oxenhams who have built a thriving business in this, a former canonry dating back to the twelfth century. John Oxenham was the first English captain to sail that most mysterious of waters, the Pacific Ocean, but was sadly captured by the Spanish and executed in Peru in the year 1580.

Admire the magnificent megalith nearby, established here by mysterious forces as long ago as 3000 BC. Deep-rooted, spiritual and symbolic of this location on the edge of the feared and loved Dartmoor, pilgrims once came as much to admire this fine stone as they do to sample the fine ales. Other lesser stones adorn this inn and its grounds too. Fear not the spirits of thy forefathers buried 'neath thy feet. A burial place this may once have been, but the dead and the dead drunk are as one in believing this place to be a worthy watering hole.

Latterly: The Oxenham Arms, Oxenham Arms, Okehampton, Devon, EX20 2JT, tel: 01837 840244, www.theoxenhamarms.co.uk.

TOPSHAM

BRIDGE INN
'To sup secretly of Spanish wine'
Topsham holds a special place in the heart of Devonshire drinkers. Not only be it flush with inns, taverns and alehouses

for a town so small, 'tis the place where the hated Lord Henry Courtenay was captured and executed for conspiracy against the Crown in 1538. His beheading and the confiscation of his land around Topsham allowed Exeter to open nearby Countess Weir for navigation. This last year, coal was imported into Topsham for the first time and be now fuelling the paper mills and foundries. Being on the Clyst, the Bridge Inn be a ride from the Exe, but be nonetheless a perfect place for traders to rest on their way to the city. A visit to the Bridge be worth a boat ride, especially if thee be smuggling, for the inn's secret passages go down to the river, as do those of other Topsham hostelries.

Made of traditional Devon red sandstone, with a malthouse of cob, its small rooms provide a cosy feel and make it harder for Her Majesty's spies to overhear suspicious conversation – though the Bridge's secret cupboards and double walls be unlikely to survive as the authorities clamp down. The beer at the Bridge be so good it supplies other inns in Topsham.

That Her Majesty hath granted a charter allowing the merchants of Exeter to import French wines and fruit hath done much for Topsham. Contrary to fears that the city would overcome the town, making Topsham nought but a suburb of Exeter, trade hath thrived. The Bridge excels in French wine whilst the occasional Spanish wine be said to be available under the counter.

Latterly: The Bridge Inn, Topsham, Exeter, Devon, EX3 0QQ, tel: 01392 873862, www.cheffers.co.uk/bridge.

Other hostelries of note ...

BRANSCOMBE

THE INN
'A most sweet ciderhouse'
Come to this cottage of 1360 for the cider not the beer, which be an irony, for 'tis near the quarry at a place called Beer, where the masons of Exeter Cathedral sculpted their wonders in stone and thence came to this drinking house to toast their efforts.

Latterly: The Masons Arms, Branscombe, Devon, EX12 3DJ
tel: 01297 680300, www.masonsarms.co.uk.

❀ DORSET

Without lovely Bridport, England's fine hangmen, all skilled, talented and ruthless in equal measure, might be bereft of the very tool they need to execute their craft. Whilst excellent rope be made elsewhere in the land, only Dorsetshire produces the renowned 'Bridport Dagger', rope of quality made from local flax it oft be said 'tis wasted on criminals.

Its fame goes back to our first Tudor monarch, Henry VII, who decreed that all rope within 5 miles of Bridport be reserved for the navy and all hemp grown within that distance be sold at the town's market. The scaffold at the county town, Dorchester, where the dagger be in regular use, be situated in the Maumbury Rings amphitheatre, first used by our Roman occupiers a millennium and more ago. It provides good views from all seats and the words of the most notorious villains can be heard from the back.

Being a coastal county subject to attacks from the Spanish, 'tis perhaps fortunate that the mariner Sir Walter Raleigh be the member of parliament for the county; the queen rewarding him with the castle at Sherborne. A string of Catholics from the village of Chideock were put to death as traitors in 1594, the same year in which Sir Walter be investigated for upsetting the vicar in Winterborne in this county with his atheistic nonsense.

BRIDPORT

THE SHAVE CROSS INN
'Of good rest and relics'
A drink, meal and shorn hair, what more can be the traveller's desire? In the 1530s and earlier, hair be worn at this inn in the traditional monkish style under the scissors of the then innkeeper

Johannes of Shaw, which means 'shave'. No short back and sides here though, as back and sides be left on whilst the pate be exposed to the elements in the fashion they call tonsure. Accommodation was oft taken at The Shave Cross by pilgrims to the tomb of St Wite, spending eternity in Whitchurch Canonicorum some 5 miles hence. Somehow Whitchurch survived the Reformation when Henry's men looked the other way. 'Tis worth a visit as it be now second only to Westminster Abbey in holding the remains of a saint, even though no one in the inn seems to knows the first thing about her. More than three centuries hath passed since this fine clay, cobb, flint, wattle-and-daub building started welcoming the pilgrims. Indeed, the doorway and blue lias floor be careworn from the thousands who visit. Skittles they play here in the old skittle alley outside the main inn. Game and other meats for dinner include deer and wild boar freshly killed in Bridport forest, where once Her Majesty's father hunted.

Latterly: The Shave Cross Inn, Bridport, DT6 6HW,
tel: 01308 868358, www.theshavecrossinn.co.uk.

CHRISTCHURCH

GEORGE AND DRAGON
'A haven in barren country'
Once thee find the George and Dragon thee will disabuse the writer who said of the area in 1538 that 'tis 'situated in a desolate place in very barren country, out and far from all highways, in an angle or a corner between two rivers, having no woods or commodious country about it, no good town near but only the said poor town of Christchurch which be a very poor town and slenderly inhabited'. Slanderous knave!

After the Dissolution, the priory was not razed, but became the church. The leper hostel survived too and for all this give thanks or commiseration at the George and Dragon. Neither Henry's men nor Mary's tracked down many priests here for the lofts and holes of the inn are numerous, opaque and hard to find between the timber frame. Space for coaches and horses be expansive, for Christchurch be rural. A change of horses can be arranged, especially for those travelling 'twixt London and Poole for the distance be long.

Latterly: Ye Olde George Inn, 2A Castle Street, Christchurch, Dorset, BH23 1DT, tel: 01202 479383, www.piddlepubs.co.uk.

EVERSHOT

KINGS ARMS
'Beer and wild boar'

Near here roam wild boars, which the inn turns into tasty stews and sausages. The tippler here brews excellent ale, employing the water drawn from St John's Spring from which the River Frome springs at the village, which be anciently known as Theuershet. The water be known to be fresh and good and free from disease. The village be a climb from other settlements, so the warming fire be welcome in winter. Whilst fiddlers encourage dancing and singing and making merrie, to do so on the Sabbath here be folly. As a warning, stones of Three Dumb Sisters are located nearby, megaliths of old that are said to be made of the bones of maidens who, upon dancing on the Lord's Day, were turned to stone forever.

Latterly: The Acorn Inn, 28 Fore Street, Evershot, Dorset, DT2 0JW, tel: 01935 83228, www.acorn-inn.co.uk.

Other hostelries of note ...

CORFE CASTLE

THE GREYHOUND
Established some twenty years ago and much used by messengers to the impressive castle.

Latterly: The Greyhound, The Square Corfe Castle, Wareham, Dorset, BH20 5EZ, tel: 01929 480205, www.greyhoundcorfe.co.uk.

DORCHESTER

THE ANTELOPE

A fine inn, but thee will find it hard to find suitable weed if thee desire to fill thy pipe. Local constables frown upon the practice of smoking tobacco as the town's jostling buildings are feared susceptible to fires.

Latterly: Antelope Walk, a shopping mall.

POOLE

ANTELOPE INN

The best place to lay in this port, famous for its wool exports. It hath a wonderful fireplace that goes back to 1465, excellent for warming the cockles in filthy weather.

Latterly: The Antelope Inn, 8 High Street, Poole, Dorset, BH15 1BP, tel: 01202 672029, www.oldenglishinns.co.uk.

SHAFTESBURY

THE NEW INN

Serving since at least 1533, 'tis well placed for the markets, which bring fare in from around this lush county.

Latterly: The Grosvenor, High Street, Shaftesbury, Dorset, SP7 8JA, tel: 01747 850580, www.bespokehotels.com.

❀ DURHAM

The Church be still a dominant force in this county, which be run by the bishop of the ancient city. Indeed, 'tis known as the land of the Prince Bishops and their Palatine extends from the River Tees in the south to the River Tyne in the north.

Historically the area had much independence from the rest of the kingdom, with its own parliament and tax raising powers. Henry VIII curtailed some of these rights and, while the great cathedral remains, he ordered the destruction of the shrine of St Cuthbert.

In 1523 the future Lord Chancellor, Thomas Wolsey, was Prince-Bishop and since the 1560s all superstitious books and idols have been removed, though a witch from Hartlepool was recently made to do penance by sitting in the market square wearing a special hat – humiliating to be sure, but a better fate than some.

Set on a sharp meander of the river, the city of Durham be a stoutly defended place and its castle hath never been breached. Other towns include the agricultural centre of Darlington, where weaving and tanning be important trades, but like many of the small towns the streets are unpaved. Other important places include the stronghold of Barnard Castle. In recent years the plague hath been a frequent visitor to these towns decimating the population. There are some 28 inns, 9 taverns and 495 alehouses in total through the shire.

BISHOP AUCKLAND

BAY HORSE
'Heady ales'
In this humble market town, which stands in the shadow of the Bishop of Durham's residence, be an alehouse on the street known as Fore Bondgate. It hath been locally famed for its ales and good humour since 1530 and provided a place to enjoy a reviving drink after five of those who had risen up against Henry VIII's reforms of the Church were publicly hanged for their treason.
Latterly: The Bay Horse, 38–40 Fore Bondgate, Bishop Auckland, County Durham, DL14 7PE, tel: 01388 609765.

Other hostelries of note ...

PIERCEBRIDGE

THE GEORGE

A sturdy stopping point where an ancient Roman road crosses the River Tees. The bridge here hath been used down the centuries by armies going to and coming from Scotland, again and again.
Latterly: The George Hotel, Piercebridge, Darlington, DL2 3SW, tel: 01325 374576, www.george-ontees.co.uk.

BOWES

GEORGE INN

At a court leet in 1440 'twas decided that an inn was maintained and beer brewed in Bowes. The George now provides good respite from the terrible roads hereabouts.
Latterly: Ancient Unicorn, Bowes, Barnard Castle, County Durham, DL12 9HL, tel: 01833 628321, www.ancient-unicorn.com.

✿ ESSEX

'The shire be most fatt, frutefull and full of profitable things exceeding anie other shire,' wrote John Norden in 1594.

Much loved by Her Majesty Queen Elizabeth as a place of play and stirring speeches, the county of Essex gets its name from the ancient Kingdom of East Seaxe which came into being in AD 527. 'Tis bordered by the River Stour in the north, the River Lea in the west, the Thames in the south and the sea to the east.

'Tis rich in agriculture, supplying everything from hops to 'great cheeses'. It also supplies saffron, from which the market town of Saffron Walden gets its name.

One of the features of the county be Royal Waltham Forest, also known as Epping Forest. Both Henry VIII and Queen Elizabeth enjoy hunting here and have a famous lodge in it, built in 1543. It hath a high platform which allows guests to view the hunt and even shoot their crossbows from the upper floor.

Another feature of the county be its great houses, including the royal palace at Havering, high on its hill overlooking London and Essex. Essex was also the venue for one of Queen Elizabeth's early progresses around her kingdom in 1561, during which she visited Sir William Petre at Ingatestone Hall, just one of the lavish new houses being built by the new men of wealth whose riches have come to them in part from the late Dissolution of the Monasteries. During her progress Elizabeth travelled for sixty-eight days, with hosts spending £2,500 a time to entertain her and her retinue with food and drink.

Colchester be the largest town in the county and famed for its wool, weaving and oysters, while Chelmsford be the county town. Beware of staying too long in the creeks of the coast where 'marsh fever' and 'marsh ague' are known to kill.

Finally, 'tis useful to know a local drinking custom, in case the sudden drawing of arms may cause concern – in Essex, there be a habit of tipplers drawing their swords and mock knighting fellow drinkers.

As of 1577 there were 399 alehouses, 77 inns and 17 taverns within the county of Essex. Just last year the Colchester Town Assembly found that there were a 'multitude of alehouses which have been suffered to be kept within the town of Colchester' some of which are 'harbourers of Theves ... and other lewd persones'.

The price of beer here be three pints for a penny.

COGGESHALL

WHITE HART
'Warm wool and chilling velvet'
This wonderful jumble of a building makes it a pleasing place to stay and sup. Part of it was first built as a house in 1526 for

the wool merchant Robert Paycocke – his family have been the leading merchants in the town, with much of their wealth built on the famous white cloth for which 'tis known. The same family own other richly carved houses in Coggeshall.

The White Hart may also be built on the site of an old guildhall and the inn hath its own ghoul – a mysterious figure dressed in blue velvet.

Note that the gruesome game of football be popular hereabouts. Just this year 'twas reported that Thomas Whistock in the nearby village of White Notleye with 'nyne other of his fellowes ... did play at an unlawfull game called fotebale whereon grew bludshedd'.
Latterly: The White Hart Hotel, Market End, Coggeshall, Colchester, Essex, CO6 1NH, tel: 01376 561654, www.oldenglishinns.co.uk.

Wicked temptations

Take note that some alehouses will offer more than a jug of beer. In 1567 the magistrates at Chelmsford, Essex, brought to the bench twelve unlicensed alehouse keepers and four of them were charged with keeping brothels. One, known as Mother Bowden, kept a sole prostitute who was found to be her daughter.

❧

COLCHESTER

WHITE LION
'Grand dinners at the sign of St George'

That esteemed writer John Leland wrote of Colchester, 'It is a proper towne ... thowght to have flourished in Roman times.' 'Tis certainly well endowed with inns and alehouses today, many of them new and exciting additions to the town's drinking scene. There be the Crown at the town's port, where plays are oft performed and, since 1554, there also be the Maidenhead near the town gates – though this be known as a more disorderly place.

It's along the High Street where thee will find the finest of the inns, which was once called the New Inn and now the White Lion. 'Twas built upon a Roman dwelling (a portion of a mosaic can still be seen) in 1470, as a family house for John Howard, who became Duke of Norfolk, and was turned into the inn we know today around 1515. Its vittles are so good that the nearby Crown and Bell have already become mere houses though The White Hart, George and Angel still compete with the White Lion to lay on lavish celebratory dinners.

The three-storey building features wonderful mouldings and carved timberwork as well as a great entrance for carriages, with a stirring George and Dragon carved over the archway. We hear talk that the name may be changed to the Red Lion, a symbol of King James of Scotland, who, 'tis rumoured, may become monarch if our current queen passes on. Long may she reign, be all we have to say.

Another inn in the town, The King's Head, in Head Street, hath, since 1565, been licensed to keep a 'tennis play' as recreation for gentlemen and 'other fit persons'.

Latterly: The Red Lion Hotel, High Street, Colchester, Essex, CO1 1DJ, tel: 01206 577986, www.red-lion-hotel.co.uk.

The White Lion, now the Red Lion Hotel, Colchester. (Courtesy of Brook Hotels)

A bedchamber at the White Lion. (Courtesy of Brook Hotels)

GREAT LEIGHS

ST ANNE'S
'Hermitage turned hostelry'

This hath been a place of refuge for many centuries, but these days there be better company to help console thee on the weary road between Braintree and Chelmsford.

St Anne's was mentioned in the Domesday Book of 1086 and until 1571 'twas connected to the Church and served as a hermitage, but was also believed to have served ale to pilgrims making their way to the shrine of St Thomas Becket in Canterbury. Indeed, the building's cellars contain remains of tunnels, which link it to Leez Priory, and Great Leigh's church. In 1571 'twas given to one Thomas Jennings and soon became a proper inn.

Given the ancient history of this inn, 'tis of no surprise that there be tales of ghouls associated with it, from the spirit of a witch to ghostly monks and a mysterious black cat.

Look out for Richard Rich who hath lived up to his name as one of the upwardly mobile 'new men'. The Dissolution was a blessing and a great opportunity to him and he managed to gain at least 100 manors in Essex while administering the monastic 'spoils', and built himself a mansion in the ruins of Leez Priory.

Latterly: The St Anne's Castle, Main Road, Great Leighs, Essex, CM3 1NE, tel: 01245 361253, www.stannescastle.co.uk.

HORNDON-ON-THE-HILL

THE BELL
'Burned at the stake – in the inn's yard'

There be delicious food to be had at The Bell, but the smell of cooking flesh be a reminder that this very spot hath been the scene of a most grizzly event. For here, in the very yard of the inn, the bell once tolled for one Thomas Higbed, a gentleman of Horndon House, who was put to death for heresy on 26 March 1555.

Taken to London by 'Bloody' Bishop Bonner as part of the persecution of Protestant heretics during the reign of Queen

The Essex Witch Trials

Since the first law against witchcraft was passed in 1542 there have been many culprits identified. During the years of Elizabeth's reign there are reckoned to have been 270 trials alone of 247 women and 23 men across the whole land. The county of Essex hath been witness to many of them. At Chelmsford in 1566 the first major trial saw Elizabeth Frances accused of using a cat called Satan to harm people. Imprisoned for a year, she was again tried in 1579 and hanged for using her powers to kill two women. The town was once more the scene of a public hanging in 1589 when three witches, Joan Prentice, Joan Upney and Joan Cunny, were put to death.

❦

Mary, he refused to recant his beliefs saying: 'I will not abjure. For I have been of this mind and opinion that I am now these sixteen years, and do what thee can.'

Being found guilty, he was taken from the capital, fast bound in a cart to Horndon, where sentence was carried out – burning at the stake. Higbed was just one of 120 put to death by Bonner. So as thee enjoy thy dinner, spare a thought for the callously cooked Thomas.

Latterly: The Bell Inn, High Road, Horndon-on-the-Hill, Essex, SS17 8LD, tel: 01375 642463, www.bell-inn.co.uk.

SAFFRON WALDEN

ROSE AND CROWN
'Haunt of poets'

This grand inn hath a great literary history. It's said that the Rose and Crown was known to William Shakespeare and 'tis just a few doors from where the famous poet Gabriel Harvey lives and he be sure to drink here. Harvey be the son of a local ropemaker and became known as a great speaker who was brought before Queen

The heart and stomach of a king

In 1588, the year of the nation's victory over the Spanish Armada, Queen Bess came ashore at Tilbury in Essex to review her army. Her famous words to the soldiers still ring in the ears of every proud Englishman:

I know I have the body of a weak and feeble woman, but I have the heart and stomach of a king, and of a king of England too, and think foul scorn that Parma or Spain, or any prince of Europe should dare to invade the borders of my realm.

❀

Elizabeth in 1578 at the nearby Audley End House when she was being hosted by Sir Thomas Smith.

Sadly his reputation hath suffered of late from a fierce quarrel with another writer, the wit Thomas Nashe, who hath mocked his verse in a pamphlet called 'Have With Thee To Saffron Walden'. In it he teased Harvey for needing to rush to the privy at the thought of his mocking publication.
Latterly: Sadly burned down in 1969.

Other hostelries of note ...

CHIGWELL

KING'S HEAD
Built in the year 1547, legend hath it that Queen Elizabeth once stayed here while on a hunting trip and even scolded an unlucky page while mounting her horse.
Latterly: Sheesh at Ye Olde Kings Head, High Road, Chigwell, Essex, IG7 6QA, sheeshrestaurant.co.uk.

BRAINTREE

WHITE HART

Thee be unlikely to be served short measures here. The inn, first built some decades ago and with even more ancient cellars, be now a place where local court hearings are heard.

Latterly: White Hart Hotel, Bocking End, Braintree, Essex, CM7 9AB, tel: 01376 321401, www.oldenglishinns.co.uk.

BRENTWOOD

WHITE HART

The leading inn in this town, with a jettied upper storey. It hath been here since at least 1480 but rumoured to have hosted Richard II in 1392.

Latterly: Sugar Hut Brentwood, 93–95 High Street, Brentwood, Essex, CM14 4RR, tel: 0845 5190019, www.sugarhutbrentwood.com.

MALDON

BLUE BOAR

Parts date back to the second half of the fourteenth century.

Latterly: The Blue Boar Hotel, Silver Street, Maldon, Essex, CM9 4QE, tel: 01621 855888, www.blueboarhotel.com.

❀ GLOUCESTERSHIRE

Each of its towns hath many inns, taverns and alehouses, so thy will never go thirsty in Gloucestershire.

The road betwixt Wales and London passes through Gloucester, so where better for accommodation to spring up? This once-prosperous county town endeavours to maintain its status by trading with others across England, but its position hath been under threat from upstart locations elsewhere in Gloucestershire. Tewkesbury be especially to blame, though happily for those of Gloucester, Tewkesbury be declared but a 'creek' of the county town in 1580. Trade though is moving elsewhere on the Severn and away from Gloucester. Even Bristol on the Avon benefits as Gloucester declines. This hath made times hard for the hostelries, even though previously they thrived. Owing to poor crops these past years, the beds be oft better than the beer.

Tewkesbury be plentiful in hostelries and the food here be of such repute that even Mister Shakespeare, through the voice of his famed Falstaff, hath commented on the condiments. 'His wit be as thick as Tewkesbury mustard,' quoth he. The Tewkesburians hath had their noses disjointed by the queen's import to them to join with Gloucester to procure a large vessel for her navy at the height of the Armada crisis. That the burghers refused go down not well, though many went unpunished. Instead they provided a 25-ton pinnace that atoned for their disobedience, until 'twas realised that this vessel be poorly equipped and could not give service. Though in maritime matters Tewkesbury be lacking, in malting it excels, procuring so much that quantities be exported to intoxicate the Welsh. Visit the historic horse-driven brewing mill in Quay Lane to witness beverage-making at its finest. There be many clerics in Tewkesbury too, oft in drink.

The famous port of Bristol be also included here under Gloucestershire due to its long association with the county. Yet the city, with a population now of 12,000, really be a county in its own right. Bristol be famous for importing hundreds of thousands of gallons of wines every year, as well as olive oil and figs from hotter climes, along with fish and hides from Ireland. Some cargoes are not so profitable. In 1557 the unfortunate Sir Martin Frobisher returned from the New World with tons of what he thought was gold, but which turned out to be worthless iron pyrites. More successfully, from Bristol in 1496, John Cabot made his voyage to the Americas. Queen Elizabeth graced the city with her presence in 1574, where she will have marvelled at the petrified kidneys under her feet, a nickname for the marvellous paving stones for which the streets are well known. She also admired the architecture, saying of the city's St Mary Redcliffe that it be: 'the fairest, godliest and most famous parish church in England'.

BRISTOL

NEW INN OR 'JONAS'
'Of mad monikers and marauding military'
In Mister Shakespeare's new play to be called, our spies tell us, *Hamlet*, a character warns: 'never a borrower nor a lender be'. Thankfully Mister Thomas Abyndon ignored this advice and borrowed £100 and this inn proudly facing the high street, restored in 1440, be the most lovely result. The inn's history, in fact, goes back to 1241, when part of it was called ye Green Lattis, for this be the colour used upon its window lattices and door posts. This was incorporated in 1565 into a larger inn called Jonas and in that very year a Captain Gilbert, who lodged here, had to rush out with his sword and intervene when some soldiers, billeted in Bristol on their way to quell a rebellion in Ireland, got into a rumpus with some locals.

The New Inn be currently one of six worthy inns in Bristol and the perfect place to sup and quench thy thirst after thy toil of the day or finishing the shopping in this market haven. The inn yard be extensive and the stabling fine. Thee may say a small prayer and think of one of the inn's former owners, Alice Hayle, who donated this fine building to the church of All Saints in the hope that her soul would rest easy in heaven for eternity.

Latterly: The Rummer Hotel, All Saints Lane, Bristol, BS1 1JH, tel: 0117 929 0111, www.therummer.net.

Beware being blown to smithereens at the Pelican

Of a summer's evening Bristol be a pleasant place to wander for a drink admiring the ships and bridge, which gave the city its name. 'Tis set with houses much like a smaller version of London Bridge. A note of caution though; on thy meanderings thee may want to avoid the Pelican on Thomas Street where there be a good chance that thee will be blown up. This was the sad fate of ten men at the Pelican, who, on Queen Elizabeth's visit to the city in 1574, were mysteriously killed by an explosion of gunpowder. Though said to be an accident we wonder if 'twas something to do with the mock battle with which Her Majesty was later entertained, part of £1,000 spent on entertainments. A better bet for a quiet drink be ye Swan in St Mary-le-Port Street, with its quaint overhanging gables, fine mullioned windows and tapestries.

❧

GLOUCESTER

NEW INN
'Famed for players and queens'
Serving beer since 1455, when ten hostelries bunched together on this one short road, rebuilding work hath done much to rejuvenate the tired, three-storeyed property. The timber frame today be carved from massive oak, with lathe and plaster noggin. The courtyard, entered from Northgate Street on its western side, hath been retained and receives travelling players who attract customers to this inn in a manner in which its neighbouring inns cannot compete. The inn hopes to book Mister Shakespeare for his company. The Chamberlain's Men, have played here, though no one knows if the man himself attended. Stabling be to the rear of the courtyard; the parlour in the centre of the north range. The large upper hall be suitable for large parties.

The open gallery from the first floor offers the best seats in the house for performances. The inn be steeped in modern history, for pretty Lady Jane Grey was proclaimed to be queen from this very gallery in July 1553. The innkeeper was very proud to have such a guest, though not for long. Nine days later, thanks to a confusion in King Edward VI's will, she was unproclaimed monarch and soon went for execution. Recently innkeepers speak little of this embarrassing episode and point to another royal guest, Henry VIII, believed to have stayed at the inn to oversee the abbey burning at the Dissolution – a fact that *Ye Olde Good Inn Guide* hath not been able to verify.

The original inn be associated with the Benedictine Abbey of St Peter after being constructed by Brother John Twyning and was handy for those paying homage at the tomb of Edward II, though this be not widely spoken of nowadays. Yet the New Inn be still leased by the Dean and Chapter of the cathedral. The inn be hard to locate for it hath little frontage to the street.

Latterly: The New Inn, 16 Northgate Street, Gloucester, GL1 1SF, tel: 01452 522177, www.newinn-hotel.co.uk.

STOW-ON-THE-WOLD

KINGS ARMS
'Warm fires at this hilly spot'

By whichever highway thy enter Stow-on-the-Wold, thy will find the Kings Arms easily for the roads converge here. Rest thy horses at the rear whilst thee enjoy the hospitality of the Kings Arms and change horses if thy wish. At last in Gloucestershire, this be an inn where a tall gentleman need not fear for his head, for the beams be high and the doorways ample. Thee will likely need to seat thyself in front of the roaring fires here though, for Stow-on-the-Wold be famously hostile and the winds rush through the body.

Latterly: Kings Arms, Market Square, Stow-on-the-Wold, Gloucestershire, GL54 1AF, tel: 01451 830364, www.kingsarmsstow.co.uk.

TEWKESBURY

THE BEARE

'Handy for salted duck'

On one of the most prominent high roads in the west of England, look out for the sign of the bear and the ragged staff that mark this inn of aged construct, some say from 1308. 'Tis sited against the Avon, so the stables are to the fore, accessible to the road, as the river sometimes laps around the ankles of customers, so frequent doth flooding occur. Many horses did drown hereabouts attempting to jump the Avon in the Roses war, for this be the house to which injured Lancastrians were transported in 1471, marking the inn with death, of man and beast.

However, the river being so near makes the inn accessible by both track and boat. Feasting on duck be a speciality here. Horses conveying salt from Droitwich to Bristol stop too, so seasoned food and cured meat be always on the menu too.

Avoid ye Swan Inn nearby if thee take a stroll through the town. Here five people died of the plague as recently as 1579.

Latterly: Ye Olde Black Bear, Tewkesbury, Gloucestershire, GL20 5BJ, tel: 01684 292202.

Other hostelries of note ...

LECHLADE

YE SYGNE OF ST JOHN BAPTIST HEAD

This inn catered for those that built the stone bridge across the Thames in 1220, where the local priory prospered. When 'twas closed in the reign of Edward IV the inn survived.

Latterly: The Trout Inn, Faringdon Road, Lechlade-on-Thames, Gloucestershire, GL7 3HA, tel: 01367 252313, thetroutinn.com.

TEWKESBURY

THE ANGEL
Once the guest house to the impressive abbey, whose church survives, there was a whiff of decay about this place as a hostelry – for a time it became a tannery. Now, thee may see some of its former grandeur in the wall paintings retained and some of the solid wood panelling.
Latterly: The Bell Hotel, 52 Church Street, Tewkesbury, Gloucestershire, GL20 5SA, tel: 01684 293293.

❦ HAMPSHIRE & THE ISLE OF WIGHT

The fact that Hampshire hath many more inns than most counties, some sixty-seven, shows how important it be as a place for travellers making their way from London and other places in England and on to the high seas. There be also fourteen taverns and 324 alehouses in the county.

Southampton, with a population of some 4,000, be a port known for its privateers, the sea dogs who take to the high seas in pursuit of riches, fame and to defend the honour of Her Majesty. The town itself be somewhat decayed of late. Until 1531 it had a monopoly on the trade in tin and lead and lately it hath been an important entry point for sweet wine from the Mediterranean countries, but its economic fortunes are unsteady, not helped by the plagues of 1563 and 1581.

Winchester be famous for its cathedral which was the venue, in 1554, for the marriage of Queen Mary to King Philip of Spain. Portsmouth be much fortified and hath become the focus of our navy's defences against the Spanish. It even hath its own military brewhouse.

To the south of the county there be the Isle of Wight, included here as a traveller must usually travel from Hampshire to make landfall on the island, an important bastion in itself against our dastardly Catholic foes.

ALTON

THE SWAN
'Rub shoulders with privateers'

The roll call of those who have chosen this fine hostelry as a resting point upon the London to Southampton road includes many of the greatest names of our age. As well as the present queen, the poet Edmund Spenser, who lived in the town, be known to have drunk here right royally. Thee may even find that the innkeeper can furnish thee with a copy of his greatest work, *The Faerie Queene*, an epic poem which cleverly links our present monarch to that legendary figure, King Arthur and thoroughly celebrates our current dynasty.

That great explorer of the seas Sir Francis Drake hath been a guest too. Indeed, he may well have stopped here with some of his booty upon his return to Southampton in 1580 aboard the *Golden Hind* before presenting his Spanish treasure to the queen herself.

The Swan, which dates back to 1377, makes lingering in this town, which also hath a famous market, very worthwhile.
Latterly: The Swan Hotel, High Street, Alton, Hampshire, GU34 1AT, tel: 01420 83777, www.oldenglishinns.co.uk.

ANDOVER

THE ANGEL
'A school for drinkers?'

The present building here be old enough, having been re-built in 1445 after a fire, but the inn dates back to much earlier times, having once been The College Inn. 'Twas frequented by King John when he stayed here in 1201 and gave the goodly town its charter. Edward I and Edward II both found it convenient too, when travelling about their kingdom.

Its old name came from Winchester College, that school which owned it. And 'twas the college which laid down the new structure of the inn with its fine flagged floors. Its timbers were designed by master carpenters Richard Holnerst and John Harding.

Now known as The Angel, it hath continued to receive royal patronage. Henry VII stayed here too. One Richard Pope be now the leaseholder and, while its connection with the school may have gone, the very variety of the wines on offer from as far afield as the continent still provide lessons for thy taste buds.

If The Angel be too full, or somewhat fusty to thy tastes, then The George, established in 1576, and the Star and Garter, also known as The White Hart, which opened in 1582, provide all a modern traveller could wish for.

Latterly: The Angel Inn, 95 High Street, Andover, Hampshire, SP10 1ND, tel: 01264 365464.

The Angel, Andover, Hampshire. (© Mr James Moore)

LIPHOOK

THE ANCHOR

'Of fine fireplaces and fighting fire-ships'

Set high up on the hilly route from London to Portsmouth, The Anchor be the perfect place to make thy port in any storm, for it boasts large, modern inglenook fireplaces with one showing the date 1588 proudly on its fireback. This be, of course, the very year that the Spanish Armada threatened English shores with the prospect of invasion. 'Tis fitting therefore that 'twas past The Anchor that the mail was sent during the year of that emergency, when our sailors were famously fuelled to victory by a gallon of beer a day.

As thee gaze at the flames at this inn, nursing thy own brew, it might be fitting to toast the cunning of our navy, which managed to disperse the brooding Spanish fleet with the help of fire-ships, packed with burning tar, panicking the would-be invader into a flight from which he never recovered.

Latterly: The Royal Anchor, 9–11 The Square, Liphook, Hampshire, GU30 7AD, tel: 01428 722244, www.royalanchor-liphook.co.uk.

Part of the fireback found in the cellar at The Anchor, Liphook, Hampshire. (© Mr James Moore)

NEWPORT

CASTLE INN
'Fortify thyself at thy peril'
For those that like a taste of adventure and are bold enough to make the journey to the Isle of Wight, the Castle Inn be a goodly place to start after landing at the town's quay on the River Medina.

First licensed in 1550, but with walls that date to 1300, this alehouse be certainly old. But beware, there are always new ways to be parted from thy purse in this part of town, for the Castle Inn be found in an area called Castlehold, famous for its thieves and vagabonds, as historically 'twas not subject to the same jurisdiction as the other parts of town. If thee enjoy the thrill of danger it might be worth venturing here for the cockfighting – another way to lose thy monies.

The nearby fortifications of Carisbrooke Castle be truly magnificent and newly embellished in defence against the cannon of the Spanish. Overseeing these improvements hath been Sir George Carey, captain-general of the island during the Armada threat of 1588.

Also of attraction in the town be a small but beautiful new archway at Church Litten, a field used both for archery practice and for burying those who died when the plague hit the town in 1582. *Latterly: The Castle Inn, 91 High Street, Newport, PO30 1BQ, tel: 01983 522528, www.thecastleiow.co.uk.*

ODIHAM

THE GEORGE
'Perfect for lovers'
The jettied front of this wattle-and-daub building be unmissable, poking out into the high street of the town which lies halfway betwixt Windsor and Winchester, making it an important stopping point.

The George hath been here since 1540 and one of the bedrooms be decorated with wall paintings said to illustrate the poem 'Parliament of Fowls', a little-known work written by Geoffrey Chaucer in around 1382. If thee are staying with thy beloved it may well be worth requesting that thee stay in this room. After all, 'tis one of the first odes ever written which marks out St Valentine's Day as special for lovers. Also romantic be the ruin of Odiham's castle, built by King John.

Latterly: The George Hotel, 101–102 High Street, Odiham, Hook, Hampshire, RG29 1LP, tel: 01256 702081, www.georgehotelodiham.com.

Home of the Royal Navy

'A great dok for shippes' was how the writer John Leland described the town of Portsmouth, which was made headquarters of our Royal Navy by Henry VIII. 'Twas here, in 1545, that he sadly saw his flagship, the *Mary Rose*, founder and sink with the loss of 500 souls. Portsmouth itself be now much expanded and fortified and Queen Elizabeth visited in 1591 to inspect her fleet of forty ships.

A word of warning before embarking on a voyage: 'tis recommended that the traveller call at The Greyhound Inn or one of the other drinking establishments near the water's edge in order to settle his stomach.

❦

ROMSEY

WHITE HORSE
'Decked out with dragons and Tudor roses'
'Tis, perhaps, befitting that inside the White Horse thee will find wonderful painted dragons on the beams, since the town hath had a reputation for many years as a place where roaring be in vogue – in the form of drunken revellers.

Originally a guesthouse to Romsey Abbey, there be ancient wine cellars at the White Horse which still house the finest wines. It hath been an inn since at least the 1400s and as well as a narrow courtyard and open galleries it be stirring to the eye thanks to its high artistic merit. As well as the dragons already mentioned,

there are black and ochre roses linked together on the plaster walls of the place and much fine oak furniture too to be admired.
Latterly: The White Horse, Market Place, Romsey, SO51 8ZJ, tel: 01794 512431, thewhitehorseromsey.co.uk.

SOUTHAMPTON

THE DOLPHIN
'Where plans were laid to conquer the New World'
Henry VIII be reckoned to have visited The Dolphin, famous for its fine stone-mullioned windows and serving up great platters of food to sailors suffering scurvy as well as charismatic adventurers. It hath been an inn since at least 1506, when its tenant was brought before the authorities for the shabby nature of the place.

It hath seen better times since then and sent one owner, Edward Wilmott, to parliament; though this may surprise some he was, in his time, fined for overcharging for wine and selling hay at short weight.

Perhaps The Dolphin's most interesting claim to fame be that 'twas here that Sir Humphrey Gilbert dined in 1582 while planning voyages to North America, hoping to establish new colonies. In 1583 he claimed Newfoundland as a possession of the queen, one of our bright new colonies, being presented with a celebratory dog by the locals for his efforts.

Sadly on the journey home, he perished in the seas aboard his ship *The Squirrel*, last seen reading *Utopia*, that sensational book by the late Sir Thomas More.
Latterly: The Dolphin Hotel, 34–35 High Street, Hampshire, Southampton, SO14 2HN, tel: 023 8033 9955, www.dolphin-southampton.com.

THE RED LION
'Court room for traitors'
The fact that this building dates all the way back to 1148, when 'twas used as a cellar, might be enough reason for it to be full of ghosts. But there be another reason for the ghouls (which drinkers

say plague the creaky timbers of The Red Lion), for it boasts a great half-timbered hall, with a magnificent fireplace which was chosen as the venue for a famous trial that took place on 2 August 1415, and which be much covered in William Shakespeare's latest play *Henry V*.

It saw Richard, Earl of Cambridge, Lord Scrope of Masham and Sir Thomas Grey of Heton accused of plotting against the aforementioned king, conspiring to have Edmund Mortimer, a claimant to the throne, made monarch in his place. Unsportingly, Edmund himself had informed on them and at hastily arranged proceedings the treasonable trio were found guilty. Two were beheaded as befitted their class, while Grey, a commoner, was hung, drawn and quartered in front of the town's Bargate.

Having dispatched his domestic enemies, King Henry immediately set sail for France where, in October that same year, he would famously defeat the French at the Battle of Agincourt. *Latterly: The Red Lion, 55 High Street, Southampton, SO14 2NS, tel: 023 8033 3595, www.theredlionsouthampton.com.*

Other hostelries of note ...

LYMINGTON

THE ANGEL
Freshly caught fish be on the menu at this inn, first erected in the thirteenth century.
Latterly: The Angel, High Street, Lymington, SO41 9AP, tel: 01590 672050, www.angel-lymington.com.

RINGWOOD

THE WHITE HART
Named after Henry VII, who, on a hunting trip nearby, spared the life of a white hart, giving it a fine gold collar and making a pet of the animal.

Latterly: Original White Hart, 4 Market Place, Ringwood, BH24 1AW, tel: 01425 472702, www.originalwhitehartpub.co.uk.

WHITCHURCH

THE WHITE HART
A well-placed watering hole, established in 1461, located at a crossing point of the London to Exeter and Oxford to Southampton roads.
Latterly: The White Hart, Newbury Street, Whitchurch, Hampshire, RG28 7DN, tel: 01256 892900, www.whiteharthotelwhitchurch.co.uk.

WINCHESTER

HYDE TAVERN
Worship can be thirsty work. If thee have the need of an ale after visiting Winchester's famous cathedral then this be a most trustworthy destination.
Latterly: The Hyde Tavern, 57 Hyde Street, Winchester, SO23 7DY, tel: 01962 862592, www.hydetavern.co.uk.

❀ HEREFORDSHIRE

Danger lay in the county of Herefordshire for those kings who came before our good Majesty. Her great-great-grandfather, Owen Tudor, was executed at the county town of Hereford after the Battle of Mortimer's Cross. 'Tis famed as ancient, large and strong walled, under the protectorate of a dyke filled with water, its castle hard by the river. The cathedral stands tall and magnificent; its tower a wonder, its windows soaring and pictured. Visitors may warm themselves here; the fire burns long, rare for such a holy house, normally riddled with draughts. Admire here the 'Adoration of the Magi', a carving from 1530 that be famed for showing St Ursula and St Gabriel on its side panels, then take refreshment in one of the many alehouses.

Ledbury be the place for cloth and gloves. In the 1580s, Her Majesty acquired its bishop's palace. Moreover, her kind permission gave the town two new fairs each year, making Ledbury a bit of a tourist trap on the feasts of St Philip and James (1 May) and St Barnabas (11 June). Stay thy distance then if thee fancy not paying vexatious prices for a bed.

Pembridge be a thriving village. Most houses have stood here for a hundred years or more and are large and much admired, though thy will need many purses of gold to purchase one. The new market hall hath been more recently built and hath done much to improve the countenance of the fayre. English woolsellers here meet the Welshmen in relative harmony, for the border be near.

FOWNHOPE

THE NAKED BOY
'A curious moniker'

From the first year of the first Tudor king, Her Majesty's grandfather Henry VII, this fine inn hath served drinkers through the dynasty and long may it be so, though it may not be looking good for a Tudor heir now the queen ages much.

We know not why the first innkeeper here named his inn with such moral depravity – or sweet innocence – in 1485, only that he built a place with a reputation for comfort and goodly food and drink.

Ceilings are low, which may be adequate for the average man in the 1480s, but better diets surely cause men to be bigger these days and many patrons here now must stoop.

Latterly: The Green Man Inn, Fownhope, Herefordshire, HR1 4PE, tel: 01432 860243, www.thegreenman.co.

HEREFORD

THE GREEN DRAGON
'Owen Tudor's last resting place before the chop'
'Tis an irony that this most comforting inn hath such a chilling
tale to tell of the death of a nobleman, for this be where Owen
Tudor, that early casualty of the War of the Roses, spent his last
night as a prisoner after defeat at the Battle of Mortimer's Cross
in 1461. Fortunately for the condemned Lancastrian he did not
realise that he was about to die when he lay his head on one of the
inn's fine featherbeds. He still believed that his royal links would
see him reprieved. 'Twas not until he saw the axe, block and crowd
awaiting him the next morning that the reality became clear. His
red collar was said to have been torn off as he quickly quipped
that 'the head that was wont to lie on Queen Katherine's lap' was
now to lie in a basket. Unlike some beheaded folk, his head was
given a wash and brush up after being cut off and placed on the
steps of the market cross surrounded with candles.
Latterly: The Green Dragon Hotel, 44–46 Broad Street,
Herefordshire, HR4 9BG, tel: 01432 272506,
www.greendragon-hereford.co.uk.

LEDBURY

THE FEATHERS
'Named after a sickly king'
The most famous inn in all Herefordshire, near the historic
Booth Hall, from which justice be dispensed in Ledbury. The
Feathers be oft described as the best place for horses in the town.
Once thy man hath seen to the stabling, he can be accommodated
and fed at the rear. The public rooms be impressive to behold,
with a hallway of extravagant proportions. The three bays of the
windows are from different times of history, a mark most curious
as The Feathers be not yet eighty years old. It hath been an inn
since the building was erected in 1521, being then named after
the man who would have been king, Prince Arthur, Prince of

Wales, sickly elder brother of Henry VIII. The innkeeper hath exciting plans to construct a greater level to the inn, so 1599 may be the perfect year to stay here before the banging and thumping of builders commences.

Latterly: Plume of Feathers, 25 High Street, Ledbury, Herefordshire, HR8 1DS, tel: 01544 388427.

THE TALBOT

'For upstanding gentlefolk'

The Talbot be one of the newer establishments much favoured by those fresh of face and ignorant of the world. In the three years since its doors opened it hath forged a reputation beyond Ledbury as a place to go for a goodly night out, its ladies being very accommodating. Parts of the building have a history of nigh on fifty years. The owners have put the space to use most splendidly, with fine bedrooms upstairs and public rooms being light and pretty. The Talbot be the place for a quieter drink, being easier on the ears than The Seven Stars in the Homend of Ledbury which overlooks the cattle market and oft be noisy, smelly and full of the great unwashed. The Talbot serves a better class of person.

Latterly: The Talbot, 14 New Street, Ledbury, Herefordshire, HR8 2DX, tel: 01531 632963, www.talbotledbury.co.uk.

PEMBRIDGE

THE NEW INN

'Soaring timbers revive the soul'

A house of two gables, 'twas constructed we know not precisely when: some say 1400, others 1311. 'Twas not originally an inn but a house upon a farm. Presently as Pembridge became more populous, the farmer sold his ale in the market, soon inviting purchasers to attend his home, and thus a drinking house his home became. 'Twas the middle of this century that rebuilding gave a new look to the inn, using splendid timbers that attract many customers, though the builders may have imbibed one too many so that it looks like it might fall upon itself at any minute. The inn hath served as a courthouse and some even say that the treaty that confirmed Edward IV as king be signed within.

Latterly: The New Inn, Market Square, Pembridge, Leominster, Herefordshire, HR6 9DZ, tel: 01544 388427.

❀ HERTFORDSHIRE

William Camden, that most reliable of chroniclers, told us just a few years ago that this was a county rich in 'corne fields, pastures, medowes, woods, groves and cleere riveretes'. He continued that 'for ancient townes it may contend with the neighbours even for the best. For there is scarcely another shire in England that can shew more good townes in so small a compasse.'

A great boost to the country's towns comes from its proximity to London and its geography, with routes to the counties of the north carving through it. Towns such as Hertford, Ware, Royston and Hempstead do lately flourish.

There are mansions too. Queen Bess once lodged at the graceful Hatfield House as a girl and hath recently praised the county's men at arms for they sent some 1,000 infantry to Tilbury in the year 1588, when all England was mobilised against the threat of the sly Spanish. Perhaps they were fired up with good cheer by the many places to sup and toast Her Majesty within stirring Hertfordshire. In 1577 there were 152 inns, 16 taverns and 359 alehouses in the county, though we note that inspectors recently reported thus: 'as we find some of the keepers of these inns and alehouses of good wealth so do we find the greatest number of them very simple houses and the inhabitors of them very poor.'

BISHOP'S STORTFORD

THE GEORGE

'Where deals are done'

The town be about halfway betwixt Cambridge and London and The George be the best of the inns on offer to market-goers, those passing through, and those involved in the locally important malting industry. Established in 1417, when Thomas Petworth was the innkeeper, 'tis now in the hands of the Hawkins family of the Manor of Piggotts at Thorley, who regularly held their manorial courts here in the fifteenth century.

'Tis a place made famous for trade and thee will find plenty of merchants keen to do business. In 1482 a churchwarden paid a Richard Barlee some 8 shillings for a boat so that he and another could row to Fulham, in London, via the rivers Stort, Lea and Thames. By the time they returned from this mammoth journey they must have been in need of another reviving drink at The George.

Other well-proportioned inns include the Black Lion, Boar's Head and White Horse.

Latterly: The George Hotel, 1 North Street, Bishop's Stortford, Hertfordshire, CM23 2LD, tel: 01279 817821, www.thegeorgehotel.org.

CODICOTE

GEORGE & DRAGON

'Serving since the days of Henry III'

There hath been an inn on the site in this village since 1279, when Laurence the Taverner be known to have lived in it, paying an annual rent of 4 shillings and 2 capons to the local lord of the manor. In 1481 'twas known as the Greyhound and served pilgrims travelling to the shrine of St Alban. Some say the inn once belonged to the abbey there and had to contribute to the village's rent to the abbot of fifty fowls, a thousand eggs and one pig.

The present timbered structure, with neat overhanging upper storeys, dates from more recent times, having been built in 1550 and the drink hath improved since one former innkeeper was scolded for bad brewing. If thee find thyself in this out-of-the-way spot there be an interesting fair and weekly market held opposite the inn.

Latterly: A Chinese restaurant, As You Like It, www.wongsasyoulikeit.co.uk.

George & Dragon, Codicote, Hertfordshire, now As You Like It. (© Mr James Moore)

HITCHIN

THE SUN INN
'King Henry's narrow escape'
An ancient town, once home of the Hicca people, it boasts a number of fine inns which are currently battling for superiority. The Sun, which hath been here since 1575, seems currently to be winning. Tarry here and thee may see the work of the courts carried out by the Hitchin justices, who meet here in the upper rooms. The inn be presently owned by Trinity College, Cambridge.

Its main rival be the nearby Angel, which famously burned to the ground in 1523 whilst Henry VIII was staying there. One account reports that his Royal Highness escaped the blaze by the skin of his teeth with 'not so much as a shirt on his back'.

Interestingly, two years after this the king was nearly killed again in the area. Whilst following his hawks, he attempted to pole vault the River Hiz but nearly drowned when the pole broke and he fell in. The king was thankfully saved by a footman called Edward Moody, who was given a pension for his trouble.

Through having been rebuilt, the reputation of the Angel appears to have suffered and the newer Sun hath become the main hostelry of the town, even giving its name to the street itself. The Red Hart be another goodly choice in this town, established in 1550.

Latterly: The Sun Hotel, Sun Street, Hitchin, Hertfordshire, SG5 1AF, tel: 01462 432092, www.sunhotel-hitchin.com.

ROYSTON

THE BLACK BULL
'A cosy nook near some curious caves'
In ancient times a Lady Roisia put up a cross where the Roman Ermine Street and the Icknield Way, a famous west-to-east trading route, met. The Black Bull was built to service those travelling in all directions, oft from London to the town of Cambridge or further north to Lincoln. It sees much traffic and there be stabling for some 100 horses here.

Note thee well that the town contains a mysterious, circular cave with mysterious old carvings which are believed, by many, to have been used by the Knights Templar, that famous military order.

Latterly: The Old Bull Inn, 56 High Street, Royston, Hertfordshire, SG8 9AW, tel: 01763 242003, www.oldbullinn-royston.co.uk.

ST ALBANS

An embarrassment of riches

It would not do justice to the town of St Albans if we did not mention how particularly well-endowed the place be for inns. In 1577 St Albans had the highest proportion of inns to alehouses of any town, with twenty-seven inns, twenty-six alehouses and two taverns. This proportion be surely as a result of the proximity to London and its position along an important road to the north. Many of the town's inns stand cheek by jowl along Holywell Hill, a diversion of the old Roman road Watling Street, which carried legionnaires into the city of Verulamium. Here, seeming to support each others timbers and tottering along the road like some of their more inebriated residents, are the Cross Keys, Peahen, the Seven Stars, the White Hart, The Angel, The Mermaid, The Saracen's Head, The Dolphin and The Crane, the latter known to have been here since 1556 with its grand jet-tied frontage and open gallery giving access to the bedrooms. Perhaps the grandest be The Bull, where Queen Elizabeth, who made three visits to the town, stayed in 1577.

The Crane, St Albans, Hertfordshire. (© Mr James Moore)

Elsewhere there are more remarkable places to stay and to sup. On French Row there be The Christopher Inn and Fleur de Lys. On Church Street, leading to Romeland from the centre of the town, be The Swan with a great hall and soaring roof. Along this street be also The George, dating to at least 1446, which once had its own chapel for the saying of prayers for guests. Further down the hill be the fine galleried Antelope, once the Tabard.

In the centre of the town be a great clock tower. Though the shrine of St Alban hath fallen victim to the religious reforms of the earlier part of this century, the abbey church remains as the town's parish church. Also of attraction to those who like antiquities are the crumbling walls of the Roman city of Verulamium, a settlement famously sacked by Boudica of the Iceni tribe in AD 61, that still stand.

❁

CASTLE INN
'Scene of a bloody battle'
This was the backdrop for the first major battle which started the Wars of the Roses – that thirty-year tussle which eventually ushered in our present 'Tudor' age.

The day of 22 May 1455 was the date of the First Battle of St Albans. Some 2,000 Lancastrians held the town, and the Yorkists, despite numbering 3,000, were at first repelled from barricades erected across the streets. The Yorkists then regrouped and pulled off a surprise attack by approaching from a meadow called Keyfield and through gardens and down small lanes. In the ensuing melee around the town's market place and in front of the Castle Inn, Edmund, Duke of Somerset fell, mortally wounded, into the doorway of the hostelry and King Henry VI was captured.

The Castle itself be not of great stature, as William Shakespeare alludes when he wrote about Somerset's dying moments in the second part of his play *Henry VI*. Richard, Duke of York says to his dying foe:

So, lie thou there;—
For, underneath an alehouse' paltry sign,

The Castle in Saint Albans, Somerset
Hath made the wizard famous in his death.

*Latterly: Skipton Building Society on the corner of St Peter's Street
and Victoria Street. A plaque marks the spot.*

CROSS KEYS
'Last resting place of a martyr'
There be a story linked to this inn, dating back to 1437, of
one sorry fellow called George Tankerfield, a humble cook
of Yorkshire who was put to death in the city's Romeland on
26 August 1555.

George had refuted the idea that the Holy Eucharist changes
into the very body of Jesus – a dangerous thing to do during the
reign of Catholic Queen Mary. One day, whilst living in London,
he was asked to prepare the feast at a banquet. But 'twas a trap set
by some Catholics who found his Protestant views abhorrent and
brought him to trial.

After being found guilty he was brought from Newgate Prison
in London to St Albans as it had been decided to burn heretics
in prominent places around the kingdom. Kept a prisoner in the
town's Cross Keys inn before the fateful day, a great throng was said
to have turned out to catch sight of the supposed wrongdoer. While
at the inn he be said to have asked for a stick of fire and pulling
up his hose put a flame to his skin to see how it could be endured
during his subsequent ordeal. The next day, as the fagots or sticks
were assembled about him he continued to deny the Catholic faith,
despite those beseeching him to convert and save himself.
*Latterly: Demolished to make way for the new London Road in
1794, the name lives on in a pub nearby: The Cross Keys, 2 Chequer
Street, St Albans, Hertfordshire, AL1 3XZ, tel: 01727 839917,
www.jdwetherspoon.co.uk.*

FLEUR DE LYS
'Where a king was kept prisoner'
The French name of this inn, in existence since 1420, links it to
a curious tradition about the place which says that a house on

the site, once owned by Simon the vintner, was used as a prison for King John of France in 1356. The king had been brought as a captive to England after the Battle of Poitiers, a great victory in the Hundred Years War, where the English Black Prince had vanquished his French foe. The *fleur de lys* be of course a stylised lily used by the French kings in their coat of arms – though 'tis also used by many aristocrats around the courts of Europe too.
Latterly: The Fleur de Lys, French Row, St Albans, Hertfordshire, AL3 5DU, tel: 01727 851439.

THE PEAHEN
'The myth of King Henry's secret marriage'
Known as Le Pehenne in 1480, 'twas kept in 1568 by Alice Thomson who left it to her son, John. There be a legend, put about by troublemakers no doubt, that Henry VIII did conduct a secret marriage with Anne Boleyn here in 1533. This be surely a preposterous myth. Today the inn be not the grandest in the town – and certainly more of a dullish peahen than glamorous peacock, which incidentally be a name given to an inn along Church Street, near The George. We hear tell that 'tis likely to join forces with its neighbour The Woolpack.
Latterly: The Peahen, 14 London Road, St Albans, Hertfordshire, AL1 1NG, tel: 01727 853669, www.peahen.co.uk.

THE OLD ROUND HOUSE
'Pigeon coop turned hostelry'
Lying near the great cathedral of St Alban, this may not be the most comfortable of watering holes but it surely be one of the most whimsical of drinking follies in our isles. For, despite the name, 'tis not round at all, but octagonal in shape being once, 'tis mooted, the pigeon house of the former abbey, dissolved in 1539. 'Tis suggested that in 1485 this coop-shaped building was moved from the immediate vicinity of the abbey to its present location a few hundred yards away, by the side of the gently meandering River Ver, though this be disputed by others who claim a drinking place hath stood here since the eleventh century. A rudimentary, but charming alehouse, 'tis now certainly out of site of those

churchmen who might frown upon its temptations. Yet there are still rumoured to be tunnels between itself and the abbey, suggesting that, in the past, some of the less devout monks may have given in to the urge for refreshment after vespers.

Be aware that if thee are of a squeamish disposition thee may encounter cock-fights in the evenings here. If thee require a more comfortable place to lay thy head than nestling amongst the confusion of feathers and droppings upon the floor, thee might be better off seeking out one of the inns in the city before inebriation takes hold or the River Ver suddenly floods, which 'tis prone to do. *Latterly: Ye Olde Fighting Cocks, 16 Abbey Mill Lane, St Albans, Hertfordshire, AL3 4HE, tel: 01727 869152, www.yeoldefightingcocks.co.uk.*

The Old Round House, later Ye Olde Fighting Cocks, St Albans, Hertfordshire. (© Mr James Moore)

WHITE HART
'A tribute to Mr Shakespeare?'

Also known as the Hartshorn, this be one of our favourite places to stay. It boasts wonderful wall paintings in the bed chambers which include birds and foliage. Most exciting be the new painting of Adonis, thought to be based upon Mister William Shakespeare's poem, 'Venus and Adonis', written in 1593, though this hath been used by some naysayers to put about rumours that the real author of his works be the much-admired philosopher Francis Bacon who hath his home near St Albans.

For many years the inn hath been making its own excellent brews. We are told that as long ago as 1535 the inn was leased by the Abbot of St Albans to John Broke and his wife Elizabeth 'with a brewing lede, one growte lede, one tabyll with a peyer of trescells standing in the hall and in the parlour one tabyll with a peyer of trescells and ten bedsteddes'. So it hath always been a comfortable place. The present owner be a John Moseley, much admired in the town for his godly attitude towards the poor, to whom he sometimes distributes spare foodstuffs.

Latterly: The White Hart Hotel, 23-25 Holywell Hill, St Albans, AL1 1EZ, tel: 01727 853624, whiteharthotelstalbans.co.uk.

WARE

WHITE HART INN
'Home of the Great Bed of Ware'

No other inn possesses such an amusing and acclaimed item of furniture as the great bed of Ware. 'Tis a marvel and true to its name – for it can accommodate twelve people for a comfortable night's sleep. 'Twas made in 1590 by Jonas Fosbrooke as an attraction for travellers, designed to tempt them into the White Hart rather than one of the other inns in the town, such as The George, Saracen's Head, Bear or Crown, for Ware be on an important road to Cambridge.

The four-poster bed be not made of walnut, the wood considered finest in our age, but of good oak at least. The elaborate carving upon it, considered 'middling grand', be certainly striking to the eye, but 'tis its size, not its style, that will most surprise thee. In July 1596 Prince Ludwig of Anholt-Kohten, in Germany, stayed here, writing: 'At Ware was a bed of dimensions so wide, four couples might cosily lie side by side, and thus without touching each other abide.' We have no reports of just how many have ever shared the bed or what depravity might have ensued.

Nicholas Bleake be the current keeper of the White Hart, which hath a history dating back to 1426 when 'twas owned by the Guild of Corpus Christi, but he be no ordinary hostelryman; as well as being the possessor of this most interesting artefact, which hath made him wealthy, he be also a mapmaker.

We hear a rumour that William Shakespeare may include the Great Bed in a play he be considering, called (appropriately) *Twelfth Night*.

Latterly: An HSBC bank branch at 75 High Street.

Other hostelries of note ...

BALDOCK

GEORGE AND DRAGON
Another inn which owes its position to trade along the north road. It hath been here since 1465 and the archdeacon of Huntingdon's ecclesiastical court meets here.
Latterly: On Hitchin Street, recently closed.

HERTFORD

THE BELL
Here since 1431, this be the best place to stay in a town which hath a castle much favoured by royals, including Henry VIII and Queen Elizabeth.
Latterly: Salisbury Arms Hotel, Fore Street, Hertford, Hertfordshire, SG14 1BZ, tel: 01992 583091, salisburyarmshotel.co.uk.

REDBOURN

THE BULL
Owned by the Finch family since as long as anyone can remember, this be set upon the old road to the north-west. William Finch be the present innkeeper.
Latterly: The Bull Inn, 43 High Street, Redbourn, Hertfordshire, AL3 7LW, www.bullinnredbourn.co.uk.

❧ HUNTINGDONSHIRE

Mister William Camden describes Huntingdonshire as a 'country for corne and tillage and towards the East where it be fenny, verie rich and plentifull for the feeding of cataille; elsewhere right pleasant by reason of rising hills and shady groves'.

As well as Huntingdon, a town of importance as a crossing place on one of the main north to south routes across the realm, other important towns be St Ives, Godmanchester, St Neots, and Ramsey.

Be advised that despite loose talk, this be not a wholly puritanical county, for clergy are known to frequent the most tawdry of alehouses, with one rector reported as going to the alehouse after every service.

BUCKDEN

LAMB AND FLAG
'Lofty beams and the brews of bishops'
The wonderful moulded oak beams lend this place an ecclesiastical air which be unsurprising when thee learned that 'tis a former guesthouse of the Bishop of Lincoln's palace, built in 1492. In the middle of the five beams be a boss in the shape of a rose with a carving of the lamb and the words '*Ecce, Agnus, Dei*' which means to us common folk 'behold the Lamb of God'. The inn hath two

grand wings and a great chimney breast spanning 10ft which also features lovely, carved rose decorations.

The inn be located some 50 miles north of London, halfway between the great capital and the city of Lincoln. Next to the inn be Buckden Palace, residence of the bishops. This was one of the places where Henry VIII's first wife Catherine of Aragon was shut up after the annulment of their marriage before being allowed to live out her days at the nearby Kimbolton Castle.

Latterly: The Lion, High Street, Buckden, Cambridgeshire, PE19 5XA, tel: 01480 810313, www.thelionbuckden.com.

HUNTINGDON

THE GEORGE
'Of Cromwells and witchcraft'

Once the property of the Druel family, The George hath been here since 1510, but, in 1574, one Henry Cromwell became the owner, who we congratulate on the very recent birth of his grandson – Oliver. We wonder if the child will make as big a mark on the country as his grandfather who runs this, the chief inn of the town, as a conurbation which owes its position to the bridge across the Great Ouse which carries traffic north and south along the great northern highway.

A word of warning: do not stay at The George if thee are easily spooked. Guests report apparitions on the staircases and invisible forces pushing them down. Despite being well-trodden ground, Huntingdon be still a superstitious place. In 1593 when Henry's wife Lady Weeks died of a horrible disease John Samuel, his wife Alice and his daughter Agnes were all executed for witchcraft – believed to have killed her with their evil spells.

Latterly: The George Hotel, George Street, Huntingdon, Cambridgeshire, PE29 3AB, www.oldenglishinns.co.uk.

STILTON

THE BELL
'Partake thyself of the cheese'

'Tis reckoned that The Bell dates back to at least the year 1437 and from 1500 to 1515 'twas in the keep of Edward Tebald and his wife Alice. It hath a somewhat troubled past, for the Tebald's daughter Margaret and her husband William Redehede were forced to sue the tenant for possession, who, it seemed, would not leave.

Things have now settled down and the food be excellent, sure to fuel any journey along the northern highway which passes directly through the village along the course of the old Roman road known as Ermine Street. There sometimes be a choice blue cheese on offer, not ever having been made in the hamlet itself, but brought in from a mysterious source in Leicestershire. This hath, frankly, an awful appearance, sometimes being surrounded by maggots, but be surprisingly delicious when eaten with a spoon.
Latterly: The Bell Inn Hotel, Great North Road, Stilton, Peterborough, PE7 3RA, www.thebellstilton.co.uk.

WANSFORD

THE SWAN
'Rest by the bridge'

In the year 1571 storms led to the flooding of the river here and caused devastation to Wansford. Good weather for ducks but not those staying at the elegant three-storeyed inn nearby which carries the name of The Swan. A chronicler tells us that:

> At Wansford three arches of the bridge were washed away and so rapid and violent was the rising of the Nene that at the Swan Inn, three storeys high, the water flowed into the bedrooms. Walls of the stables were broken down and horses tied to the manger were drowned.

The damage having been repaired, The Swan, another hostelry that owes its existence to the Great North Road, still be a good place to tarry if thee want news of the conditions ahead.

Since those egregious floods, maintaining the bridge hath been recognised as vital for those bringing goods or news from the north or vice versa. The crossing hath been here since the thirteenth century and was at first built of oak. Since 1577 it hath been made of stone and now carries a considerable amount of traffic. Indeed, in 1581, 'twas considered so important as to be brought under the ownership of Her Majesty.

Latterly: The Haycock Hotel, Wansford, Peterborough, PE8 6JA, tel: 01780 782223.

❀ KENT

Already known as the garden of England, this county be famed for its agricultural produce, boasting bounteous orchards that bear fine apples and plums. Cherries, first grown here as recently as 1540, are now plentiful and new vegetables, such as that peppery stick called celery, are also to be found. Barley be grown for malt in the eastern part of the county and hops be grown around Maidstone, having first been cultivated in England, as legend hath it, in the village of Westbere. The county also be famous for its cattle and poultry. In the Weald iron making be an important industry, while Faversham hath become renowned for the making of gunpowder.

The city of Canterbury hath suffered in stature since the Dissolution of the Monasteries and though not now a place of pilgrimage 'tis still on an important trade route. The county also be famous for its ports, vital for defence against the French and Spanish, though many of the more ancient harbours are silting up and not oft used by our larger warships. Dover hath now recovered from the earthquake of 1580 that caused much damage. At Chatham there be a new royal dockyard, instituted by Her Majesty Queen Elizabeth, for the fitting out of ships.

Kent be home to some of the most important royal residences and castles. The queen was born at Greenwich Palace while King Henry VIII grew up at Eltham. Hever Castle was the home of Anne Boleyn and where Henry VIII courted his future wife. After her treason and beheading 'twas given to his fourth wife, Anne of Cleves, on their divorce in 1540. Henry also enjoyed staying at Leeds Castle both on his way to the Field of the Cloth of Gold, his meeting with the King of France in 1520, and to escape periods of pestilence in London.

Other fine sights for the traveller include Sissinghurst Castle, a fine moated manor house in a contemporary style, and the *Golden Hind*, the famous ship of Sir Francis Drake which be now permanently kept on display at a creek near Deptford, though be quick if thee want to pluck a souvenir, they are going fast.

Kent hath many fine inns, forty-five as of 1577. However, there be presently much worry about how much crime be fermented by the lower sort of alehouse, for in the courts of the county offences linked to tippling houses make up the largest number of misdemeanours.

CANTERBURY

THE FOUNTAIN
'The best in England'
A very ancient inn indeed, for it hath been handed down to us that in the year 1029 Gytha, the wife of Earl Godwin, lodged here and Archbishop Lanfranc found it a comfortable place to put up while his palace in the city was rebuilt in the year 1070. Indeed, it may have been the last plotting place of those infamous four knights, who believing they were doing the king's will, murdered Thomas Becket in the cathedral in 1170.

In 1299 an ambassador from Germany attending the marriage of Edward I, then aged 60, to Margaret of France, just 16 years of age, wrote: 'The inns in England are the best in Europe, those of Canterbury are the best in England and The Fountain wherein I am now lodged as handsomely as I were in the King's Palace the best in Canterbury.'

Since Becket's shrine was destroyed in 1538, clergy stay less at The Fountain, which now caters mainly to merchants who travel to the continent via the coastal ports.

Latterly: Became The Royal Fountain Hotel on St Margaret's Street which was destroyed in an air raid during the Second World War.

THE WHITE HART
'A place to beat the curfew'

Of the twenty or so inns in this commodious city The White Hart now rivals The Fountain for fame and comfort. Situated near the Westgate, it hath, since 1403, been a convenient stopping point on the road from London, but in times past hath also been useful to those who arrived in the city after curfew, but needing a place to stay.

The White Hart caters to those cashing in on the recently arrived weavers and silk makers from the Low Countries. 'Twas surely also visited by that notorious playwright Christopher Marlowe, who was born to a shoemaker in the city but rose to become one of the greatest writers of our age, famous for works like *The Jew of Malta* and *Doctor Faustus*.

Mystery still surrounds his death with some asserting that he was killed in a drunken brawl in Deptford. He be known to have spent liberally on food and drink and The White Hart would certainly have suited his lavish appetite.

Note also that for those travelling to Dover the Flying Horse, established since 1574, be a good similar prospect on the eastern edge of the city.

Latterly: The Falstaff, 10 St Dunstan's Street, Canterbury, Kent, CT2 8AF, tel: 01227 462138, www.thefalstaffincanterbury.com.

THE CROWN INN
'Where our virgin queen was wooed'

Queen Elizabeth spent three days here in 1573 on the occasion of her 40th birthday, during her progress to the county and this fine inn hath since been decorated in style to celebrate the occasion with a plaster ceiling in a first floor chamber which includes a Tudor rose and her royal monogram. Whilst here she be said to have received one of her suitors, the French Duke of Anjou. Though the match came to nothing the queen for a time, wore a frog-shaped earring that he gave her.

Latterly: 43–45 High Street, Canterbury. Now Thorntons and Caffe Nero.

Beer, not ale, be the fashion

Hop growing be now most popular here in Kent, which hath a long tradition of brewing. Supping beer instead of ale hath taken some time to catch on as the fashion. For, in 1426 in the town of Maidstone, a person was decried for 'putting into beer an unwholesome weed called hoppe'. But today beer be reckoned the superior drink. In the 1570s Reginald Scott wrote that most men in Kent 'do abhor and abandon ale as a loathsome drink'.

As the old saying goes: 'herisie and beere came hopping into England both in a yeere.'

❁

CRANBROOK

THE GEORGE
'A mile of cloth for the queen'
Queen Elizabeth's visit to the town in 1573 was much celebrated by local folk who presented a silver gilt cup engraved with a lion to the monarch for troubling to call at this sleepy place high in the Kentish Weald. Cranbrook be known for its broadcloth and so 'tis no surprise that on the occasion of her visit part of the celebrations saw her walking along a mile-long piece of locally made cloth.

The George, first constructed in around 1300, was built, in part, to cater for the merchants who trade this much sought-after commodity. And 'twas here that the queen slept. For a sum, thee may still stay in the room in which she lay.

Latterly: The George Hotel, Stone Street, Cranbrook, Kent, TN17 3HE, tel: 01580 713348, www.thegeorgehotelkent.co.uk.

Marlowe's grizzly end

'Twas in the neighbourhood of Deptford that the renowned playwright Christopher Marlowe met his grizzly end at the young age of 29, in the year 1593. 'Tis oft said that he died in a tavern brawl over the bill. Another account, published just last year, says that he was 'stabbed to death by a bawdy serving-man, a rival of his in his lewd love'. And yet another says that he was in a boarding house kept by one Eleanor Bull, smoking and playing backgammon before a quarrel between himself and another man, Ingram Frizer, over who was to pay the tab. Marlowe grabbed Frizer's dagger and slashed at him, but the blade was driven into Marlowe's head, above his eye. What be certain was that death was swift. Some have countered this account, instead attributing Marlowe's death to his stealthy life as a spy for the good English state. The report that he died swearing, fitting for this denier of God, be surely true.

❖

DARTFORD

THE BULL
'Chaucer's muse'
Like many of the greatest inns, this began life as a hospice attached to the local Augustinian priory of St Mary and St Margaret. Situated in Watling Street on the way between London and Canterbury, 'twas a regular stopping point for Geoffrey Chaucer who was friends with the innkeeper Urban Baldock. Urban gave him many suggestions for characters in his famous work *The Canterbury Tales*. The galleried Bull, known in 1508 by the curious name of Le Hole Bole, be now a pleasant place to steel thyself for the rigours of the road or the throbbing streets of the capital.
Latterly: The Royal Victoria and Bull Hotel, 1 High Street, Dartford, Kent, DA1 1DU, tel: 01322 224415.

GRAVESEND

THREE CORNISH CHOUGHS
'Of prayers and smuggler's prey'
There hath been a drinking place licensed here since 1565 and the present building was converted from a row of timber cottages into the hostelry we know today. Weather-boarded against the elements, 'tis sited at an important crossing point used in times past by pilgrims coming from Essex across the Thames Estuary and on to Canterbury. Many travellers still favour this method, preferring the perils of the sea to the banditry of the rough roads.

The choughs in the inn's title are birds featured on Canterbury's coat of arms, and of its martyred archbishop and saint, Thomas Becket. Legend hath it that it also be a very mischievous bird, known to steal small items and trinkets. Since thee may well encounter smugglers here, who use the waterside inns as their dens and hawking places, perhaps its name hath a subtle double meaning.

Latterly: Three Daws, Town Pier, Gravesend, Kent, DA11 0BJ, tel: 01474 566869, www.threedaws.co.uk.

Beware Gad's Hill

A word of warning about Gad's Hill, between Gravesend and Rochester. 'Tis a notorious place for highway robberies, immortalised in the famous ballad of 1558 called 'The Robbers of Gad's Hill.' The place hath become so linked with roguery on the roads that 'tis included in William Shakespeare's new play *Henry IV* as the spot in which his character Falstaff organises a botched robbery.

ROCHESTER

THE CROWN INN

'When Henry VIII met Anne of Cleves'

Set upon the main street of the city, famed for its cathedral and great castle, near the place where a fine old stone bridge crosses the Medway, this graceful inn was founded by at least 1316. In that year one Simon Potyn was the innkeeper, a godly sort who found a hospital locally for lepers. 'Twas probably at this inn that the writer Geoffrey Chaucer and the pilgrims of his tales stayed as they made their way between London and Canterbury.

The Crown be certainly well named, for its association with royal visitors be perhaps unparalleled in all the land. Indeed, Francis Thynne, a well-known Kentish man of our age, states that 'tis the 'only place to intertaine princes coming thither'.

Both King Philip of Spain and Queen Mary were guests, as was Queen Elizabeth who stayed here for four days during a 'cold and wet progress' in the September of 1573. She also stayed with Richard Watts, a man who set up a place to stay in the city for poorer travellers. Good to know if thee have been robbed on thy way here.

Perhaps the most memorable story surrounding The Crown involves Henry VIII's first meeting with his fourth wife, Anne of Cleves. The king was said to have stayed in The Crown so that he could go incognito to catch sight of his pockmarked, German-born intended who was staying at the city's Bishop's Palace.

It seems that the beer at the inn, despite being well hopped, cannot have had that effect, which it sometimes does, of giving the eyes more pleasure in beholding members of the opposite sex than they deserve, for the king branded her a great 'Flanders mare' and, as history tells us, their subsequent marriage was not a success.

Latterly: The Crown Freehouse, 2 High Street, Rochester, Kent, ME1 1PT, tel: 01634 814874, www.thecrownrochester.co.uk.

SANDWICH

THE QUEEN'S ARMS
'The latest thing'

The town itself be old, being near the place where the Romans first arrived in England and one of the ancient Cinque Ports, long fortified against the threat of invasion. In 1255 Sandwich saw the first elephant landed in England, brought as a gift for Henry III. Its port hath suffered from silting up with sand in recent decades.

Against this historical backdrop, with its fine Barbican gate, the town boasts a very modern addition: The Queen's Arms, built in 1580, commemorates Queen Elizabeth's visit to the town a few years before, when she was entertained with a banquet and mock battle. The inn comes with every modern convenience thee could want. It also sports some daring architectural flashes, including a carving of a cloven satyr on its frontage and the queen's coat of arms in iron.

If The Queen's Arms be too flashy for thy liking, the Bell Inn, a much older establishment dating from around 1300, will be sure to cater to thy needs.

Latterly: The King's Arms Hotel, Strand Street, Sandwich, Kent, CT13 9HN, tel: 01304 617330, www.kingsarms-sandwich.co.uk.

TONBRIDGE

THE CHEQUERS INN
'Drinks and the gibbet'

There hath been an inn here, below the castle, since around 1264, when it faced the market square with its stocks and whipping post. In its time it hath been used as a place to try felons and, as testimony, a gibbet juts out of a strong oak post over the main street. 'Twas here that Wat Tyler's brother reputedly faced the noose after the former's failed rebellion of 1381 which began in the county.

In more recent times this hath been the setting for further grizzly events. In 1555 Margery Polley was burned here for heresy and in 1575 a woman was burned for poisoning her husband.

The present, recently constructed, inn commands great respect, with its fresh timbers and gables, giving this town on the River Medway an air of sophistication, which its paltry population of 500 inhabitants would not lead thee to expect.

No one be sure where the inn gets its name but in ancient Rome the Chequers moniker was said to indicate that a wine tavern also provided banking facilities to its customers. It could also be linked to the fee gatherers for the exchequer of the local castle.

Latterly: Ye Olde Chequers, 122 High Street, Town Centre, Tonbridge, TN9 1AS, tel: 01732 358957.

Other hostelries of note ...

BOUGHTON-UNDER-BLEAN

WHITE HORSE

Set upon the pilgrim's route in a village mentioned by Chaucer and the first place where his pilgrims would have been able to see Canterbury Cathedral.

Latterly: The White Horse, Boughton-under-Blean, The Street, Boughton, ME13 9AL, tel: 01227 751343, www.whitehorsecanterbury.co.uk.

IGHTHAM

GEORGE AND DRAGON

Dating from 1515, this be a perfect stopping-off point for those lucky enough to be visiting the moated manor house of Ightham Mote.

Latterly: The George & Dragon, The Street, Ightham, Kent, TN15 9HH, tel: 01732 882440.

SARRE

CROWN INN
Situated at the main crossing point to the Isle of Thanet, it hath served travellers since 1500.
Latterly: The Crown Inn, Ramsgate Road, Sarre, Kent, CT7 0LF, tel: 01843 847808, www.crownsarre.co.uk.

SPELDHURST

GEORGE AND DRAGON
Originally built in 1212, some of its beams come from one of Henry VIII's old ships.
Latterly: The George & Dragon, Speldhurst Hill, Speldhurst, Kent, TN3 0NN, tel: 01892 863125, www.speldhurst.com.

❧ LANCASHIRE

Fine inns be hard to come by on the bleak, high expanse of moss and moor that covers much of the land in this county, causing woeful melancholy in those who seek good company. The county be still among the poorest in the land, except for prosperous Manchester. Even some decades ago, John Leland told us that 'twas the 'fairest, best built, quietest and most populous town in Lancashire. Here a small number of people own fortunes of more than £100! The town hath become a centre for woollens and already hath a very worthy school.'

Linen be good in Eccles, Wigan and Ormskirk and such be the repute of the Lancastrian cloth that 'tis sold at London's Blackwell Hall. Though carding, spinning and weaving employ many hands, coal, say some, will be the future of Lancashire. To the north of the county, Preston be up and coming, but in the west, the Liverpudlians lament they inhabit a 'poor, decayed' town, and wrote such to Her Majesty in 1571. Yet some speak well of Liverpool, predicting an upturn now that the River Dee be silting up, causing trade to be taken from Chester. Lancaster's castle hath been improved in the reign of Queen Elizabeth and the city hath a reputation for entertaining hangings of felons.

In Manchester, houses for drinking are not allowed unless the innkeeper provides two honest beds and in Preston he must permit at least four men and horses to bed afore ale he may sell.

BOLTON

OLDE MAN & SCYTHE

'Don't mention the war'

The town name comes from the Old English which means 'settlement with a special building' and this inn be certainly this. 'Tis not known on exactly what date this inn was constructed but its musty, barrel-vaulted cellars have been harbouring good wine and ale since before 1200. By 1251 a charter permitting a market in the town of Bolton – most excellent for provisions – mentioned the inn by name. Its unusual title stems from its ownership by the Pilkington family a century or so ago. This family hath oft come into trouble and the crest which hath become the inn's sign shows a mower and scythe in recognition of an ancient family member who escaped punishment in the time of the Norman Conquest by disguising himself as a common labourer of the land. Sadly for the Pilkington family the inn hath now fallen out of their hands and into that of the Stanleys, for the Pilkingtons, strangely, fought on the wrong side at the Battle of Bosworth, that culmination of the battle between the House of Lancaster and York, which the Lancastrians won. The sign hath been retained but it might be best not to mention the old family.

Latterly: Ye Old Man & Scythe, 6–8 Churchgate, Bolton, Lancashire, BL1 1HL, tel: 01204 451237.

MANCHESTER

SEVEN STARS
'A buxom mistress'
Yet another that claims to be one of the oldest licensed premises in the land, the Seven Stars hath served ale since at least 1356, around the time Edward III required inns and taverns to be regulated. When the Collegiate Church was founded in 1422, a passageway was constructed betwixt the two buildings, so men of the cloth could get to the inn without falling foul of the vagaries of the weather or attracting the attention of the bishop. The churchman who in 1571 did not take this precaution and stepped into the street to reach the inn was caught, and the court leets show that he did so whilst his colleague mounted the pulpit to address his congregation.

Travellers must mount Smithy Bank to reach this tavern, where the smell of good home cooking, by the worthy widow who keeps the house, will waft o'er the hills. This buxom mistress, Dame Sutcliffe, declares her intent to keep the Seven Stars for many years.

The vestry here be the meeting place of the watch and ward of Manchester who adjourn to this picturesque and comfortable tavern to talk of issues of import to the town.
Latterly: The site was at the entrance to the Arndale Centre, Withy Grove, Manchester.

MITTON

THREE FISHES
'Named by an abbot'
Take the ferry to Mitton to enjoy the hospitality of the Three Fishes, just upstream from the new bridge at Lower Hodder that provides access if thy ride here. Mitton be a place of pilgrimage for those who come to All Hallows' church, and this inn be a place for rest and refreshment. The company be mixed between those with wealth and those with none and the Three Fishes be oft a

Drunken clergy and their fuzzy flock

Chronicles report that many clergy misbehave here. George Dobson, vicar of Whalley, be said by his flock to be a 'common drunkard and such an ale-knight as the like be not in our parish'. Many be the vicar that keep an alehouse to supplement their stipend. Worse, alehouses are oft better attended than church.

'Tis not only the clergy who seek to top up wages by selling sack, wine and spirits. Widows, labourers and the poor in general hath opened alehouses in Lancashire. Though unlicensed they may mostly be, justices have overlooked this in order that the proprietors do not become a burden on their neighbours or turn to vagrancy.

hiding place for ne'r-do-wells, though they risk much when taking shelter here for the inn also holds the annual court leet, where worthy appointments be made, including for the Ale Taster of Mitton, oft a member of the clergy.

Many think the Three Fishes a foolish name, others that it makes sense given the three rivers of Hodder, Calder and Ribble that lap its door and converge here. But the last Abbot of Whalley Abbey named the inn such, and he being a man of God, knows the old story of how much can be made out of a few fishes. Abbot Paslew's own arms that show three fishes are carved above the door.

Latterly: The Three Fishes, Mitton Road, Mitton, Near Whalley, Lancashire, BB7 9PQ, tel: 01254 826888, www.thethreefishes.com.

HORNBY

CASTLE INN
'Fortify thyself'
Opposite the gates of the castle and handy for market day, which hath latterly switched from Fridays to Mondays, be the Castle Inn, which we believe the finest of the several hostelries in this

small town. Henry Chatburn, innkeeper here, be a man of many talents, trading linen and acting as deputy bailiff for the castle of Hornby. The castle hath recently added a new tower, which be much to behold. Many come to admire it and yet, as they be not allowed in, go instead to the Castle Inn, and this hath made Mr Chatburn much content, especially if he can sell linen as well as ale. The Castle Inn be handy for travellers from Lancaster to Kirkby Lonsdale as the inn rests at a crossing point by the River Wenning. The village be quaint, with four shops, in the market place near to the smithys, so thy can sup whilst thy horse be shod.
Latterly: The Castle Inn, Main Street, Hornby, Lancashire, LA2 8JT, tel: 01524 222279, www.thecastleinnhornby.co.uk.

Other hostelries of note ...

STANDISH

BOAR'S HEAD
Established as an inn since at least 1450. Do not venture in if thee are not bold of heart, for ghouls are said to walk its corridors. Here prisoners from the Chester Assizes have been shut up on their way to be hanged at Lancaster.
Latterly: The Boar's Head, Wigan Road, Standish, Wigan, Lancashire, WN6 0AD, tel: 01942 749747, www.boarsheadstandish.co.uk.

❧ LEICESTERSHIRE & RUTLAND

This landlocked county in the very heart of England and 'bearing corne in great plenty' hath also been at the centre of history these past hundred years or so for 'tis here that the Battle of Bosworth was fought in 1485 which did, as every scholar should know, usher in the reign of the battle's Lancastrian victor, Henry Tudor, as Henry VII. His dynasty, of course, endureth to this very day.

In 1087 came the first reference to the county as Laegrecastrescir. Chief among the settlements be the revered city of Leicester, on the River Soar. 'Tis a Roman city which once boasted baths and pavements and centurions marching along that great cross-country road, the Fosse Way. Today 'tis a city of some 600 families with a growing wealthy group of tanners, butchers and drapers. There are other important towns in the county too, like Loughborough and Melton Mowbray.

Also of note be that Leicestershire was the burial place of Cardinal Thomas Wolsey, who famously fell out with King Henry VIII, not, by any account, a wise thing to do. Already having been liberated from his former palace at Hampton Court, he was, in November 1530 ordered to go to London, from York where he had fled, accused of high treason. On the way he fell ill and his party was forced to stop at Leicester Abbey. He told the abbot that night: 'I am come to leave my bones among thee', and swiftly did as much. Just a few years later the Dissolution would bring the walls of the abbey crumbling down around those mouldering bones as if cursed by their presence.

With much to-ing and fro-ing about the county by such folk, 'tis at least good to know that Leicestershire today hath enough inns to stable a thousand horses. Rutland, considered in this entry also on account of coming within the compass of Leicestershire, hath 100 alehouses of its very own, despite its smallness.

LEICESTER

BLUE BOAR
'King Richard's last night before Bosworth'
History tells us that in August 1485 King Richard III stopped here, when the inn was known as The White Boar, being his emblem. 'Twas to be his last resting place before the Battle of Bosworth Field on the 22nd of the month, the culmination of that conflict between the houses of York and Lancaster.

We know that Richard came into Leicester from Nottingham upon a white steed with his crown proudly upon his head.

The Blue Boar, Leicester. (© Leicester Arts and Museums Service)

Stopping at the gabled front of the Boar, with its ornate oak balcony, he paused for the night. It's said that he slept in the main chamber in a great gothic bed covered in gold.

In the morning he set out to meet his foes across the city's Bow Bridge. On the way his spur struck the bridge and a soothsayer predicted that his broken head would strike the same spot. That bloody battle would see the king killed and, with the victory of the subsequent Henry VII, usher in a new dynasty. The drama of that struggle hath been captured by the bard William Shakespeare, who hath the king utter the last line:'A horse, a horse, my kingdom for a horse!'

Later Richard's mutilated and stripped body would be carried back across the same bridge where his head did brush against the parapet, thus fulfilling the soothsayer's prophecy. His body was paraded in the city and hung for good measure, before being finally buried at Grey Friars church.

'Tis rumoured that the king left treasure in the form of £300 in gold coins at the Boar which he expected to collect on his return, victorious. But the current innkeeper, one Thomas Clarke, stayed tight-lipped about the subject upon our enquiries. The legend hath certainly helped him fill his own coffers and if thee decide to enjoy the comfort of the Boar remember that thee will be charged a premium for its interesting history.

Another inn, The Angel on Cheapside, also hath a story to tell of a royal end – Mary, Queen of Scots stayed here in 1586 on her way to her subsequent execution at Fotheringhay Castle.

Latterly: Sited on the corner of Highcross Street and Blue Boar Lane it was demolished in the nineteenth century.

MARKET HARBOROUGH

SWANNES
'Of the roasted kind'

Harborough be a pleasant town serious about its trade and its inns. 'Tis well known in the region for its market and fair, where there be hard haggling over horses, sheep and cattle, but there be trade in the making of shoes too. Harborough be also placed upon important roads and near the ancient Rockingham Forest, long used as a royal hunting ground. The Swan here dates from at least 1517, when 'twas known as 'Ye Sygne of Swanne' and was run by a Richard Cade. More swans have been added as the inn hath increased in size – it now features an archway to carry traffic through to the courtyard.

The Swan be of course a bird with great association to the monarch, but the Worshipful Companies of Dyers and of Vintners are also allowed to own them. Roasted swan be a delicacy and many an inn hath adopted the name to signify fine dining within.

Latterly: The Three Swans Hotel, 21 High Street, Market Harborough, Leicestershire, LE16 7NJ, tel: 01858 466644, www.bw-threeswanshotel.co.uk.

Other hostelries of note ...

ASHBY-DE-LA-ZOUCH

THE BULL

A new alehouse which be frequented by those who ply their trade at the town's ancient and well-fortified stronghold.

Latterly: The Bull, 67 Market Street, Ashby-de-la-Zouch, Leicestershire, LE65 1AH, tel: 01530 564815, www.bullsheadashby-de-la-zouch.co.uk.

NEWTON BURGOLAND

SHEPHERD AND SHEPHERDESS

A humble place but serving since 1290 and worth a detour.

Latterly: The Belper Arms, Main Street, Newton Burgoland, LE67 2SE, tel: 01530 270530, www.thebelperarms.co.uk.

❀ LINCOLNSHIRE

Our late king Henry VIII was perhaps a little harsh when, in his reign, he called the county of Lincolnshire 'one of the most brute and beastly'. 'Tis true, however, that much of the county be remote and unforgiving. A roaring hearth and a hearty ale are certainly much in demand in the largely flat landscape, where winds sometimes seem to blow sharp enough to cut a man in two.

Splicing through the western side of Lincolnshire, passing through the towns of Stamford and Grantham, be the Great North Road. But travel in other parts of the county be not easy. The River Trent, in the west, be unbanked and wide, with the lowest bridge at Newark many miles from the sea. Those that want to travel north or south through Lincolnshire should be aware that only a ferry will carry them across the Humber – the best being between Barton-on-Humber and Hull, established since the fourteenth century.

Lincoln, with its great cathedral, dominates the centre of the county being some four or more days' ride from London. Boggy marshes and fens, believed to be prone to fevers and which at times turn into little inland seas, dominate the south. Watery inlets pepper the coastline, providing cover for many a smuggler, while the town of Boston provides the main trading harbour. Yet this vast county, numbering around 115,000 souls, also hath several wondrous ports of call for the tavern and inn lover, thanks to its prime situation halfway betwixt the north and south of England. Furthermore it produces great quantities of barley, much of which be taken to London for brewing in the capital city. There are fifty-four inns and over 700 alehouses here.

BOSTON

RED LION
'Beer and bowls'
Known in 1515 as the 'hospitium of the Red Lion in Bargate' and

owned by the Guild of St Mary, this well-stocked house hath been licensed as recently as 1586 to sell 'Lincoln and other beer brewed out of the borough'. Run by a local family called the Sibseys, both its own tipples and those brought in from other quarters of the county are thought to be excellent. There be not only good stabling and a smithy here but we understand a fine bowling green at the back of the property too – perfect for relaxing after a heavy day squelching through the boggy landscape or when hailing in from a stormy trip on the Northern Sea.

The game of bowls hath, of course, been banned in recent times among the lower orders, due to the interference 'twas deemed to have in stopping good men practising their archery. But of course our late, great, mariner Sir Francis Drake was a fan and those of good standing may find an exception to this old decree if staying at the inn.

Latterly: Demolished in 1959 to make way for Woolworths.

GRANTHAM

ANGEL
'Knights Templar and heavenly hosts'
Built of warm-coloured stone and bearing a gold-painted, carved figure of an angel above its great archway, the appearance of this venerated inn must be like that of a heavenly refuge to those who ply this lonely section of the Great North Road. With its stately rooms and solid poise the magnificent property stirs the soul of the traveller, enveloping he or she in its welcoming arms. As long, of course, as the said wayfarer can afford a bed in it!

The Angel be no mere wayside drinking den. Dating back to the twelfth century, the lodging was once a hostel owned by the legendary Knights Templar, that brotherhood of crusaders, before 'twas seized by the king in 1308. The house was certainly once used by pilgrims visiting a relic of St Wulfram in the town's parish church.

By 1213, and just two years before the signing of Magna Carta, the Angel was already a place for regal travellers to tarry. For we

The Angel
Grantham

The Angel, Grantham, Lincolnshire. (Courtesy of the Angel & Royal Hotel, Grantham)

Interior of the Angel, Grantham. (Courtesy of the Angel & Royal Hotel, Grantham)

know that King John held court at the inn on 23 February in that year. The hosts would surely have made sure the service was good, for by this time King John had a fearsome reputation having, in 1212, summarily hung twenty-eight sons of rebellious Welsh nobles in nearby Nottingham.

Next among its royal visitors were Edward III and Queen Philippa in the fourteenth century, whose carved heads adorn either side of the gateway arch.

Only the most esteemed of modern-day guests can afford to stay in *La Chambre le Roi*, or the King's Chamber, which, by the time of Richard III, was the name for the large room over the gateway of the inn. 'Twas in this room in October 1483 that Richard III summoned the Great Seal of State used for issuing a death warrant. 'Twas delivered to the king by messenger and here he signed orders for the execution of his cousin and rival the Duke of Buckingham. The sentence was carried out near another inn, The Bull's Head, in Salisbury.

Grantham be a town of about 2,000 souls. Here thee may marvel at the lavish Grantham House and at one of the much-famed Eleanor Crosses, built in a line down the East of England by King Edward I in the thirteenth century to mark the funeral procession of his wife, Queen Eleanor.

Latterly: Angel & Royal Hotel, High Street, Grantham,
Lincolnshire, NG31 6PN, tel: 01476 565816,
www.angelandroyal.co.uk.

A note on local temperament

The recently late Privy Councillor Thomas Wilson, himself from Lincolnshire, reported that it be much better to be 'born in London than in Lincoln for that both the ayre be better, people more civill and the wealth much greater and the men for the most part more wise'.

❧

LINCOLN

WHITE HART
'Of fallen spires … and tottering men'

In a city which seems a little down on its luck due to the decline of its former friaries, the cosy comforts of the White Hart bring a note of good cheer and not merely because thee may be lucky enough to glimpse, hereabouts, a great composer of our age, William Byrd, on a visit to the city of his birth.

In 1549 Lincoln suffered a tragedy when its cathedral spire, which once made the building the tallest in Christendom, collapsed in a storm. Due to the poverty of the church here in recent times, the spire hath not been replaced.

It seems that 'twas not the only sudden collapse likely to occur about the town. In 1553 the city's tippling houses were restricted to thirty on the grounds of the disorder from those who had overindulged.

The White Hart on the city's Bailgate be much the most salubrious place to quench one's thirst. Established since the fourteenth century, it gained its name from the insignia of Richard II, who reputedly stayed here. The White Hart be one of the most popular names for inns thanks to reverence for the king, who, history tells us, came to the throne aged just 10.

Those that visit the city should not miss the High Bridge over the River Witham, which hath a row of shops upon it. 'Twas built in the year 1160. Thee may also want to drop in at the Cardinal's Hat, a three-storey inn on Steep Hill, named originally after Cardinal Thomas Wolsey of King Henry VIII's reign who was once Bishop of Lincoln.

Latterly: White Hart Hotel, Bailgate, Lincoln, LN1 3AR,
tel: 01522 526222, www.whitehart-lincoln.co.uk.

SPALDING

WHITE HART
'A queen's sad journey'

Another inn named after King Richard's stag of choice. Spalding's White Hart was first mentioned in 1337, the year the king came to the throne, but the moulded timberwork here hath provided the backdrop for its own regal goings on. Legend hath it that in 1586 Mary, Queen of Scots lodged here on her sad journey to Fotheringhay Castle in Northamptonshire, where she would, as history tells us, later be executed. As she resided in what hath become the inn's Crown Room, we wonder if she knew she was making one of her last journeys.

There be talk that the inn was once the local priory guesthouse and that its other famous guests have included that great author Geoffrey Chaucer.

As far as the neat town of Spalding goes, this be a place on the up. It hath just got its own drains.

Latterly: A Chinese restaurant, www.shanghaigarden.co.uk.

STAMFORD

THE GEORGE
'Monarch of the inns'

'Tis possible that this grand resting and drinking place hath already been standing here, at the point where the Great North Road crosses the River Welland, for over 500 years. For there be talk of a hostelry belonging to the abbots of Croyland dating back as far as the year of our Lord 947.

But it be its connection with Lord Burghley, our great statesman so recently dead, that be worth noting. As recently as 1597 he had the place rebuilt as its remarkable new stone mullioned lattice windows and his coat of arms on the building testify. The restoration was much needed since the town suffered from a great flood in 1570, which ripped off the north end of the bridge.

The George was already of great importance back in the 1400s when the man in charge, one John Dickens, was elected Chief Magistrate of the town. Through his daughter Alice the ownership of the inn can be traced directly down to Richard Cissell, father to William Cecil, later Lord Burghley, who made the present house keeper one William Scarre. Who knows if Burghley's famous spies have ever been briefed within?

The inn hath a great reputation for its wine, stored in its ancient vaults, while fresh fruit be plucked from its own orchards. Here groups of travellers will set out together to avoid bandits along the great northern highway.

The town be noted for its travelling players and market. But of great majesty be Burghley House, a stone's throw from the inn and one of the finest examples of modern architecture.

Latterly: The George Hotel, 71 St Martins, Stamford, Lincolnshire, PE9 2LB, tel: 01780 750750, www.georgehotelofstamford.com.

❀ NORFOLK

The county, once home to the Iceni tribe and the infamous warrior queen Boudica, stretches from The Wash and the port of King's Lynn to the town of Yarmouth in the east. Rye be the predominant crop but of chief interest to the traveller be Norwich, our nation's second largest city, with its mighty walls, which numbers around 20,000 souls, despite a nasty dose of the plague in 1597 which be believed to have killed several thousand persons.

The city, dotted with orchards but dominated by its great castle and cathedral, throngs with merchants and weavers who have, in recent decades, fled religious troubles in the Low Countries. These new inhabitants now make up a third of the populous and are known locally as 'strangers'. With such a trade the city be peppered with hostelries which rank from the occasional great inn to many tawdry alehouses.

As such, in 1577, 'twas reported that there were 480 inns, taverns and alehouses in all Norfolk and that most of those who ran them were 'of the poorest class of people in the county'.

NORWICH

ADAM AND EVE
'Blessed ale and rebellious locals'

There be an old saying that along with a church for every Sunday, this fine city hath an inn, alehouse or tavern for every day of the year. But among its tippling places be a difficult-to-find gem – the Adam and Eve, located behind the great cathedral. Beneath the ancient floor be a well from Saxon times, but 'tis first recorded as a brewhouse in 1249 when the building was owned by the monks. Its ales helped both quench the thirst of stonemasons working on that great religious edifice and restored the health of patients at the nearby Great Hospital, or, if not, at least eased their passing.

'Tis in the shadow of the Adam and Eve's fine gabled ends that much of the drama surrounding Kett's rebellion of 1549 was played out. Robert Kett and his rebels rose up against the enclosure of common land by wealthy folk and marched on Norwich, camping out at nearby Mousehold Heath before briefly taking the city.

Their revolt was to be short lived. An army of some 13,000, dispatched under the Earl of Warwick, defeated them and Kett was hung from the battlements of Norwich Castle. But 'tis the ghost of the loyal Lord Sheffield, cut down by the rebels, who be said to haunt the Adam and Eve still.

Latterly: Adam and Eve, 17 Bishopsgate, Norwich, Norfolk, NR3 1RZ, tel: 01603 667423.

Cuckolds and courtesans

We hear tell of Margaret Molle, an alewife in Norfolk, who kept a lover in her brewhouse despite her husband's protestations and be known to beat away local folk who intervene with burning sticks. Yet some alewives appear to object to their bawdy reputation. One Margaret Fiske in 1578 said, 'there cannot be any alewife thrive without she be a whore or have a whore in her house'.

Adam and Eve, Norwich, Norfolk. (Courtesy of Dr Claire Nesbitt)

MAID'S HEAD
'Fishy tales and fine lodgings'

The Maid's Head was once a tavern known as the Molde Fishe or Murtil Fish, serving wine to city gentlefolk. But its old, gruff names disguise a present inn with great stature. First mentioned in 1287, 'tis one of the finest in England and another house in which our good Queen Bess hath rested, this time on her five-day-long visit to the city in 1578.

During this tour of the region Queen Elizabeth was presented with many gifts, such as a riding crop made from a whale fin. But on her tour the weather was awful and the great fireplaces, beams and carvings of the Maid's Head must have provided a welcome respite.

The inn already had a long-standing reputation. As far back as the year 1472 local John Paston wrote to his wife of an impending visitor: 'I praye yow make hym good cheer … it were best to set hys horse at the Maydes Hedde and I shall be content for ther expenses.'

The Black Prince also stayed here in 1359, to attend a joust, as well as the late Cardinal Wolsey of King Henry VIII's reign. 'Twas here, too, that Lord Sheffield breakfasted on 22 July 1549, before being slain by a rebel butcher during Kett's rebellion.

It's suggested that the name of the inn comes from a fishwife in the nearby Tombland called Mathilde, who, in 1349, became widowed and was offered the tenancy of the inn in order to make a living.

Latterly: Maids Head Hotel, Tombland, Norwich, Norfolk, NR3 1LB, tel: 01603 613688, www.maidsheadhotel.co.uk.

The Nine Days' Wonder

We must remark upon a very recently completed merriment – William Kemp's celebrated 'nine daies wonder'. For a wager the acclaimed actor danced the morris continually from London to Norwich in nine days. On arriving in the city he promptly jumped over the wall of St John Maddermarket Church to celebrate his achievement.

❀

THETFORD

THE BELL
'Pleasantly plastered'

Since at least 1493 The Bell hath been here, first as a seminary linked to the local priory and since 1540 solely as an inn – and a very fine one at that, giving good succour to the traveller who makes their way through the flat, gorse-covered sandy heath known as the Breckland, which surrounds the town.

Inside the inn there are welcoming fireplaces and an open gallery which gives way to lavish rooms adorned with magnificent paintings. One shows a series of great arches in extraordinary perspective – the modern manner.

By a local bye-law fish caught in the local rivers may only be traded from the corner of The Bell, and a great attraction of the town, which hath some score of alehouses, be its market. Here thee will find a great variety of produce for sale, from cheese and timber to meat, corn, hay and leather.

Proclamations to the townspeople of Thetford, thought to be the ancient royal residence of warrior Iceni queen Boudica, are also posted on the inn's corner post where the number of old nails tell the tale.

They certainly do things with great pomp in this town. When Thomas Howard, 2nd Duke of Norfolk's funeral took place in Thetford in 1524 'twas said to have cost £1,300 and included a procession of 400 hooded men, 100 wax effigies and 700 candles.
Latterly: Bell Inn, King Street, Thetford, Norfolk, IP24 2AZ, tel: 01842 754455, www.oldenglishinns.co.uk.

WYMONDHAM

GREEN DRAGON
'Kett and some curious carvings'

Like many of our oldest inns, the foundations of the Green Dragon were laid down by monks – the place served as a hostel for the now ruined Benedictine monastery and there was even a tunnel, which still exists, linking the two.

These days there be no need for religious influence to cloud the beer. The Green Dragon, which hath also been known as The White Swan, simply provides a welcome stop on the great road to Norwich. But perhaps 'tis best not to tarry too long admiring its flint walls or mulling over its curious carvings, for 'tis in this town – pronounced Windham – that the rebel Kett originated. Who knows what rebellious plots one might get caught up in once again if thee loiter. A famous oak tree where Kett and his band of ne'r-do-wells first plotted be still to be seen along the Norwich to London road.

Latterly: The Green Dragon, 6 Church Street, Wymondham, Norfolk, NR18 0PH, tel: 01953 607907, www.wymondhamgreendragon.co.uk.

Other hostelries of note ...

HARLESTON

THE SWAN
A lovely airy courtyard be a feature of this inn, which must have pleased its builder, one Robert Cook, who was lucky to see the light of day at all after his part in Kett's rebellion (see Adam and Eve entry). Pardoned, he sought out a quieter life, constructing the inn here in 1551.

Latterly: The Swan Hotel, The Thoroughfare, Harleston, Norfolk, IP20 9AS, tel: 01379 852221, www.harlestonswanhotel.co.uk.

NORWICH

THE BLUE BELL INN
Dating from 1485, this famous inn be a comfortable alternative to the Maid's Head.

Latterly: The Bell Hotel, 5 Orford Hill, Norwich, Norfolk, NR1 3QB, tel: 01603 630017, www.jdwetherspoon.co.uk.

❀ NORTHAMPTONSHIRE

First noted in 1011 as Hamtunscire, with the 'north' later added to differentiate it from the southern county, it hath since been dubbed a county of 'spires and squires' and hath been described by the writer William Camden as 'exceedingly populous' as well as being 'beset with sheepe'. The map maker John Norden told us that it hath 'great herds of swine' but there be modern industry afoot in the county too. For the town of Northampton, boasting as many as seventeen inns as of 1577, be famed for its shoe and boot making. Production be rising in line with the fashion in our Elizabethan times for heels of 2 or 3 inches. Brick and tile making are other important industries locally. The soke of Peterborough, with its great cathedral, be also associated with the county at this time, while great new houses to admire include the classical Kirby Hall, begun in the year 1570 and owned by the late Sir Christopher Hatton, Lord Chancellor to Queen Elizabeth. Her Majesty be also known to be fond of the manor at Castle Ashby, built in the popular E-shaped style in her honour. The castle at Fotheringhay, where Mary, Queen of Scots was imprisoned in her last days and executed, has lately fallen into much disrepair. There are, we believe, some 300 inns and 400 alehouses in all Northamptonshire, making it a place where, if thee linger for a moment, thee may end up staying too long.

FINEDON OR TINGDENE

BELL INN
'A Saxon alehouse'
A new face was given to this hostelry in 1598 but it goes back many centuries. For an alehouse hath been here since Saxon times. There was a royal manor in Finedon held by Queen Edith in the tenth century, the widowed wife of that ancient Saxon king, Edward the Confessor. The village be small but was once one of the most important places in the county. Indeed, there be a corny

rhyme here which goes: 'Queen Edith, Lady Once of Finedon, Where at the Bell good fare be dined on.' Excruciating it may be, but still true today.

Latterly: The Bell, Bell Hill, Finedon, Wellingborough, Northamptonshire, NN9 5ND, tel: 01933 680332.

OUNDLE

THE TABRET

'Pigeon pie for Mary's Executioner'

No one seems sure if the name be associated with a kind of musical instrument like a tambourine; 'tis more likely that this inn was named after a tabard, a kind of sleeveless coat worn by heralds.

'Tis certain though that this stout inn will shield thee well from the weather for Oundle be a solidly built place. As John Leland told us in his survey, 'The town hath a very good market and be all builded of stone.' Though the town's bridge across the River Nene did fall down in 1570 it hath since been rebuilt.

The Tabret, now free from Papist influence, can claim to have been serving ale since the year AD 638 – 'twas once a hospitium attached to the monastery built by Bishop Wilfred, giving succour to travellers and pilgrims who passed by. There be a chill about the place, perhaps due to its association with Mary, Queen of the Scots, who was executed in nearby Fotheringhay Castle. Indeed, the inn claims that her executioner lodged here the night before his task and 'partook of pigeon pie, drank a quart of best ale and made a merry discourse with the serving girl till an early hour of the morning'. Nice work if thee can get it.

Latterly: The Talbot Hotel, New Street, Oundle, Northamptonshire, PE8 4EA, tel: 01832 273621, www.thetalbot-oundle.com.

TOWCESTER

TABARD
'For the benefit of the town'
The old Roman town of Lactodorum be the setting for a number of inns catering to those travelling along the old Watling Street. In the last century the local rector, one Archdeacon Sponne, clearly believed that selling ale could be of great benefit to the people, for, in 1440, he bought the Tabard Inn and used the profits therewith to help repair the town's roadways and help the poor of the town. 'Tis to this day a comfortable place, with a warming inglenook fireplace and still used for charitable purposes, providing peace of mind to any well-to-do traveller that their monies are going to a good cause, whichever side of the religious divide from which they may come.
Latterly: The Sponne Shopping Centre, Towcester.

❦ NORTHUMBERLAND

At the most remote point of England lies this beautiful but thinly populated county. It extends from the heavily fortified town of Berwick, upon the River Tweed in the north next to Scotland, to the port of Newcastle towards the south. The traveller William Camden described Newcastle as the 'eye of the North, the hearth that warmeth the south parts of this kingdom with fire'. Started by the Romans who built the first bridge across the Tyne, 'tis a fine city of some 10,000 people but his words also refer to the centre of the new coal industry, producing some 300,000 tonnes of black gold each year. So famous hath the region become that the quip taking 'coals to Newcastle' was coined in 1538. Unfortunately the city hath sadly suffered several attacks of the plague over the last few decades.

Newcastle's main inns have always been along the way known as Pilgrim Street, which lead to the quayside and the single stone bridge across the river. The street was so called after those who came to worship at Our Lady's Chapel in Jesmond. Here be the famous hostelry once known as the Pilgrim's Inn or St Cuthbert's Inn in the time of King Henry VIII, along with others such as The George and Queen's Head. 'Twas not always a salubrious street, for we hear whispers of counterfeiters, active here.

Other important towns in Northumberland include Alnwick, Morpeth and Hartlepool. To the north-west lies the Cheviot Hills. Towards them thee will find the remains of the Roman Hadrian's Wall, though don't linger too long staring in wonder at this relic as this region be feared as a haunt of robbers. Another warning: The county be also known for its numerous Roman Catholics and gave much support to the thwarted, infamous 'Rising of the North' in 1569.

Beer on the Sabbath?

Sunday be a day of rest and some in our land have interpreted this as being the chance to languish in the alehouse rather than reflect on our Lord or attend church. Lately Edward Harvye and his wife in Berwick-upon-Tweed were brought up before the bench for 'disordered and unlawful company who use drinking, gaming, playing at cards, and other misdemeanours as well in service time on the Sabbath day as at other times'.

❀

ALNWICK

THE QUEEN'S HEAD
'Beer in a barren land'
Named in honour of Queen Elizabeth, the inn be just one of a group of fine hostelries which also include The Griffin. Many travellers seek solace here upon the Great North Road – for Alnwick be something of a last outpost of civilisation and comfort before setting out across the wild border lands which Camden described as 'lean, hungry and waste'.

The town's walls provide an air of security which be welcome in a region ravaged by wars between the Scots and the English and which hath been the victim of wild border raiders. But the castle hath been left in disrepair after Thomas Percy, Earl of Northumberland, was recently executed for his part in the infamous 1569 Catholic plot against Her Majesty.

Latterly: The Queen's Head Hotel, 25 Market Street, Alnwick, NE66 1SS, tel: 01655 604691, www.alnwickqueensheadhotel.co.uk.

Other hostelries of note ...

CORBRIDGE

THE ANGEL

Once a hospice within the remit of the abbey at Hexham, there be an irony in that this was the place where the king's officers rested while overseeing the aforesaid religious house's surrender. Either side of the Dissolution this hath always been a good place to get an ale.

Latterly: The Angel, Main Street, Corbridge, Northumberland, NE45 5LA, tel: 01434 632119, www.theangelofcorbridge.com.

✿ NOTTINGHAMSHIRE

A county renowned throughout the kingdom for the quality of its ale. The malting of grain be one of the biggest industries. United with Derby under one sheriff until 1568, the county's political importance hath long centred on the stronghold at Nottingham Castle. But there are other fine buildings; Wollaton Hall be of note, a spectacular new mansion built by Sir Francis Willoughby between 1580 and 1588 with lofty towers, a great central hall and glass windows so large they do assault the eyes.

The county be dominated by the great River Trent and Sherwood Forest, famed for the legendary outlaw Robin Hood. Who knows whether he was real or even a humble thief or a lord in disguise, but what be sure, tales and ballads about him abound.

Thee may hear them in the enormous number of hostelries which exist throughout Nottinghamshire. The great survey of 1577 tells us that there are some 1,023 in the county, with Nottingham seeming to have more than its fair share of well-established boozing establishments compared to other counties. Thee may find some of the locals clad in fine stockings, as hosiery be a budding industry here since the invention of the stocking frame by William Lee in the county in the year 1589.

BLYTH

THE ANGEL
'Where bishops imbibe'

We know much of this inn's early heritage because of an historic bill left by two of its earliest visitors which hath been miraculously preserved. In October 1274, Robert de Insula, the new Bishop of Durham, and Richard Claxton, prior, were travelling along a spur of the Great North Road, returning from an audience with the king in London. They decided to stop for the night at Blyth, some 150 miles north of the city and 50 miles from York. It seems that after a long day on the road they let their hair down.

The yellowing tariff tells us that their party enjoyed copious portions of bread, lots of wine and other food as well as hay and litter for their horses, totalling some £4 9s 7d – a huge sum in those days and even today. The Angel be still serving good food and remains a decent resting point when travelling north or south.

In former times the village, on the River Ryton, was a venue for jousting. Blyth was one of a handful of places in the nation which were licensed for such tournaments, now, largely a thing of the past.

Latterly: The Angel Inn, Bawtry Road, Blyth, Nottinghamshire, tel: 01909 591213.

NEWARK

SARACEN'S HEAD
'Beware a poleaxing'

A sound fellow called John Twentyman be the owner of this, one of the principal inns in a town which hath an embarrassment of fine lodgings for the traveller. There be a fascinating story behind his name. Tradition has it that the surname was given to a man who, in less peaceful times, had poleaxed twenty men in battle.

A merry evening at Mr Twentyman's establishment, which he purchased from Bryan Lucas in 1590, can see a similar number of men knocked sideways.

The inn itself was here at least as early as 1341, the name being linked to the Crusades. Today, whether thee are travelling to the Holy Land or simply to market thee are assured of a comfortable night's rest. Each chamber hath its own pleasing name such as the 'Corne Chamber' or 'The Tapistry'.

Latterly: A row of colonnaded shops in the market place which still bear the bust of a Saracen's Head.

WHITE HART
'A timber masterpiece'

Newark be a prosperous town thanks to its wool trade, important market and situation by the River Trent over which 'tis the principal crossing point for miles around. So 'tis perhaps unsurprising that this town, on the Great North Road, hath more than one great inn. The White Hart, which began serving customers as far back as 1413, must be one of the architectural masterpieces of our age. Chief among its glories be the timber facade that faces on to the market place which sports two rows of plaster-cast figurines set within little canopies. These hold different emblems and their feet stand on hog's masks.

Along the top storey there be a glazed gallery, a now fashionable feature of well-to-do houses, while at the rear there be a fine courtyard with plenty of stabling and more beautiful half-timbered accommodation. The popularity and convenience of the White Hart means 'tis oft full. Be advised that the Talbot, established in the 1300s, and the Swan and Salmon from 1521, also have excellent reputations.

Note that Newark be not a place to fall into disagreements easily as the town be oft brimming with armed men. Large numbers of troops stayed in the town during their march northwards to confront the rebels in the 1569 Rising of the North against Her Majesty.

Latterly: A branch of the Nottingham Building Society.

NOTTINGHAM

YE OLDE TRIP TO JERUSALEM
'Crusaders, caverns and ale casks'

Dug into the very rocks beneath the stronghold of Nottingham Castle, this lively alehouse may have been serving flagons of the finest ale as far back as the year 1189. Near this spot men were roused to follow King Richard the Lionheart in the crusades to the Holy Land, hence the alehouse's name.

Here thee can play ringing the bull, that ancient game where one must cast a bull's nose ring in an arc so that it lands upon a hook. Beware the bloody nose from players who, drunk with passion, do not like to lose in their own backyard and have been known to pawn their own shirts in pursuit of wagered purse on the outcome. The ale here be of an excellent type, brewed, as it be, in the caves, rendering an even temperature and giving a goodly glow to the insides which counter the chill and damp arising from these ancient stone walls.

Ask the keeper if there be bear-baiting to see during thy stay in the city.

Latterly: Ye Olde Trip to Jerusalem, Brewhouse Yard, Nottingham, NG1 6AD, www.triptojerusalem.com.

THE BELL
'Reminders of Friar Tuck & Robin Hood'

Claiming to be the city's oldest inn, there be certainly much history here and a link, if tenuous, to that legendary robber of the rich and defender of the poor, Robin Hood.

A Carmelite Friary with a guesthouse was established in this area of the city in the thirteenth century and account for the cellars beneath the inn that stands here today. Dating to 1437 the name of the inn be reckoned to be linked to angelus bell, an old call to prayer. A curious feature of the place be its leprosy holes where scraps of spare food were once passed to these unfortunates.

The monastic associations of The Bell have led some to imagine that this was a hang-out for Robin Hood's bibulous companion Friar Tuck. If the famed pair did once roam these parts then surely he would have stopped at this fine inn for a quick beer and a feast before hoodwinking the hapless sheriff once again.

Latterly: The Bell Inn, 18 Angel Row, Nottingham, NG1 6HL, tel: 0115 947 5241, www.bellinnnottingham.co.uk.

Old Rhyme of Nottingham

In good King Stephen's Days, the Ram
An ancient Inn in Nottingham,
Was kept as all good people knows
By a buxom wife called old Rose

❀

THE SALUTATION
'Ale and hearty'

This rambling old place gets its name from the Archangel Gabriel saluting the Virgin Mary – an ancient sign used for drinking places.

Here the ale and entertainment, not the beds, are the main draw. Dating back to 1240, 'twas originally a tannery and then a private dwelling. Now 'tis a place for those a bit bolder to seek out for merriment.

The alehouse hath caves beneath it that are believed to have been used to brew ale in Saxon times.

Latterly: Ye Old Salutation Inn, 54 Hounds Gate, Maid Marian Way, www.salutationpub.com.

SOUTHWELL

SARACEN'S HEAD

'Art lover's haven'

Southwell be famous for its twelfth-century minster and Archbishop's Palace, where Cardinal Wolsey once stayed. An important church hath been here since the first archbishop, Paulinus, baptised Christians in the River Trent.

However its second most esteemed set of buildings are those which make up the Saracen's Head, also known as the King's Arms, which hath been here since 1396. In that year the Archbishop of York, Thomas Arundel, gave it to John Fysher, his wife Margaret and their heirs.

The present building, which was constructed in 1463, hath beautiful rooms which have recently been redecorated with lavish paintings. This be fitting as the inn hath hosted many royal visitors, including King John Edward I, Edward II and Richard II.

Latterly: The Saracens Head Hotel, Market Place, Southwell, Nottinghamshire, NG25 0HE, tel: 01636 812701, www.saracensheadhotel.com.

Other hostelries of note ...

NOTTINGHAM

FLYING HORSE

Said to have been an inn by 1483, 'twas built on the site of an older house owned by the locally famous Plumtre family and its name be said to derive from a swinging horse game that featured in medieval fairs.

Latterly: Now part of Flying Horse Walk Arcade, South Parade, Nottingham, NG1 2HN.

❀ OXFORDSHIRE

Though its open fields be bursting with wheat, this county be chiefly famous, not for its agriculture, but for the city of Oxford. Its population be now much recovered from the sweating sickness that killed half its number in 1517 and though the plague still visits from time to time Oxford now boasts some 4,000 souls. Many of these are occupied with the university – one of only two in England, and founded in 1100s. King Henry VIII expanded the subjects its scholars studied from mainly religious matters to Greek, law and medicine. The city hath not been spared from the religious strife of these last decades. Indeed, thee may still see the scorch marks where famous Protestant martyrs Hugh Latimer, Nicholas Ridley and later Thomas Cranmer, were burned to death outside the doors of Balliol College in October 1555.

That be not the only source of dissent. Town and gown relations are oft the source of much conflict. As far back as 1355, a disagreement broke out at the Swyndlestock Tavern, now The Mermaid, between two students and the taverner John Croidon over the quality of the drinks. The two students ended up pouring a jug of wine over Croidon and the incident led to a full-scale riot between students and locals. It left sixty-three scholars and thirty townsfolk dead. Thee may expect to find today's Oxford equally rowdy.

BANBURY

REINDEER INN
'Bread and beer'
Banbury's prosperity be built on wool and the trade in salt. But its best inn be built on bread. For a recent addition to the town's

hostelries hath been constructed by John Knight a local baker. John be no ordinary baker. He set up the inn after extending his property in 1570 and, with his wife Joan, extended a property he owned to build the solid timber and stone structure known as the Reindeer. The Knights' fortunes have since risen as quickly as the dough in their ovens. There be good cheese to be had here too.
Latterly: Ye Olde Reindeer Inn, 47 Parson's Street, Banbury, OX16 5NA, tel: 01295 264031, www.yeoldereindeer.co.uk.

CHIPPING NORTON

WHITE HART
'Homely and hospitable'
On the main road from London to Worcester, this inn sits proudly in the market place and in the centre of this high town in the Cotswold hills, an area where fortunes have been built on wool.

The White Hart, named in honour of Richard II, hath been here for at least a century and hath a wonderful wooden gallery and bedchambers, each with its own name, including the Queen's Chamber and the Harrford Chamber, as well as its own brewhouse. There be a fine stone staircase leading to the rooms, magnificent wood panelling throughout and sumptuous fireplaces.

'Tis oft bursting at the seams thanks to its fame, which spreads far and wide. If it be full try the Crown and Cushion.
Latterly: Converted into flats.

DORCHESTER-ON-THAMES

THE GEORGE
'In the footsteps of Romans'
It may only be home to a few score people today but Dorchester hath a long history – being important since Roman times and once being the capital of that old kingdom of Wessex. It lies near the Thames, which be still navigable here.

The George, Dorchester, Oxfordshire, now The George Hotel. (© Mr James Moore and Mr Paul Nero)

The inn lies across from the abbey, which was founded in 1140 on a religious site which hath been of note since St Birinus was here in the seventh century. The George, like many of our grandest inns, was once hospice and brewhouse to the abbey which hath now, since the Dissolution, become an everyman's inn thanks to Richard Bewforest who bought the Church lands for £150 and now enjoys the profits from the place. The abbey church survived destruction in the ensuing melee and became the parish church. Its glories are only echoed in The George with its joyfully jettied floors protruding into the street, fine open galleried yard to the rear and inglenook fireplaces.

Serving since 1495, it commands the main thoroughfare and thus the attention of those passing through. The George might be seen to compete with the White Hart, but we hear that there be something of a monopoly in the town with the owner of the local manor having bagged all the biggest inns for his own profit.
Latterly: The George Inn, High Street, Dorchester-on-Thames, Oxfordshire, OX10 7HH, www.thegeorgedorchester.co.uk.

The show must go on

Queen Elizabeth visited Oxford University in 1566 and 1592. Our well-read Majesty enjoyed lectures put on at the colleges and was regaled by countless poems in her honour. She also attended many theatrical performances. On one occasion, during her 1566 visit, she was watching a play called Palamon and Arcite. The crush was so great, which we wager was to see the regal visage rather than the work, that a wall collapsed, killing a student, cook ... and a brewer. A concerned queen sent her own physicians to help. Despite the deaths, the play duly proceeded. Once 'twas finished the queen sent for the author and gave him 'great thanks with the promise of reward'.

❀

OXFORD

THE CROSS INN
'Of burnings and the bard'

There hath been a hostelry here, off the city's Cornmarket, since at least the last century, where it hath long jostled with shops for trade in one of the busiest parts of the city. There was a building here in 1193, when the canons of Osney Abbey sold it to Mauger, a vintner. 'Twas in 1390 or thereabouts that William of Wykeham bought it for New College. Those poor martyrs Latimer, Cranmer and Ridley were held in this inn for some time in 1555, before being imprisoned in the infamous Bocardo Prison and then burned for heresy. The rooms they stayed in have now become somewhat revered as the religious mood hath altered.

The inn hath around fifteen bedchambers and some of its rooms are painted. There be a squash in this part of the city, with pressure on space, so stabling can be a problem, but for entertainment The Cross be a good spot – there be a pillory just a stone's throw from the inn's facade. If this sort of spectacle does not amuse, The Star Inn be another good place to rest on the same street.

Note thee well that adjacent to The Cross be a tavern not only decorated with equally fine paintings but be rumoured as a place in which William Shakespeare calls on his travels between London and Warwickshire. Inside the paintings include beautiful fruit and flowers but also the warning: 'Serve god Devoutlye … Feare god above anythyng.'

Latterly: The Cross Inn became the Golden Cross, now Pizza Express in the Golden Cross Shopping Centre. The tavern associated with Shakespeare was The Bull and became the Crown. Some say he had a son by the wife of the owner there John Davenant. It is now a shop. The Star Inn became the Clarendon Hotel and was demolished in 1955.

THE BEAR
'Wall to wall drinkers'

In Oxford a local be said to be 'cup sprung' when they have taken too much ale. We wonder if 'twas at the intimate Bear inn where records tell us that in one Oxford alehouse the throng was once so great that a drinker – no doubt a scholar of the local university – did fall backwards out of his chair and through one of the thin plaster walls of the establishment, into the room of a house adjoining.

The Bear hath certainly been a popular haunt since 1242, albeit in a slightly different location and it hath been known as Le Tabard before its present moniker, linked it would seem to bear baiting, which sometimes livens up the academic tedium in the vicinity. It may also be associated with the crest of Richard Neville, Earl of Warwick, known for his exploits in the Wars of the Roses and nicknamed the Kingmaker.

Latterly: The Bear Inn, 6 Alfred Street, Oxford, OX1 4EH, tel: 01865 728164, www.bearoxford.co.uk.

WALLINGFORD

THE GEORGE AND DRAGON
'A right royal rumpus'

Though technically in Berkshire at the time, the proximity of the town to routes to Oxford mean that we have included it here. In 1517 Geoffrey and Elizabeth Baynton established The George and Dragon in the High Street in a building which was once associated with the town's castle.

So 'twas here in the following year when King Henry VIII brought his court and new queen, Catherine of Aragon, to Wallingford and was used to house many of the party. 'Twas also a place where many must have supped and talked of Sir Henry Norris, the man who, in 1536, was executed on a charge of adultery with King Henry's wife Anne. It's said that at a jousting tournament in Greenwich the queen dropped her handkerchief in front of Norris, who picked it up, wiped his face on it and handed it back to her on the end of his lance. He denied the romance to his grizzly end.

Thee would have thought that in the town of Wallingford this might be a lesson to the inhabitants to keep their heads down. Not so; in 1537, a man who unwisely and ten years too soon suggested that the king was dead promptly had his ears cut off and was whipped around the town before being thrown in Reading dungeon.

The castle, soon left ruined, was shunned by royalty henceforth and great, moulded wooden doors from it used at The George instead.

Latterly: The George Hotel, High Street, Wallingford, Oxfordshire, OX10 0BS, tel: 01491 836665, www.peelhotels.co.uk.

Other hostelries of note ...

SHIPTON-UNDER-WYCHWOOD

THE CROWN
Once used as a hunting lodge, 'twas gifted to the people of the village in 1580, by her generous Majesty the Queen. The proceeds are to be used for the benefit of the poor.

Latterly: The Shaven Crown, High Street, Shipton-Under-Wychwood, Oxfordshire, OX7 6BA, tel: 01993 830330, www.shavencrown.co.uk.

❧ SHROPSHIRE

Shropshire hath some of the finest manors of the land and good lords who take care of their people. Welsh flax and wool have brought prosperity to these parts and many excellent houses have been built upon the trade ensuing.

If splendid architecture be the measure, surely Shrewsbury hath strong claim to be the greatest town of England. The market be much thronged, but the traveller turning up when the market be closed will find great ease venturing through the many streets that happily state the name of the produce to be chanced upon there: Milk Street, Fish Street, Butcher Row ... Grope Lane.

Drovers have long taken cattle from Wales to Shrewsbury, by way of Bishops Castle, along the route passing Church Stretton, causing many good inns and taverns to spring up to take their shillings. Though many be laid waste by the great fires of 1593 that destroyed much of Church Stretton the rebuilding, hath, in fact, been a boon to the place.

Sweet be the food of Shropshire, for they add sugar to most everything when 'tis available and the savouries do not escape the sweetening. Shrewsbury cakes be so good they play the role of diplomatic aid, for the council of that town presents them as gifts to visiting knights and peers. As a circular drafted by Shrewsbury proclaims, the cakes are: 'a particularly delicious shortbread with a flavour all their own, the secret of which be jealously preserved'. They certainly go down well with ale, for which the town also be famed.

LUDLOW

BULL INN
'See dogs bait a beast'
Drinkers at Ludlow have much choice, but few inns are surely so accommodating as The Bull. Parts of this building be 400 years old or more, and much be unchanged since that time. The latrines remain outside some distance from the building, which is to be commended.

Entertainment be frequent in the courtyard to the rear. Visiting players and strolling minstrels have plenty of space and audiences can be large. As the name of the inn suggests, the place simply cries out for bovine battles. Bull baiting be a big crowd puller. Thou should get there early to bag a spot and stock up with beer so as not to lose thy place.

Latterly: The Bull Hotel, 14 Bullring, Ludlow, Shropshire, SY8 1AD, tel: 01584 879339, www.thebullhotelludlow.com.

How famous Old Parr of Shropshire lived to 100

That green cheese was most wholesome (with an onion)
Coarse maslin bread and for his daily swig
Milk, butter-milk and water whey and whig,
Sometimes methaglin and by fortune happy
He sometimes sipp'd a cup of ale most nappy.

❀

SHREWSBURY

THE LION
'A lair of kings'

One king and one future king are reputed to have stayed here of yore. Henry IV bedded down before the Battle of Shrewsbury in 1403, while Henry Tudor stayed in 1485, before marching to meet his destiny on the field of Bosworth.

The amount of wood employed in the build of The Lion would surely bankrupt a king. The floors, the fireplaces, the wardrobes and cupboards, all crafted from local timber, are a sight to behold; dark, brooding and gloomy. Rooms be small, so thee are likely to bang thy head if thy by tall; and narrow too, so by extending arms, thee can press both walls. Windows be bayed, jutting out into the street below, so fun may be had emptying thy chamber pot; and the street be a myriad of confusion in its construction, so 'tis a place of character.

Tapestries are exhibited in the drinking rooms, unless they be taken for a beating, much be the smoke from both fire and pipe. The Lion be a stopping place for those London-bound, with extensive stabling.

Latterly: The Lion, 73 Wyle Cop, Shrewsbury, Shropshire, SY1 1UY, tel: 01743 353107, www.thelionhotelshrewsbury.com.

To make Shrewsbury cakes

Take a quart of very fine flower, eight ounces of fine sugar, beaten and sieved, twelve ounces of sweete butter, a nutmegge grated, three spoonsful of damaske rose-water. Worke all these together with thy hands hard for the space of halfe an houre, then roule it in little round cakes about the thickness of 3 shillings one upon another. Then take a silver cup some foure or three inches over and cut the cakes in them. Then strowe some flower upon white appers and lay them upon them and bake them in an oven as hot as for Manchet, set upon thy lid till thee may tell a hundred. Then thee shall see them white. If any of them rise up clap them downe with some cleane thing and if thee oven be not too hot set up thy lid again. In a quarter of an hour they will be baked, but heede thy oven be not too hot for they must not looke browne but white, and so draw them forth and lay them upon one another till they be cold, and thy may keep them halfe a year, though the new baked be best.

❦

YE POSTE HOUSE
'Good steeds and horseplay'

Let not the situation on Milk Street confuse, for liquor be flowing freely in five licensed premises here. Finding the front door of this inn can be burdensome, for 'tis discreetly situated off a passageway, away from the interests of passing constables, yet still in the heart of the town and near the castle.

The choice of hostelry be many in Milk Street, but Ye Poste House be favoured by travellers for the accommodation. Horses may be changed and hired here.

The Angel, The Beehive, The Mug House and The Sun be set upon the same row, so the tavern crawl be a popular occupation and of all five Ye Poste House be the newest and possessing of the modern amenities.

Latterly: The Old Post Office, 1 Milk Street, Shrewsbury,
tel: 01743 236019, www.oldpostofficepub.co.uk.

Other hostelries of note ...

CLEOBURY MORTIMER

THE TALBOT
Rest here between Ludlow and Bewdley, as did the body of Arthur, that much-lamented prince who would be king and brother to Henry VIII. The Talbot be set in the centre of the village, being busiest on market days. Find it by the sign of the market cross.
Latterly: Talbot Hotel, 29 High Street, Cleobury Mortimer, Shropshire, DY14 8DQ, tel: 01299 272898, www.thetalbothotelcleobury.co.uk.

SHREWSBURY

THE GOLDEN CROSS
Once known as the Sextry, a corruption of the word Sacristy, a place where the church plate and vestments from St Chad's church were kept, it be long used to brew the church ale. It hath been serving since at least 1495, when an old bill shows that 13*s* 2*d* was spent upon 'The King's gentlemen in sextre at the comyng home of Mr Prynce from London'.
Latterly: The Golden Cross Hotel, 14 Princess Street, Shrewsbury, Shropshire, SY1 1LP, tel: 01743 362507, www.goldencrosshotel.co.uk.

❀ SOMERSET

Times have been hard in Somersetshire of late, with many a poor harvest. As Mister Shakespeare reflected in one of his new plays, *A Midsummer Night's Dream*: 'The ox hath therefore stretched his yoke in vain'. Indeed, the county's starving took to crime, making the alehouses and taverns places of ill repute, with 400 'wandring souldiers and other stout rogues' roaming the county. Good Justice of the Peace Edward Hext wrote to Lord Burghley in the service of Her Majesty that 'rapynes and thefts multiplye daylye'.

Thankfully, in Somersetshire the harvests have now returned better fruits and, we hope, the county's hostelries to better humour. Beer be not as fashionable as cider, the apples here create a most excellent sort and, some say, better than Devonshire. The land when 'tis fulsome be fertile indeed. Around the populous town of Taunton the country be 'most delectable on every side, with green meadows, flourishing with pleasant gardens and orchards' according to the chronicler Camden. The deer hereabouts also make such fine venison that can be made into a hundred pasties. Leather goods, especially gloves, are best bought at Yeovil, an excellent stopping place for travellers betwixt Exeter and London. There be a quay at Bridgwater while the formerly Roman town of Bath hath recently been given city status by Her Majesty and be becoming popular again for its healing waters. For those who admire architecture, Montacute House, in the parish of the same name, be a very grand place, having just been completed by its owner Sir Edward Phelips. But one can now only admire the ruins of Glastonbury Abbey, torn down in the Dissolution. The town be a mystical place with rumours that its famous hill, Glastonbury Tor, was once Avalon, the seat of King Arthur. There are some 100 inns in the county and more than 200 alehouses where thee can contemplate the legend.

CASTLE CARY

THE GEORGE
'Ale and hearty against the Armada'
Church and inn rest easy together in Castle Cary, being constructed at around the same time in 1470 and serving customers and worshippers of the town ever since. In the 1580s, Castle Cary prepared well for the Spanish invasion, with seventeen billmen, eight archers, four pikemen and plenty of

people providing armour, all of whom were in need of good food and drink and many of whom found it at The George.

Latterly: The George Hotel, Market Place, Castle Cary, BA7 7AH, tel: 01963 350761, www.thegeorgehotelcastlecary.co.uk.

Roast venison – a Somersetshire delicacy

For a fresher flavour, Somersetshire inns take special pride from cleansing all the blood from venison before roasting. Ask thy host if mutton lard or pork lard hath been used, for mutton be best. The best hostelries will roast the venison on an open fire for all to see that the hosts are not trimming the finest cuts for their own enjoyment. See that vinegar, breadcrumbs and some of the gravy from the venison hath been boiled well and seasoned with sugar, cinnamon, ginger and salt and that the meat be brought forth upon the sauce when 'tis roasted enough. Beware of imports as Exmoor beast be superior to those of other moorlands.

❉

GLASTONBURY

THE GEORGE

'Where King Henry watched while the abbey was pulled down?'
This stone hostelry be more than a century and a score old, built by Abbot John de Selwood as a *novum hospitium* for pilgrims to the Benedictine abbey. Important guests to the abbey rested here, though 'twas pricier than the ordinary hospice next door, which used to give board and lodging without consideration to worthy pilgrims. Even today the inn hath a better class of guest, even if their souls may struggle to reach heaven, much be the merriment made.

'Tis, for certain, a lovely building. Central archway and three-storey bays rest on either side with mullioned windows, cupped and glazed, which hath been helped by the reduced cost of glass. Three carved shields are present above the grand entrance, one adorned with the armorial bearings of the abbey and one with the arms of Edward IV. The third still awaits the arms of the patron builder, though it hath been 125 years since he left to pick up some tools. His initials, BE, can however be seen on shields at the cornices. A corbel of dimensions no ordinary mortal could carry be atop a stone column in the entrance.

'Twas from one of the grand chambers, accessed by a spiral staircase, that in 1539, rumour hath it, Henry VIII watched as the abbey was torn down. Richard Whiting, the last abbot, resisted the abbey's destruction and was hanged. Whether Henry was here, or no, the inn, being seen as a place much better for the soul, was kept and ownership passed to the Crown. It hath certainly kept its standards with some of the bedsteads being carved and gilded. *Latterly: George & Pilgrim Hotel, 1 High Street, Glastonbury, BA6 9DP, tel: 0845 8053478, www.relaxinnz.co.uk.*

A festival of drink

Eager maltworms have always seethed in Glastonbury. In 1314 as many as sixty-eight ale sellers were in breach of regulations in the town, some forty-five ale sellers were fined in 1378, and in 1417 two innkeepers and twenty ale sellers were also had up for misdemeanours. Today, thee will find no less pleasure in the comfort that a tankard can bring for as well as The George, there be the Pelican and the Hart, both good for a booze.

❖

MELLS

THE TALBOT
'Enjoy a pie at the home of Jack Horner'
Wells be known for its cathedral, but Mells be superior for this tavern. It hath been accommodating travellers between London and Wells for more than a century. Fine Somersetshire forest hath gone into the building and furniture.

Children will delight to know that their friend Little Jack Horner, the stupid boy who stuck in his thumb and pulled out a plum, used to live nearby, and his family were likely to frequent this place. 'Tis believed that Little Jack was in fact a person of mature years but possibly not of great height, who was not as innocent as suggested by the popular rhyme. Jack was in fact one Thomas Horner, steward to the late Abbot of Glastonbury. The abbey was the last remaining in the region after the others had succumbed to King Henry's wrath. The story goes that Thomas was dispatched to the king with a Christmas pie, with the deeds to twelve manor houses carefully secreted within it, the plan being to placate the monarch and save the abbey. Horner be alleged to have arrived with only eleven deeds, taking that relating to Mells Manor for himself. To this day his progeny say that this be slander. What be certain be that the other deeds, if delivered to His Majesty, did nothing to save the abbey.

Latterly: The Talbot Inn, Mells, Near Frome, Somerset, BA11 3PN, tel: 01373 812254, www.talbotinn.com.

A worse for wear Wolsey

Son of a humble Ipswich butcher, Thomas Wolsey would rise to become Cardinal and Lord Chancellor in the time of Henry VIII. But he began his career in the Church as a rector in Limington. One day at a local fair he was found to be drunk and placed in the stocks by a local sheriff Amias Poulet. The sheriff later rued the day, when Wolsey had him imprisoned for six years.

❁

NORTON ST PHILIP

THE GEORGE
'Cosy beds for wool merchants'
Located betwixt Frome and Bath, this village may not seem much to the uninitiated but it boasts an inn that carries much fame across these parts.

'Twas at first built as a wool store by Carthusian monks at Hinton, but since the Dissolution the place hath been converted

The George, Norton St Philip, Somerset. (Courtesy of Wadworth)

most commodiously into an inn, providing a convenient guest house for traders who visit the wool fair here in August.

Built of sturdy stone in 1397, timber floors have since been added and its beams are a marvel to behold. There are exquisite oriel windows on the upper floor and a gallery which runs alongside the courtyard. An interesting feature be the octagonal stair turret which provides access to some of the excellent accommodation.

Latterly: The George, High Street, Norton St Philip, Bath & North-East Somerset, BA2 7LH, tel: 01373 834224,
www.georgeinnnsp.co.uk.

WELLS

THE CROWN
'In the shadow of the cathedral'
Men of the cloth, yeomen and the husbandry rub shoulders at The Crown. Travellers too hath been resting here for more than 100 years, though the building be older still, being constructed as a house in 1450.

Toast Robin Hood for the sake of the parish

Yeovil hath much to offer, especially at Whitsun when the Robin Hood play be performed. More than £20 oft be collected for the parish by the ale especially made for it in years past. The names of those locals playing Robin Hood hath not been disclosed since 1578, out of fear that Her Majesty disapprove of the performance, but the day carries much merriment with minstrels, dancing and the carrying of men aloft. Hostelries refresh those participating in the Robin Hood Whitsun procession; a crawl between alehouses that gets more raucous as the day wears on. Beware: join the locals, or risk ridicule or even beating. Taking part be expected.

❧

This inn be but a short hop to the cathedral and indeed a former bishop who ordered this building to be made, linking inn with church in the traditional fashion, be said to have made the journey nightly.

Latterly: The Crown Hotel, Market Place, Wells, Somerset, BA5 2RP, tel: 01749 673457, www.crownatwells.co.uk.

Other hostelries of note ...

DUNSTER

THE SHIP
With a great gothic hall boasting a high hammer-beam roof, this was once the guest house to the abbey at Cleeve, now in ruins. Now 'tis in the remit of the Luttrell family, bigwigs hereabouts. A convenient spot if thee have business at the castle.

Latterly: Luttrell Arms, Dunster, TA24 6SG, tel: 08444 119 486, www.legacy-hotels.co.uk.

❀ STAFFORDSHIRE

Pots be especially fine in this county, which makes drinking vessels of excellent quality. Stafford, the county town, hath some fine buildings, including a stout castle. Lichfield, with its fine cathedral, also had a castle, now long gone, where Richard II spent the Christmas of 1397 – his party consuming a weighty 200 tons of wine. Two years later he was imprisoned here, failing to escape after jumping through a castle window, before being overthrown by his cousin Henry Bolingbroke.

There be coalmining and metal working at the town of Walsall in the 1570s and 1580s, but most lasted not long, sending miners back to the land. West Bromwich hath iron mines which led to a boom in nailing, with skilled men slaking their thirst after a day metalworking at the town's inns. Leather making be thriving at Lichfield and a tanners' company hath been established to match the cordwainers and saddlers, whilst clothmakers and weavers vie for dominance too. Yet the finest industry by far here be the manufacture of food and drink. Naysayers wish to put an end to this happy situation, saying that Lichfield alehouses be excessive in number and raucous in nature.

The town of Burton-upon-Trent hath been famed for its ale since the abbey made excellent brews in Richard I's time. Indeed, whilst a prisoner in the county's Tutbury Castle, Mary, Queen of Scots was supplied with her beer from 'Burton three myles off'. No prisoner can have been treated more fairly we feel. Yet the ungrateful royal made a mockery of herself by trying to pass messages to her Catholic supporters outside in the beer barrels in which her refreshment was brought. Sadly for the hapless queen, the brewer was a double agent working for that most excellent of spymasters, Sir Francis Walsingham and her treasonable activities were rumbled.

BAGNALL

KINGS ARMS
'Small … but perfectly fermented'
On the edge of a village green rests a snug inn crafted from local sandstone many hundreds of years ago. This be the inn on the hill of Bagnall. Kept in excellent condition by the present innkeepers, the Kings Arms be dark for the windows are small. The building be older than nearby Hulton Abbey in parts, so 'tis possible that good Bagnall people drank here before 1223, but records do not go back so far, so that we know it only as an inn from around the time of Bolingbroke's usurping of the throne in 1399 and declare that this still be old. The inn hath a small amount of stabling, though if this be full, grazing be available nearby at the risk of the traveller. The villagers do not like horses to graze on the green.
Latterly: Stafford Arms, The Green, Bagnall, Stoke-on-Trent, Staffordshire, ST9 9JR, tel: 01782 502266, www.staffordarms.com.

PENKRIDGE

WHITE HART
'Where Queen Elizabeth rested'
A restorative sight be this three-storeyed, three-gabled timber-framed building which was built by the Earl of Warwick in 1565, but the inn sign, linked to Richard II – much associated with the county – suggests that there hath been an inn here for many a century.

There be a charming herringbone design upon the plaster and a graceful carriageway through the centre takes travellers to their rest. Among those who are said to have passed through are Queen Elizabeth in 1575 and even Mary, Queen of Scots was supposed to have lodged here for a night, though many make this claim. With stabling for forty horses, a small royal retinue could certainly be accommodated.
Latterly: The building be still at Stone Cross, Penkridge, ST19 5AS.

Trouble at the alehouse

In this very year we hear of the malign influence that the alehouse can have upon a local community. For one Thomas Jackson, an alehouse keeper from Eccleshall in Staffordshire, hath recently been brought before the courts on a charge that he had denounced the Puritan minister during church services and on Ascension Day had led 100 revellers and three minstrels over the minister's grass with the purpose of destroying it.

❀

SALT

HOLLY BUSH
'Flavoursome meals at an ancient hostelry'
The tippler here claims a heritage of more than 400 years and to be the second oldest drinking place of its kind in the whole land. We are doubtful and this be not verified by facts. Indeed, he be known to claim it even more ancient when in drink.

At the Holly Bush, the alewife's fair hand be expressed in floral tributes. She adorns windows with flowers of the brightest hue, and such windows be both leaded and glazed, for the inn be popular and makes much profit to spend on glass, so ponder this when thy be handing over thy pennies.

Smoked meals be much recommended, being baked in a glorious charcoal oven that hath lasted more than a hundred years. The salt not be from local salt pits, despite the village's name, for there now be none, though in times past this was collected from local places. In fine weather, travellers take their drinks and food and eat on the banks of the Trent for the position of Salt, also known as Selte, be shielded from harsh winds.
Latterly: Holly Bush Inn, Salt, Near Stafford, Staffordshire, ST18 0BX, tel: 01889 508234, www.hollybushinn.co.uk.

Other hostelries of note ...

LICHFIELD

THE ANTELOPE
Known as far back as 1495, the inn, also trading as the Bush, be a place known to be frequented by men at arms.
Latterly: The Kings Head, 21 Bird Street, Lichfield, Staffordshire, WS13 6PW, tel: 01543 256822.

❀ SUFFOLK

With its access to the sea, proximity to London and good farming country, the county be most prosperous. From wool to milk it sees trade in almost every commodity and many hops are now grown, making all sorts of beer available. The writer William Camden tells us that it be 'full of havens and fertile solie ... whereof there are in every place most rich and godly corne fields. And great store of cheeses are there made which to the great commodity of the inhabitants after vented into all parts of England, nay in to Germanie, France and Spain also ...'

'Tis regarded as the seventh wealthiest county in England. Indeed, Suffolk's success in trade can be seen in the fortunes of towns like the timbered loveliness of Lavenham and the impressive bustle of Ipswich. Other well-to-do towns include Sunbury, Long Melford, Clare and St Edmund's Bury. Sadly, the once great town of Dunwich is much cast down for it be slowly falling into the sea.

There are ancient castles too, with Framlingham being the most famous. 'Twas the place where Mary Tudor mustered her forces in 1553 before successfully storming London to win the throne.

There were 119 inns in the county in 1577 so for those who are well-endowed with groats, enjoying Suffolk's pleasant pasture can be done in comfort.

BURY ST EDMUNDS

ANGEL
'A very "public" house'

Occupying a fine position across one side of the market square, the Angel faces the old abbey of Edmundsbury, to whose visitors in past times it offered refreshment.

Known to have been here since at least 1452, the inn once sat between two other hostelries called The White Bear and The Castle. The Castle hath now been incorporated into the Angel to make a much grander resting and drinking place. Indeed, the Angel's high standards have been celebrated for some time. In 1526 'twas sold for the princely sum of £133 6s 8d!

One of the curious facts about this inn be that it hath, for a good period of its life, been owned publicly for the benefit of the town. For, in 1557, a fine fellow called William Tassel gave it to the 'guildhall feoffees' so that it should provide an income for the relief of soldiers and the people of the town as well as for the upkeep of two churches.

Bury St Edmunds hath been a place of worship for hundreds of years, with an abbey dedicated to Edmund, King of the East Angles, killed by Danish invaders in the year of our Lord 869. Today the church of St James be still an architectural feat worthy of a few minutes of prayer.

Latterly: The Angel Hotel, Angel Hill, Bury St Edmunds, Suffolk, IP33 1LT, tel: 01284 714000, www.theangel.co.uk.

Beware witches!

As elsewhere in the counties of East Anglia, the traveller should be aware of weird folk in the town and surrounding countryside. For in a series of recent trials several witches have been identified by the authorities. In one strange case, tried in Bury this very year, an Oliffe Bartham of Shadbrook was executed for 'sending three toads to destroy the sleep of Joan Jordan'.

❁

IPSWICH

THE WHITE HORSE
'Top of the taverns'
While surely not the first place to serve ale or wine in the town, The White Horse was no doubt its first formal hostelry and hath been mentioned in glowing terms since at least the year 1518. At first 'twas known as simply The Tavern, giving its name to the street in which it lies, and more recently The White Horse.

Ipswich, birthplace of Cardinal Wolsey, son of a local butcher, hath been booming of late thanks to sail making and the wool trade. And the inhabitants of the town are known to enjoy a celebration. On the anniversary of the coronation day of Queen Elizabeth one set of parish churchwarden accounts show that some 40 shillings was spent in three Ipswich inns, toasting her health.

A special tax was even levied in 1561 to celebrate a visit of Her Majesty, during one of her great perambulations. A shame then, perhaps, that the queen found the local clergy not up to scratch and complained of the filthy condition of the streets.

There are by now plenty of other inns in the town, which numbers some 4,000 people and which contributed two ships to fighting the Spanish in 1588. Travellers will find The King's Head, George, Tabard, Griffin, Assumption, Turke, Angel, Dolphin and The Cross should satisfy their needs.
Latterly: 41–49 Tavern Street, Ipswich, now Starbucks.

LAVENHAM

ANGEL
'Pints and pitch penny'
The population of the town of Lavenham be now more than 2,000, but as recently as 1524 'twas listed as the fourteenth wealthiest in the kingdom. This be in large part due to its famous cloth making, though this trade hath recently been dented by Dutch weavers in Colchester.

The riches of the town also mean that it hath many fine buildings, including the great Guildhall of the wool guild of Corpus Christi. Near this, in the market place, be the Angel Inn, with its lofty gable ends, first licensed in 1420. As well as good lodgings, this be a great place to enjoy a game of pitch penny.

If the Angel be full thee will find equally good service at The Swan, another magnificent inn with good stabling, wonderful old beams and a minstrel's gallery from which thee may be serenaded while thee dine. There be good moulded decoration on the plasterwork, including a Tudor rose.

Latterly: The Angel Hotel, Market Place, Lavenham, Suffolk, CO10 9QZ, tel: 01787 247388, www.wheelersangel.com and The Swan Hotel, Lavenham, Suffolk, CO10 9QA, tel: 01787 247477, www.theswanatlavenham.co.uk.

LONG MELFORD

THE BULL INN
'A wonder of wood'

This former house of a wealthy wool merchant, built around 1450, must be praised to the rafters – for its massive beams are beautifully moulded and the whole wooden solidness of the place gives residents at the inn a wonderful sense of wellbeing. The inn's 18in beams are carved with whimsical foliage and one of the upright timbers displays a great 'green man' – an ancient symbol of nature and rebirth. It also boasts a breath-taking 12ft-wide fireplace as well as other interesting decorations to marvel at.

The Bull hath been known as an inn since 1580, the year in which Sir Francis Drake returned to these shores on the *Golden Hind* after successfully circumnavigating the globe.

Queen Elizabeth came this way on her tour of East Anglia in 1578 and visited the local Melford Hall where 'tis said she had been 'graciously pleased to express her great content'. Since her host, Sir William Cordell, was known for his 'sumptuous feastings' and laid on '200 young gentlemen in white velvet, 300 in black and 1500 serving men' to see to her party's needs we are not surprised

at her satisfaction.' Twas while here that the queen received envoys from France to negotiate a marriage to the Duke of Alençon. These efforts were, it hath to be said, less successful.
Latterly: The Bull Hotel, Hall Street, Long Melford, Sudbury, Suffolk, CO10 9JG, tel: 01787 378494, www.thebull-hotel.com.

Other hostelries of note ...

CLARE

THE GREEN DRAGON
A good local inn since 1580, handy for the market.
Latterly: The Bell Hotel, Market Hill, Clare, Suffolk, CO10 8NN, tel: 01787 277741.

THE SWAN
An alehouse since at least 1498, when John Norfolk gave it to his son.
Latterly: The Swan, High Street, Clare, Suffolk, CO10 8NY.

SUDBURY

THE BULL
An inn since 1540. Aptly, thee may see bull-baiting in the yard.
Latterly: The Olde Bull Hotel, Church Street, Sudbury, Suffolk, CO10 2BL, tel: 01787 374120, www.theoldebullhotel.co.uk.

BARTON PARVA

THE OLDE BULL
A fine staging post on the long, lonely road to Norwich.
Latterly: The Olde Bull Inn, The Street, Barton Mills, Bury St Edmunds, Suffolk, IP28 6AA, tel: 01638 711001, www.bullinn-bartonmills.com.

FRAMLINGHAM

THE CROWN
Standing in 1553 when an army of 13,000 men mustered here in support of Queen Mary.
Latterly: The Crown, Market Hill, Framlingham, Suffolk, IP13 9AP, tel: 01728 723521, www.framlinghamcrown.co.uk.

✿ SURREY

This much wooded county extends along the southern side of the River Thames and includes the playgrounds of the metropolis around Southwark as well as the important towns of Kingston, Guildford, Reigate and Dorking.

There are many fine houses and palaces. Chief among its glories must surely be the magnificent Nonsuch Palace, begun by Henry VIII though not finished when he died and recently returned to royal hands. There also be Richmond Palace, where Henry VII passed away and which be a favourite of Queen Elizabeth who enjoys stag hunting in the grounds.

Important industries in Surrey include brewing, leather making and iron working. But it also serves to provide London with many of its daily needs, including fruit and vegetables and also chickens, which are fattened up in the county and loaded up on waggons to be taken to the city's meat markets. This hath led to the nickname for a Surrey-born person – a Surrey Capon.

Here also be Southwark, the great gateway to London, filled with fleshpots and famous for its inns, brothels, theatres and bull baiting. As of 1577 there were some seventy-seven inns in the county of Surrey and a mighty 369 alehouses.

CHIDDINGFOLD

THE CROWN
'Royal largesse and short measures'

Originally built as a place of rest for monks making their way between Salisbury and Canterbury, this beautiful timbered place was once a simple alehouse. During its early history it seems to have been kept by shrewd if not villainous types, for, the records tell us, in 1353, 'twas being used as an alehouse by one Stephen Guleham whose own mother had already been fined for selling ale at more than the set price of the day. He himself was sued in 1372 for not paying 12*d* for a barrel of ale by a Robert Shurtere. And in 1383, when Richard and Agnes Gofayre became the alehouse keepers, they were fined four times for overcharging their good customers and for selling ale without displaying a proper sign.

Thankfully in the more recent past this wayward alehouse hath been transformed into an honest-to-God inn which be both an architectural wonder and a cosy place in which to lie.

'Tis built throughout with great oak timbers and can boast a great king-post roof, with many fireplaces, including one that hath a massive arched beam across its chimney opening. There are also some finely painted walls.

Its attractions have come to the attention of royal blood. Edward VI and his retinue of some 4,000 men camped on the village's green in 1552 and the king must surely have rested his head at the inn itself. Queen Elizabeth also availed herself of The Crown's charms on one of her great progresses in 1591. A George Stanton was paid 2 shillings to bring a tonne of wine up from Ripley to Chiddingfold for what must have been a very happy occasion indeed. The village be in an area well known for its glass making and The Crown was recently owned by the Dennys family, whose ancestors were once famous in France for their glassware, so we are sure they were not lost for a fine vessel to serve up a good vintage to Her Majesty.

Latterly: The Crown, The Green, Chiddingfold, Godalming, Surrey, GU8 4TX, tel: 01428 682255, www.thecrownchiddingfold.com.

GUILDFORD

THE ANGEL
'Of Drake and a sport called Kreckett'

With a fine stone-vaulted undercroft, where all kinds of provisions can be stored, The Angel be said to date back several centuries. By 1527 the inn was in the ownership of a fellow called Pancras Chamberlyn who sold it to Sir Christopher More, the father of Sir William More, a trusted minister of Queen Elizabeth and the man who built the nearby magnificent new Loseley House. Sir Christopher relinquished The Angel in 1545, to a shoemaker called John Hole, who must have been able to fill his boots with all the travellers and merchants passing through his inn. Today one John Astret be, we hear, the innkeeper and with its well-proportioned rooms and generous stabling, The Angel well serves those who travel through the town on their way to London, Southampton or Portsmouth. Indeed, that renowned explorer, Sir Francis Drake, be believed to have been one of the inn's customers.

If thee are lucky, thee may see, during thy stay in the town, a curious new pastime called 'kreckett'. This sport, played with a stick and ball, be favoured hereabouts as a way of passing the time and be even known to be played at Guildford's good school which also boasts a chained library.

Latterly: The Angel Hotel, 91 High Street, Guildford, GU1 3DP, tel: 01483 564555, www.angelpostinghouse.com.

LEATHERHEAD

THE RUMMINGS HOUSE OR RUNNING HORSE
'A lusty alewife and brews laced with hen dung'

Thanks to that great wit John Skelton, poet laureate to Henry VIII, this intriguing hostelry, established as far back as 1403, hath long been associated with a mysterious former alewife who went by the name of Elynour Rummynge. Skelton's ribald rhyme about Elynour told of her bawdy charms and of the den

Part of 'The Tunnyng of Elynour Rummynge'

And this comely dame,
I vnderstande, her name
Be Elynour Rummynge ...
... And as men say
She dwelt in Sothray,
In a certayne stede
Bysyde Lederhede ...
... She breweth noppy ale,
And maketh therof port sale
To trauellars, to tynkers,
To sweters, to swynkers,
And all good ale drynkers

❦

of iniquity which she ran here in time past, serving to all manner of customers including many base womenfolk. She, herself, we are told had a 'face all bowsy, Comely crynkled, Woundersly wrynkled, Lyke a rost pygges eare'.

In his ditty, written in the year 1521, Skelton also told us that she had an unusual method of flavouring her brews too. He tells how 'somtyme she blennes, the donge of her hennes, and the ale together'.

Today there may be less to worry about when taking a cup of beer at the establishment which serves as a good stopping-off point when crossing the bridge over the River Mole. And 'tis likely that the wenches thee set thy eyes upon may be more pleasing, for indeed Queen Elizabeth herself hath been said to have stayed at the hostelry whilst waiting for the floods, which can oft occur suddenly in these parts, to subside. 'Tis interesting to note that the town be home to Edmund Tylney, Master of the Revels.

Latterly: The Running Horse, 38 Bridge Street, Leatherhead, Surrey, KT22 8BZ, tel: 01372 372081.

The Running Horse, Leatherhead, Surrey. (© Mr James Moore)

A sign at the Running Horse, Leatherhead. (© Mr James Moore)

SOUTHWARK

Bards, brothels and beer

In his famous survey, the chronicler John Stow told us that in Southwark 'be many fair inns for receipt of travellers, by these signs: the Spurre, Christopher, Bull, Queen's Head, Tabard, George, Hart, King's Head ...'

Most of these are along the road used to enter and depart the city via London Bridge – the only crossing below Kingston. The street was made famous by the writer Geoffrey Chaucer and his pilgrims, for 'twas along this route that they began their journey to the shrine at Canterbury in his famous Tales. The inns here are towering galleried buildings, sitting cheek by jowl with one another and each boasting great yards at the back and with plentiful accommodation.

'Tis in this neighbourhood, which be also home to the notorious Clink Prison, that the playwright William Shakespeare recently made his home. With his literary friends, he be known to frequent a bawdier establishment, a Bankside alehouse known as the Falcon. His lodgings are conveniently located within easy reach of the new purpose-built theatres now rising in this area. The Rose, built in 1587, and The Globe, completed this year of 1599 in Maid Lane are the best known.

Other entertainments have become legendary in Bankside too for this area be no doubt London's honey pot across the water. Bull and bear baiting be a common sight in the gardens set aside for the practice. Patronised by Queen Elizabeth herself, 'tis even, on occasion, possible to see lions fighting too.

There also be a seedier side to the hustle and bustle of this district. For there are many brothels hereabouts. And though there have been many attempts to close down the Southwark stews, such as Henry VIII's decree in 1546, they still seethe along the banks of the river and in the back streets. 'Tis easy to mistake them for mere drinking establishments. For only last year the chronicler Stow tells how they were to be found painted white and oft sport signs painted on the walls like the Boar's Head, the Cross Keys, the Castle, the Crane and the Bell. Harlots can however be severely punished. In Southwark 'tis not uncommon to see a prostitute paraded, with her head shaved, through the streets.

And thee might not want to risk frequenting them thyself as a recent report of 1584 pointed out – a man might have to part with 40 shillings or more in a brothel for 'a bottle or two of wine, the embracement of a painted strumpet and the French welcome' or as that wit Ben Jonson hath called it 'to be bitten by the Winchester Goose' on account of the sexual disease within the land here, much of which be owned by the Bishop of Winchester.

❀

THE GEORGE
'Plays and packhorses'
This great galleried inn on the east side of the High Street, with its ever-bustling yard, was once known as the St George and also the George and Dragon but hath now become plain George.

The George, marked on maps as long ago as 1542, hath such a reputation that 'twas once owned by the local member of parliament Humfrey Collet and was left in his will of 1558 to the tenure of Nicholas Marten and now to one William Grubb.

Galleries at The George, Southwark, Surrey. (© Mr James Moore and Mr Paul Nero)

While the yard oft be full of packhorses and troops of travellers there be merriment to be had too for 'tis another of the places in the environs of the capital where thee might be lucky enough to have caught William Shakespeare perform. Who knows, if thee buy him an ale he might even divulge the topic of his latest play.
Latterly: The George Inn, George Inn Yard, 77 Borough High Street, Southwark, London, SE1 1NH, tel: 0207 4072056.

THE TABARD
'Chaucer's famous inn'
Spoken of by Stow as the 'most ancient' inn hereabouts we know for certain that The Tabard be very old indeed. 'Tis believed to have been established in the year 1306 when the Abbot of Hyde, a monastery in Winchester, built a hostel to accommodate himself and his retinue on their visits to do business in the capital.

In time it became a commonplace inn used by pilgrims on their way to the shrine of Thomas Becket at Canterbury Cathedral. 'Tis in this vein that it achieved great national fame as the starting point of Chaucer's pilgrims. His *Canterbury Tales* of 1386, charting the travels of twenty-nine 'sondry folk', may relate to a real-life journey and his Tabard inn and host, named as Harry Bailey in the tome, who was 'bold of his speche, and wys, and well y-taught', was certainly drawn from reality. Henry Bailley was member of parliament in the fourteenth century and indeed owner of The Tabard.

After the casting down of the monasteries in the reign of King Henry VIII, the inn, with its great stable and gardens, passed to John and Thomas Master and in 1542 its annual rent was a princely £9 a year. Later 'twas in the hands of a goldbeater called Robert Mabbe who had inherited it from his father John and wife Isabel. Today the battered timber building be in need of some repair but is currently being renovated under the new ownership of a Master Preston.
Latterly: A blue plaque on Copyprints Ltd marks the spot at
1 Talbot Yard, Borough High Street, London, SE1 1YP.

Part of The Canterbury Tales

In Southwerk at the Tabard as I lay
Redy to wenden on my pilgrimage
To Caunterbury with ful devout corage,
At nyght was come into that hostelrye
Wel nyne and twenty in a compaignye
Of sondry folk, by aventure yfalle
In felaweshipe, and pilgrimes were they alle,
That toward Caunterbury wolden ryde;
The chambres and the stables weren wyde,
And well we weren esed atte beste;

❧

WHITE HART
'A den of rebellion'

We can see in Southwark how important to our social life and to a great man's coffers the good inns of the present day can be. For as well as the aforementioned George, the ancient White Hart, next door, be also owned by the family of the member of parliament, Humfrey Collet. Like the George it hath also been used to perform plays though now 'tis more common for them to be seen in the local playhouses.

The inn, first recorded in 1406, hath a less light-hearted history, but one which hath provided marvellous historical grit for the leading playwright of our age, Mr Shakespeare. In July 1450 the inn was the headquarters of Jack Cade, the leader of a rebellion from Kent and Surrey against Henry VI, who marched on London with a force of 5,000 men seeking reforms. Initially successful and after killing the Lord High Treasurer and looting the city he retired to the White Hart. But during the following days the king's supporters regrouped and engaged Cade and his men in a bloody battle on London Bridge itself. Cade fled the capital but was eventually tracked down to Lewes, in Sussex, where he was killed.

Shakespeare hath immortalised the moment when his fictional Cade, in the second part of his play *Henry VI*, cries vainly to his followers:'Hath my sword therefore broke through London gates that thee should leave me at the White Hart in Southwark?'

Legend hath it that the hostess of the inn identified Cade's body when 'twas brought back to London. It certainly hasn't been damaged by its association, for it now boasts one of the largest signs in front of its premises in the city.

Latterly: There be a plaque marking the spot at 63 Borough High Street, Southwark.

THE BEAR
'The first inn before the bridge'

Set at the foot of London Bridge, this be perhaps the oldest inn of all in Southwark, poetically described by some as the 'first house in Southwark built after the flood' meaning cheekily of the Biblical flood.

In fact it hath been here since 1319 when 'twas a tavern passed from Thomas Drinkwater to James Beauflur, who purchased all the vintages and silver cups owned by the aforesaid Drinkwater who clearly did not live up to his name.

Its endurance hath been enhanced by the fact that 'tis from here that boats leave to Greenwich and Gravesend, a route once favoured by pilgrims to Canterbury who wished to avoid the annoyance of the rutted roads out of the city. Less wholesome characters have used the back door, to the riverside, as an escape route.

Today it also hath the curious quality that 'tis the only inn hereabouts where archery can be practised in the grounds.

Latterly: Swept away when London Bridge was rebuilt in 1831.

Other hostelries of note ...

CRAWLEY

THE GEORGE
An inn since at least 1579, when 'twas bequeathed by Richard

Covert. It makes a convenient and cosy place to stop halfway between London and the coast.
Latterly: Ramada Crawley Gatwick, High Street, Crawley,
West Sussex, RH10 1BS, tel: 01293 524215,
www.ramadagatwickhotel.com.

ESHER

THE BEAR
Built in 1529, the same year that Cardinal Wolsey was banished from his palace at Hampton Court and retired here.
Latterly: The Bear Hotel, 71 High Street, Esher, KT10 9RQ,
tel: 01372 469786, www.bearesher.co.uk.

GODSTONE

THE BELL
Providing comfort to travellers since 1393, it currently competes with the more recent White Hart on this busy staging post on the road between London and the port of Rye.
Latterly: The Bell Inn, High Street, Godstone, Surrey, RH9 8DX,
tel: 01883 743216, www.thebellgodstone.co.uk.

HORLEY

THE SIX BELLS
Legend hath it that there hath been an alehouse here since the year of our Lord 827. 'Tis certainly an ancient and comforting spot in which to sup.
Latterly: Ye Olde Six Bells, Church Road, Horley, RH6 8AD,
tel: 01293 825028, www.vintageinn.co.uk.

MOLESEY

THE BELL
Serving since 1460, 'tis well known to those who work at Hampton Court Palace.
Latterly: The Bell, 4 Bell Road, Town Centre, East Molesey, KT8 0SS, tel: 020 8941 0400.

The Bell, Molesey, Surrey. (© Mr James Moore)

RIPLEY

THE TALBOT OR THE DOG
Built in 1453 when there were still monks at the nearby Newark Priory, and named after the hunting dog.
Latterly: The Talbot, High Street, Ripley, Woking, Surrey, GU23 6BB, www.bespokehotels.com.

ROTHERHITHE

THE ANGEL

Haunt of many a salty seadog, this was originally built as The Salutation, by the monks at Bermondsey.
Latterly: The Angel, 101 Bermondsey Wall, East London, SE16 4NB, tel: 020 7394 3214.

THAMES DITTON

THE SWAN

Set on the opposite bank to Hampton Court Palace and near the town of Kingston, many a royal caller hath supped here.
Latterly: Ye Olde Swan, Summer Road, Thames Ditton, Surrey, KT7 0QQ, tel: 020 8398 1814,
www.yeoldeswan-thames-ditton.co.uk.

CHERTSEY

THE SWAN

A relatively new hostelry, rivalling the town's established George, it hath become popular as a place for visitors on route to the royal palace at Windsor to change horses.
Latterly: The Olde Swan, 27 Windsor Street, Chertsey, Surrey, KT16 8AY, tel: 01932 562129, www.theoldeswan.co.uk.

✿ SUSSEX

'Sowseks, full of dirt and myre,' goes the old saying. But the notably poor roads in this county belie a prosperous place where the fortunes are built on wool, iron working, glass making and, of course, the felling of oaks to build ships of war. 'Tis from here, also, that the markets of London get much of their bread corn. And, from its dense forests to its coastline the county of Sussex be peppered with all manner of inns and alehouses that will delight the traveller. Here thee might find thyself rubbing shoulders with smugglers, fishermen, soldiers, pilgrims or wealthy merchants alike.

The county, home to some 100,000 souls and able to offer up 10,000 able-bodied men at arms, hath many famous spots of note for the traveller. The Forest of Ashdown produced the iron that built Henry VIII's cannon while in the present-day great beacons have been erected at places like Ditchling and Crowborough to warn of invasion by foreign powers.

In the west of the county be Chichester, with its cathedral, magnificent Market Cross and streets – newly paved. It hath also earned a reputation for its malt which be traded up and down the coast and as far away as Ireland. Rivalling Chichester be the town of Lewes, where the county gaol be found. Here also, during the recent reign of Queen Mary, a number of Protestants, including Dirck Carver, a brewer from Brighton, were burned for heresy.

Don't be afraid to take back bad beer. In 1461 four brewers in Steyning, in the county, were warned not to brew their beer 'of any musty malt or eaten with wivels'.

ALFRISTON

THE STARRE
'Lair of smugglers & pilgrims'
Lavish carvings adorn this ancient place, first known as the Star of Bethlehem. 'Twas built originally as a hostel by the monks at the nearby Battle Abbey for pilgrims travelling to the shrine of St Richard in the city of Chichester – destroyed in 1538 – and to Canterbury.

One tradition says that 'twas here that King Alfred famously burned the cakes, though there seems scant evidence for this half-baked claim.

Outside 'tis decorated with carvings of St Giles, St Julian, the patron saint of travellers and our national patron saint, St George, slaying the dragon. More comical of the artwork here be an inebriated figure swigging ale. Most interesting of its relics, however, be the Sanctuary Post – once indicating a spot in which those in religious plight can seek protection. Though, in the days since the fall of Rome, we fear that it might better be employed for tethering dogs or, perhaps, those local bearded boatmen who have enjoyed too much of the local ale on returning to land.

Since 1520 this hath been a general inn and a place known to be frequented by smugglers offering contraband of all kinds.

The nearby George Inn next door, itself dating back to 1397 complete with huge fireplaces, be said to have tunnels extending to the sea used by the very same bandits of the waves.

Latterly: The Star, High Street, Alfriston, East Sussex, BN26 5TA, tel: 01323 870495, www.thestaralfriston.co.uk.

All ale the king

The good people of Sussex have always had a great capacity for beer brewing. When King Edward I passed through Uckfield in Sussex in 1299 with his entourage, Arnold de Uckfield was able to speedily supply the party with a vast 82 gallons of local ale.

❀

HASTINGS

THE STAG
'Mummified cats and salty seadogs'

In a town which hath suffered badly from the plague, the last outbreak being in 1597, and from its collapsing harbour, this be a sanctuary. Winding passageways and oak beams lend a mysterious air to The Stag, which hath been open since 1547. This be unsurprising since legend hath it that within the chimneys are to be found mummified cats. These smoke-dried animals are in fact linked to a local witch who once frequented the place.

Here, on a summer evening, thee may also find a game of loggits being played by some of the local seafarers whose boats launch straight into the sea from the beach. For merriment a stake be placed in the ground while players compete to get their sticks as close to said stake as possible.

Latterly: The Stag Inn, 14 All Saints Street, Hastings, TN34 3BJ, tel: 01424 425734, www.staghastings.co.uk.

MIDHURST

THE EAGLE
'A right royal retreat'
This be a favoured haunt of travelling wool merchants, which be apt given the comfortable nature of the beds at this well-established inn. Once used as a hunting lodge, The Eagle, conveniently placed for the town's market, hath been welcoming in the weary since the year 1430 and be without doubt the best of the four inns in the town, nestled in the rolling South Downs near the River Rother. The grand hostelry's leaded-light windows, heavy oak timbers and roaring inglenook fires make this attractive building a salvation for those tramping the rough roads of Sussex.

The Eagle, which boasts good stabling and frothy brews, be rumoured to have been one of the many inns that have had the pleasure of accommodating royalty. Our noble Queen Elizabeth be believed to have looked in on her visit in 1591 and, for a paltry extra sum, thee may stay in the same room.

The magnificently crenelated Cowdray House, a superb model of our current architecture, and a site nearby that should not be missed. 'Twas raised by Sir William Fitzwilliam, Earl of Southampton and be owned by the Viscounts Montague. In the grounds there be a famous large oak tree said to have been visited by the queen when she spent five days at the house and shot four deer with a crossbow. King Henry VIII was a visitor too, in 1538, 1539 and 1545, as was Edward VI in 1552, with these esteemed guests entertained 'marvellously, nay rather excessively'. Though we have heard rumour that there be a black mark against a former footman, at the house, one Guy Fawkes, who hath since been known to have travelled abroad to fight for Catholic Spain. Who knows what evils he may get up to next?

Latterly: The Spread Eagle Hotel & Spa, South Street, Midhurst, West Sussex, GU29 9NH, tel: 01730 816911, www.hshotels.co.uk.

The Spread Eagle, Midhurst, Sussex. (© Mr James Moore)

ROBERTSBRIDGE

THE SEVEN STARS
'Beware the Red Monk'

'The red monk, he shall a walk and a rattle when the moon be new.' So goes the folklore about this drinking house. The Red Monk be not a fiery local ale but a spirit, one whose supernatural activities seem to match the inn's celestial name.

Robertsbridge gets its name from a crossing place over the River Rother, built by the abbot Robert de St Martin in the twelfth century. Perhaps the hooded figure glimpsed around the inn be a disgruntled holy man from the Cistercian monastery nearby, now pulled down and deserted.

No one quite knows when The Seven Stars started serving beer but the grand timbers go back to at least the last century. And no one be quite sure how it got its name, though some suggest it may be linked to the seven-starred celestial crown which the Virgin Mary hath sometimes been shown wearing.

Another nearby hostelry of fame be the John's Cross Inn, located at the point where Crusaders were gathered together under the banner of John the Baptist before embarking on their holy quest.

Latterly: Seven Stars Inn, High Street, Robertsbridge, TN32 5AJ, tel: 01580 880333, www.seven7stars.co.uk.

RYE

THE MERMAID

'Famous feasts and ghostly goings on'

As if washed up from the sea, the timbers of The Mermaid straggle up a hill on the main street of the town, leading from the harbour to the centre of things.

Re-built in 1426 from old ships' timbers, after a raid by the French burned down the former inn, its cellars date from as far back as 1156. In former times it built up a reputation for its own brewed well-kept ale and for lodgings that cost a penny a day. These days rooms will cost thee more as The Mermaid hath become very well-to-do in recent times, hosting functions such as the Herring Feast.

Queen Elizabeth be said to have looked in during the year 1573, when she visited the town and bestowed her favour upon the port, which hath been one of the main departure points for troops serving on the continent and in the great battle against Spain in 1588.

If thee awake at The Mermaid in the night with wet clothes about thy room 'tis less likely to be caused by some bad fishy feast thee have been served the evening before but by the spirits reported to lurk in the inn's dark nooks and crannies. Many a guest hath found their clothing damp after being left on a chair overnight, with no obvious cause, while a phantom lady dressed in white or grey hath been glimpsed about the place. Another tale tells of two spectral figures duelling in a room.

Latterly: The Mermaid Inn, Mermaid Street, Rye, East Sussex, TN31 7EY, tel: 01797 223065, www.mermaidinn.com.

Earning a crust

In the town of Rye there hath of late been a great argument brewing between the makers of the town's beer and the bakers. In 1575 the town's mayor wrote to Lord Cobham, warden of the Cinque Ports, 'by reason of the brewers, who oughte by the lawes of this realme not to be bakers also, have by our sufferance used both to bake and brewe of long time, whereby Robert Jacson be growen to good welthe and the whole company of the bakers utterly impoverished.'

❁

SEDLESCOMBE

THE QUEEN'S HEAD
'Good brews and buried treasure'
The Romans were known to tramp this route and are even said to have built a bath house in the village. Since 1523 there hath been another place to partake of some liquid refreshment. The Queen's Head be said to have taken in Her Royal Majesty Elizabeth in the year 1573, on her travels in the area, but many an alehouse hath made this claim so we cannot be entirely certain of her patronage.

'Tis also claimed that, hereabouts, there be hidden treasure thought to have been stowed by King Harold before the Battle of Hastings in 1066 – and since his death just 3 miles from the village still buried here in a mystery location.

Latterly: The Queen's Head, The Green, Sedlescombe, Hastings, TN33 0QA, tel: 01424 870228, www.queensheadsedlescombe.co.uk.

Other hostelries of note ...

FITTLEWORTH

THE SWAN
Serving reviving frothy brews since 1382.
Latterly: The Swan, Lower Fittleworth, West Sussex, RH20 1EN, tel: 01798 865429.

ROTTINGDEAN

THE BLACK HOLE
Once a forge, this alehouse purports to date from 1513 and be a known haunt of smugglers.
Latterly: The Black Horse, 65 High Street, Rottingdean, Brighton, East Sussex, BN2 7HE, tel: 01273 302581.

❁ WARWICKSHIRE

The loss of many a country tavern and inn is to be lamented. Its cause be oft the loss of villages which have disappeared completely. Forty-six proud Warwickshire villages have gone during Her Majesty's reign, lost to enclosure, or lost to landlords putting out their tenants so they can have a deer park or farming land near their estate. When the people go, hostelries go too. Too oft today, people drink at home, not socially and this cannot be good.

Yet a decent pint can still be found in this county, a favourite of Her Majesty, who brings court to Kenilworth Castle, Robert Dudley's newly renovated mansion. When the whole party comes it cost Lord Dudley a good fair purse, but that be the price of love.

Coventry be the biggest place – the eighth most populous in the country, boasting 8,000 souls which Leland told us hath 'many fayre towers in the waulle … stately churches in the harte and midle of the towne and many fayre stretes … well buyldyd with tymbar'.

Bremischam, which some do call Birmingham, comes up fast with 3,000 people in this solid market town echoing with the noise of anvils at the forges, much be the fashion for ironmongery. Warwick be a stout walled town too, with fine buildings and a famous castle.

Stratford today be much recovered after the disastrous fires of both 1594 and 1595, when more than 120 houses were destroyed by the flames, leaving a quarter of the population homeless. Vagrancy continues to be a problem, but whippings help to quell the numbers. Some brick houses have replaced those lost to the flames, all with tall chimneys, which help keep upper levels warm, but do little for health of the lungs.

Mister Shakespeare makes few visits to Stratford these days. After marrying not long out of boyhood and having several children, he tramped to London, aiming to make a living as an actor. Though this normally be the occupation of the knave he hath made good and be now well respected in the town. His connection with the alehouse be long. In his youth he joined local drinking clubs while Mister John Shakespeare, his father, was the town's ale-conner in 1556, testing the quality of each public brew before approving it for sales. Some say 'tis hard work for these men with twenty-nine inns and over 400 alehouses in the county to inspect. Interestingly we hear the Mister Shakespeare Junior even plans to lease his own house of birth over to an inn if his father should pass on.

DERITEND

THE OLDE CROWN INN
'Where Queen Bess once laid her head'

Built in 1368, this timber house be the oldest building in the hamlet of Deritend, at the crossing point over the River Rea to Bremischam. Her Majesty passed a night in the Royal Gallery Chamber here in 1575 – they thus named the room especially to take much advantage of the tourists. Behold the central *fleur de lys* symbol that adorns the ceiling of the galleried bedroom, for this be designed in honour of the queen's night under their roof and partly for the hopes of a royal wedding, which always doth much for business.

The Olde Crowne hath a chequered history, being forfeited to the Crown in the 1530s when Edward Grey, then Lord of Bremischam, played a bad political hand. Lord Dudley accused him of committing an assault and robbery, a capital crime, 'upon the niyght aftore Christmas evyn last passyd' and upon this news reaching the king, The Olde Crowne went to the Crown though Grey did not go to the block and many think this be a travesty.

Since then the place hath, we hear, become an inn, which we think the best use.

Latterly: The Old Crown, 188 High Street, Deritend, Birmingham, West Midlands, B12 0LD, tel: 0121 248 1368, www.theoldcrown.com.

Don't get caught at cards

In 1592 an order in the county forbade gaming ...
No innholders, alehouse keepers, no typlers should suffer any poor artificer, day labourer, men's servants pr prentises to sytt to gaminge in any of their howses by day or night ... ipon payne of imprisonment by the span of three days and nights.

KENILWORTH

CASTLE TAVERN
'In the shadow of the famous castle revels'

This be a good place for a break along the droving road 'twixt Balsall Common and Southam, and also for those passing from the castle at Kenilworth to Coventry. 'Tis a busy place built around an old oak tree; where strangers rub shoulders with workers and gentlemen of Kenilworth. First constructed in 1430, the tavern shows signs of age in parts; what some call historic, others may consider plain old. 'Tis a lively place on market day, when thou should take care of thy purse.

Many would have passed the gossip here as Queen Elizabeth enjoyed her customary visits to Kenilworth to be entertained by her once-favourite Robert Dudley, Earl of Leicester. In 1575 she spent most of July at the Castle as he made an attempt to win her hand in marriage. As well as great rockets thrown into the sky, he laid on a masque, Morris dancing, bear-baiting and above all lashings of liquor. Sadly, 'twas to no avail. Dudley died in 1588 on the way to the baths at Buxton.

Latterly: The Clarendon House Hotel, High Street, Kenilworth, Warwickshire, CV8 1LZ, tel: 01926 515451, www.milsomshotel.co.uk.

STRATFORD

THREE TUNS TAVERN
'Low timbers and high art'

This be Mister Shakespeare's local, if he ever be at home, for he be much occupied finishing a royal play about King Henry V who heroically and memorably beat the French. It may be that he will return to his Stratford roots for respite once the ink be dry and that to Sheep Street he will return for 'tis near his wife and children. The Three Tuns be making much of its association and calling rooms after Mister Shakespeare's characters and plays. The wattle-and-daub walls get musty from the new tobacco

Adultery in the alehouse?

We hear of a scandalous case of a man called John Petcher, who, in 1597, was accused of adultery in an alehouse at Atherstone with another man's wife one Sara Winter. The allegation was that he had fornicated with Sara at an alehouse in the town during a fair, a known place for wayward wives to find solace from poor marriages with someone they oughtn't. Fortunately for Petcher his neighbours testified that his accuser, Edward Taylor, was himself a rogue and troublemaker who had not, as he alleged, refused sixpence to keep quiet about the matter. John hath since been restored to his good name. Whether deserved, or not, we cannot tell.

❁

fashion, but this be a place of warmth and merriment. Mind thy head for the timber be low here. Interestingly we hear that John Shakespeare, William's father, be now of much infirmity and that if he dies, his house, William's birthplace on Henley Street, will be let out as an inn with a man called Lewis Hiccox interested in running it as The Maidenhead. With the bard's current fame this be surely a wise man indeed.

Latterly: The Falstaff Experience, an Elizabethan visitor attraction in the former hostelry, 40 Sheep Street, Stratford-upon-Avon, Warwickshire, CV37 6EE, tel: 01789 298070, www.falstaffexperience.co.uk.

WHITE SWAN OR THE KING'S HOUSE
'Dramatic murals that inspired the dramatist'
Another place to share a bench with the bard, when he be at home, be an inn which hath existed since 1450 and been serving since 1560 when 'twas owned by the brewer Robert Perrott and kept by his brother William. There are three wonderful wall paintings inside depicting the *Book of Tobit*, commissioned at this time by William in honour of his wife. William himself perished in the plague of 1564 but the paintings of these characters, from Biblical

times, telling the tale of a man who eventually weds a woman who hath lost seven husbands to the demon of lust, still live on. Compose thyself with a pot of ale in one of the inn's finely carved settles before a roaring fire and contemplate them as, we believe, Mister Shakespeare must have done. For he be, our spies tell us, planning to use the tale as inspiration for parts of a new play he be planning to set down which he may call *All's Well That Ends Well*.
Latterly: The White Swan Hotel, Rother Street, Stratford-upon-Avon, Warwickshire, CV37 6NH, tel: 01789 297022.

COVENTRY

THE BULL INN
'A prison for Mary, Queen of Scots'
Already here in 1485, when Henry Tudor put the reign of Plantagenet Richard III to the sword at the Battle of Bosworth. Indeed, 'tis said that The Bull, sometimes known as the Black Bull, hosted celebrations following the victory when Henry became Henry VII.

He was certainly a lover of inns. On the eve of the battle he be said to have stayed at the Three Tuns in Atherstone, receiving the sacrament in the church before the ensuing melee.

During the Rising of the North in 1569, that dastardly attempt of the Catholics to seize power from our Majesty Elizabeth, Mary, the Scottish queen was moved from Tutbury Castle in Staffordshire to the stout walls of Coventry. The castle was found to be too ruinous for the job and so, for a time she was put up at the city's best inn, The Bull, before being moved to the Guildhall. She could at least drown her sorrows as during her stay the mayor was said to have plied her and her servants with 240 gallons of wine. Beware, to this day the inn be known to be a haunt of Catholics.
Latterly: Once on Smithford Street it was demolished in 1793. Now the Upper Precinct shopping centre.

Other hostelries of note ...

COVENTRY

THE GOLDEN CROSS
Once the local mint, it hath been coining it in since 1583.
Latterly: The Golden Cross, 8 Hay Lane, Coventry, West Midlands, CV1 5RF.

The Golden Cross, Coventry, Warwickshire. (© Mr James Moore)

REDHILL

THE STAG
Variously a prison, latterly a tavern, there be a chapel to the fore, allowing patrons to atone for sins of the bottle.
Latterly: The Stag, Alcester Road, Redhill, Stratford-upon-Avon, B49 6NQ, tel: 01789 764634, www.thestagatredhill.co.uk.

❀ WESTMORLAND

Two bishops vie o'er the land here. Carlisle stares York in the eye and though the former hath jurisdiction over the largest part of Cumberland and only the north of Westmorland, he wants more. The Council of the North hath done much to stem the theft of horses, sheep and cattle, for it operates across county borders.

Almost no towns of note be here; every place be a village and not much more. Even Kendal and Appleby be not worthy of the name town, although both be royal boroughs and Kendal the birthplace of Her Majesty's step-mother, Catherine Parr, who be much lamented here still. Appleby stings still from Scots' invasions, though the pillaging be centuries old, they are long of memory. Mines extend through Borrowdale, Grasmere, Newlands and Buttermere but all the county be much blighted by famine and plague. Subsistence be hard for many, and so the purses of inns and taverns do not bulge, except on play and festival days, when they throw merrie here and forget their troubles. Members of town corporations be required to wear black caps and gowns or best gowns for those that hath them. Despite hard times, they cut back not on players here, paying 28 shillings for Sir Potter's stage play recently. It better have been good.

HAWKSHEAD

KINGS ARMS
'Comfort in a cold climate'
Hawskhead be a drinker's paradise, which be of good fortune, for this be a remote and hilly place where thy can be cut off for days. Winters be especially harsh, so warm thyself by the fires at the Kings Arms. Up the twisted staircase be a number of luxury rooms with linen which keepeth their own fires, keeping the ice at bay. If kings be not thy favourite monarch, the nearby Queens Head may suit better.
Latterly: Kings Arms, The Square, Hawkshead, Cumbria, LA22 0NZ, tel: 015394 36372, www.kingsarmshawkshead.co.uk.

AMBLESIDE

KIRKSTONE PASS INN
'Taste the lamb at this lofty retreat'
Having recently celebrated its centenary, this remote inn continues to attract shepherds and rustlers alike, for there be nowhere for miles for a meal and a drink. Try the lamb, though the venison, being local, be also excellent. This be one of the highest inns in the land and certainly in Westmorland, for it rests in the clouds on some days. Being a hike to reach, the walk will build thy appetite. Monks used to frequent this house, for this be an inn close to heaven, though now they have descended to lower grounds following the 1530s' purge of the monasteries.
Latterly: The Kirkstone Pass Inn, Ambleside, Cumbria, LA22 9LQ, tel: 01539 433888, www.kirkstonepassinn.com.

✤ WILTSHIRE

This be a county in which princesses are made. Wishing no disrespect to Her Majesty, whose mother was Anne Boleyn, a fine much-beloved lady whose honour was indisputable right to the moment of her execution for high treason, incest and adultery, Wiltshire's heart belongs to her successor as queen consort, Jane Seymour. For Mistress Seymour was born at Wulfhall at Savernake Forest and famously married to the queen's father eleven days after her mother's beheading.

In addition to its royal connections, Wiltshire be also admired for its pigs. Bacon, hams and sausages be tasty and filling and form much of the fare. Taverns double as chop houses. Porkers' feet be particularly noteworthy. At Devizes blankets are made, while Amesbury be famed for the manufacture of tobacco pipes to service the new puffing craze.

For the lover of history, a sojourn through the county will uncover delights aplenty. Mysterious Stonehenge be a sight to behold, attracting many pagans who risk severe whipping for practising dark arts. Far safer be the spire of Salisbury, England's tallest, a house of God in gothic splendour and home to the best of the four original copies of Magna Carta that remain. Malmesbury too be a fine town that stands on the very top of a great slaty rock and hath a number of excellent inns. Trade hath been light in Wiltshire of late, especially in the hitherto thriving wool and cloth industries, putting inns under pressure. Bargains may be had for those who feel no shame about driving a deal.

DEVIZES

THE BEAR
'Pause for an ale at the sign of the claws'
In 1559 John Sawter welcomed visitors along the Great West Road into this inn, with a great new sign of the bear with a bunch of grapes, set before the town's solid castle on the market place. It must surely be a fine establishment as our queen stayed here in 1574 whilst travelling between Bath and Lacock. The sign hath since been replaced with the bear and ragged staff, that crest associated with the Earls of Warwick. The sign be so large that it stands not attached to the building itself but upon a slab supported by two great pillars.
Latterly: The Bear Hotel, Market Place, Devizes, Wiltshire, SN10 1HS, tel: 01380 722444, www.thebearhotel.net.

MALMESBURY

THE BELL
'Of abbots and grey ladies'
The Dissolution did much for Malmesbury. Many of the abbey's buildings have been put to use in the woollen trade which attracts many people to the town. It hath helped The Bell thrive, another which claims to be England's oldest, being built around 1220. The then Abbot of Malmesbury had the inn built to house his guests, who warmed themselves at the hooded stone fireplace in

Jellied porkers or hogs' feet

For honest pub grub, try jellied porkers' feet. The finest porkers' feet are soaked for twenty-four hours, scraped very white and boiled in a scoured brass pot or pipkin in 3 gallons of liquor, 5 quarts of water and 3 of wine vinegar per dozen trotters. Best with nutmeg, ginger, and cinnamon added and jellied feet laid out flat and cut into wedges. Calves' feet may be used more commonly in other counties, but Wiltshire favours the hog.

❈

the great hall. This can be thy pleasure here today still. Take time to admire the artwork in the roof spaces; glory be to God in their images. Part of The Bell rests upon an old graveyard of the abbey and there be talk of hauntings here. Some guests will tell thee of a Grey Lady, poorly married at the abbey, who stalks the corridors at night. Others mention vessels rising in the air and smashing against walls as if there be life in them of their own.

Latterly: The Old Bell, Malmesbury, SN16 0BW,
tel: 01666 822344, www.oldbellhotel.co.uk.

KINGS ARMS
'*Where a flying monk fell to earth*'
Though this house hath not yet been open more than a score years it hath built a reputation for excellent hospitality. 'Tis a popular farmers' inn, where much money changes hands on market day.

The yard extends to Olivers Lane, where today the horses rest but where in 1010 flying monk Eilmer be said to have landed, after attaching wings to himself to fly from the abbey, believing too seriously in the Greek fable of Daedalus. He was said to have been lame ever after but was said to have flown a full furlong. Until his dying day Eilmer was certain that the only reason he had not gone further was because of his lack of a tail.

The town be also famous for St Aldhelm, who came to the rescue of the town from the perils of paganism, reading to the crowds stories of our Lord and Saviour. So tales of another sort than the kind Eilmer lacked, are never wanting at the Kings Arms, always a place to enjoy a good yarn.

Latterly: The Kings Arms, 29 High Street, Malmesbury, SN16 9AA, tel: 01666 823382, www.thekahotel.co.uk.

SALISBURY

THE GEORGE

'Of quarrelling royals and moonlighting Italians'

The great timbers of The George can be found in the heart of the town. 'Twas built as far back as 1314 as a hospice for pilgrims and associated with the local Guild of St George, for the patron saint be much revered in this city. It hath been owned by the city since 1414, though its trade suffered greatly in 1579 with the onset of the plague.

There be a great hall with a minstrels' gallery and wonderful hammer-beam roof with carved beams sporting likenesses of Edward II and his queen Isabella, known as the 'she-wolf', who

The George, Salisbury, Wiltshire. (© Mr James Moore)

later had her husband killed. No wonder they appear to be snarling at each other. Its enormous bay windows are a marvel too. One was built in 1453 for 20 shillings by some Italian craftsmen said to be moonlighting from their proper work at the cathedral.

The courtyard, which can stable some fifty horses, hosts plays, the only inn in the city allowed to do so. William Shakespeare be said to be considering a performance.

Latterly: The Boston Tea Party Cafe, 13 High Street, Salisbury, SP1 2NJ, tel: 01722 238116, www.bostonteaparty.co.uk.

WHITE BEAR INN
'Benches and ducking stools'

That the White Bear be a little rough around the edges should not be surprising when thee learn it first served ale to builders working on Elias of Dereham's plans for the new cathedral in 1220, and indeed provided them with kind shelter. Within a generation it hath become their hostel and not until 1320 did construction workers cease living here.

Outside the White Bear be the ducking stool, now less used than in olden times. Watching wicked prostitutes that hath short-changed their customers or those believed to be witches get a

soaking in one of the city's main open ditches gets a good crowd that then take ale to discuss the case. Sadly, a sign of the times, such punishment be in decline and the drinkers of the White Bear much lament it.

Latterly: The Red Lion, Milford Street, Salisbury, SP1 2AN, tel: 01722 323334, www.the-redlion.co.uk.

Carving at the White Bear Inn, later The Red Lion, Salisbury, Wiltshire. (© Mr James Moore)

Other hostelries of note ...

AMESBURY

THE GEORGE AND DRAGON

One of the many inns that began as a hospice to an abbey, it became Crown property after 1541.

Latterly: The George Hotel, 19 High Street, Amesbury, Salisbury, Wiltshire, SP4 7ET, tel: 01980 622108.

LACOCK

THE GEORGE

Take in a game of shovelboard at this inn, here since 1361, near the abbey which hath recently been converted into an interesting gentleman's house. Relax at the fire while a turnspit dog helps cook meat for thy dinner over a roasting fire.

Latterly: The George, 4 West Street, Lacock, Wiltshire, SN15 2LH, tel: 01249 730263, www.wadworth.co.uk.

MARLBOROUGH

THE ANTELOPE

An inn hath been here more than a hundred years. Some restoration work hath been undertaken to holdeth up the roof before the Spanish were vanquished.

Latterly: The Castle and Ball, High Street, Marlborough, Wiltshire, SN8 1LZ, tel: 01672 515201, www.oldenglishinns.co.uk.

SALISBURY

THE HAUNCH OF VENISON

It hath been an inn since the 1300s but be also rumoured to have

once hosted a brothel, popular with the less devout clergy of the nearby cathedral.
Latterly: The Haunch of Venison, 1 Minster Street, SP1 1TB, tel: 01722 411313.

QUEEN'S ARMS
Licensed in 1558 in celebration of Her Majesty ascending to the throne. The Queen's Arms be an historic building much connected with the cathedral, being bequeathed to the Dean and Chapter in 1400.
Latterly: The Queen's Arms, 9 Ivy Street, Salisbury, Wiltshire, SP1 2AY, tel: 01722 341053, www.queensarms-salisbury.co.uk.

❀ WORCESTERSHIRE

'Tis likely that no town of England makes so much cloth as Worcester upon the mighty Severn River. Spinners, weavers and dyers fill up the alehouses. After the cloth trade, beer be of much importance. And although no longer be the price of ale fixed every law-day, this be a place that looks after its own. No stranger to the borough may buy barley or malt until the resident brewers have been served. No one in the county town must sell ale without a sign at his door, upon pain of a fine. Indeed, even by the standards of today, Worcester be a strict town. For more than a century, people who broke the assizes suffered harsh punishment that may have gone unpunished elsewhere. But no thirst should go unquenched. Indeed, Worcestershire beer be recommended.

Worcester be still a place of kings, as King John rests in the cathedral. The rest of the county – wondrously rich with corn – be sparse for inns, though where they are found they are good. Try the local perry which be much admired.

Avoid Droitwich in the winter wet as that sage of a traveller John Leland tells us that the town 'be somewhat foule and dirty when any rayene faullthye with moche carriage throught the street being ill pavyd or not pavyd'.

BROADWAY

WHYTE HART INN
'Wine swigging wool merchants'

This be an inn for the wealthy, for the common man may not afford much of the menu and the price of a drink be most prohibitive. The building be extensive and of the finest Cotswold stone, with, in parts, walls which are 4ft thick.

For those with gold in their purse, the Whyte Hart be one of the finest inns in the land, with rooms of luxury where even the queen would be proud to rest her head. The inn hath been serving rich clientele, mostly wool merchants, since at least 1532. Indeed, one of these wool merchants was one of the first innkeepers, a Mister Thomas Whyte. Thomas added new facilities to the original century-old building, including chimneys and fireplaces. Farmers as well as innkeepers, the Whytes brewed with their own grown barley and kept both brewhouse and wine cellar.

Snug and warm, the Hart hath big fires throughout – a blessing after a day in the glorious countryside around, hunting perhaps. Horses may be provided for travelling along the next stage of thy journey, for the Whyte Hart be an excellent staging post 'twixt London and Worcester, or for the many sports that may be enjoyed here.

Latterly: The Lygon Arms, High Street, Broadway, Worcestershire, WR12 7DU, tel: 01386 852255, www.pumahotels.co.uk.

CLAINES

CHURCH ALE HOUSE
'Give thanks for the barley'

An old inn indeed and one that owes its origin to the church nearby to which it hath long been linked for the making of ales to celebrate religious feasts and raise money for the parish for more than a hundred years.

Thou might need much to steady thy nerve for the hauntings be many and for this the drink be reliable. The inn be built upon consecrated ground so 'tis not surprising that some of those souls that rest in the graveyard, who thought they were going to their rest, sometimes stir. The traveller can rest in peace that when he knocks back his liquor, he be contributing to God's mission and, if the number of times this place hath been affected by plague are anything to go by, getting closer to the Lord.

Latterly: The Mug House, Claines Lane, Claines, Worcestershire, WR3 7RN, tel: 01905 456649.

INKBERROW

THE BULL
'Mister Shakespeare's wedding trip'

In 1582, on his way to collect his marriage licence at Worcester the young playwright William Shakespeare, a mere 18 years of age, stayed at this modest inn on route from his home at Stratford in the neighbouring county.

He was to marry one Anne Hathaway who, 'tis said, be some years his senior and other mischievous rumours say that she was with child when the nuptials took place.

Who knows whether at Inkberrow, a rural idyll, he was first inspired to write some of those entertainments with which we are now becoming well acquainted.

Latterly: The Old Bull, Village Green, Inkberrow, Worcester, WR7 4DZ, tel: 01386 792428.

OMBERSLEY

THE KINGS ARMS
'Sagging Charms'

Looking decrepit in parts and dark throughout, this Ombersley inn hath few windows and those that it hath be small, causing danger from excessive candles at night. But the dark timbers have their charm with many a nook and cranny for intimate trysts and secret conversations.

The building pre-dates the Tudor lineage on the throne, but though 200 years it hath stood, many improvements have been made and 'tis a good lodging on this important road north of Worcester.

Latterly: The Kings Arms, Ombersley, Worcestershire, WR9 0EW, tel: 01905 620142.

Other hostelries of note ...

BEWDLEY

THE ROYAL FORESTER

A historic inn that has been taking in travellers since 1411 in the heart of the forest of Wyre. Care should be taken travelling thither at night.

Latterly: The Royal Forester, Callow Hill, Worcestershire, DY14 9XW, tel: 01299 266286, www.royalforesterinn.co.uk.

EVESHAM

THE SWAN

Here these few years since 1586 the Swan be the place to try a fruit pie, for the Vale around be famed for its fertility and fine orchards.

Latterly: The Old Swanne Inne, 66 High Street, Evesham, Worcestershire, WR11 4HG, tel: 01386 442650.

KIDDERMINSTER

SEVEN STARS

It hath been here many years and the locals vouch for its warm welcome.

Latterly: The Seven Stars, 13–14 Coventry Street, Kidderminster, Worcestershire, DY10 2BG, tel: 01562 755777.

WORCESTER

TALBOT INN
Most handy for the worshipping at the cathedral, this inn be very old, dating back to the thirteenth century.
Latterly: Ye Olde Talbot Hotel, Friar Street, Worcester, Worcestershire, WR1 2NA, tel: 01905 235730.

✿ YORKSHIRE

There be 'nowt so queere as the folke' in the inns and taverns of this vast county, England's largest. Here folk are proud of their ability to knock back twelve pints and still do the work of ten men.

York, with its fine minster, be an architectural wonder that mustn't be missed and rivals Bristol as the third most populous in the land, home to 12,000 people. As such 'tis the seat of the Council of the North, the body which governs northern England at arm's length from London. This hath been of import since the worrisome Pilgrimage of Grace of 1536, which may to uneducated ears sound innocuous, but was in reality a challenge by Catholic elements to Henry VIII's proper reformation of the Church.

The city be a fine place to find drink, with scores of inns and alehouses. A competitive race, a Yorkshireman likes to believe that he holds his beer best, though ale be still much more fashionable here thanks to the difficulty of growing hops.

Industry lies in the west of the county: wool and cloth in Leeds, Bradford and Halifax while the port of Kingston upon Hull be home to 6,000 people. Beaches and fishing be to the east, with Scarborough much frequented in the olden days by the House of York, with Richard III wishing to make Scarborough a county of its own.

Three times as much rye be grown as wheat in Yorkshire and the whole county now feeds itself in good times. As over 200 inns and more than 3,600 alehouses are licensed in the county neither inhabitant nor traveller will go thirsty.

BARDSEY

THE 'PRIESTS' INN
'A place to hide?'

Though many may stake the claim for being England's oldest hostelry, this inn hath indeed been welcoming drinkers since before King Harold's misfortune during battle in the south. 'Twas known to be popular with pilgrims and monks en route between St Mary's in York and nearby Kirkstall Abbey.

Its name, though not in tune with our times, hath somehow stuck. Though some say its underhand Catholic activities continue and that two excellent, discreet and airy priest holes have secreted heretics since 1539. Today the inn welcomes Protestants of all denominations, though discretion be required. Dinners are especially popular and the inn hath several comfortable chambers for those that need overnight accommodation.

However, in the traditional Yorkist fashion, there are no discounts for those disturbed by levitating objects, cold breezes in the night or spontaneously combusting candles that are the work of the resident spirit, believed to be a former resident trapped in purgatory.

The excellent Samson Ellis brew dates back more than 600 years. This traditional ale hath been brewed on site since at least AD 953, the inn subsequently becoming so popular that people flocked here from all over the county. Indeed, so popular did this become that a church was built next door, making it one of the few inns to pre-date the church.

Latterly: The Bingley Arms, Church Lane, Bardsey, West Yorkshire, LS17 9DR, tel: 01937 572462, www.bingleyarms.co.uk.

HELMSLEY

BLACK SWAN
'Bustling with pack horses'
More than a hundred years old, this be a busy place full of pack horses and men of trade haggling over the price of the much sought-after Ryedale fleeces. As they haggle they may sup on good brews, which are warming in the middle of the moorlands. The inn caters to travellers betwixt Cleveland, York, Scarborough and Thirsk. Men working on the extension of Helmsley Castle drink here on their days off, where they still lament the fact that Richard of York got above himself with his quest for the crown and would have been better off staying at Helmsley, running the castle and popping down the Black Swan.
Latterly: The Black Swan Hotel, Market Place, Helmsley, North Yorkshire, YO62 5BJ, tel: 01439 770466, www.blackswan-helmsley.co.uk.

A pub brawl

If thee are abroad in the town of Tadcaster take care among the rougher alehouses for these are places where fights are known to break out. A court recently heard that 'William Smyth was in a common alehouse when he made an assault on Richard Takson, upon crye made, John Horseman, being constable of the sayed towne of Tadcaster, took William Smythe and hym put in a courte house.' Those that can afford it may want to repair to the reliable inn The Red Hart, where punch ups are less commonplace.

❁

SCARBOROUGH

THE THREE MARINERS
'Of smugglers and busty lasses'
Built in 1300, this tavern be much used by smugglers off the

Yorkshire coast. 'Tis made of old 'cruck' timber framing, which means it looks as warped as the back of Richard III who be said to have stayed here. These curved beams create a supporting arch that holds up the roof and are verily, most attractive. In the narrow Quay Alley that thy must walk to reach the Mariners, grown men can touch the walls on both sides, which be handy for staying upright when trying to get home after a night here. 'Tis harder to get the bodies down to the tavern in the dark, but many be the body of a sailor or fisherman carried here after departing this earth in the wrecks off Scarborough.

The Mariners be possessed of many secret passages and concealed cupboards used by smugglers. Rope ladders are provided in secret recesses in some rooms to hasten thy escape to the cellars if thee be mistaken for one of these fellows and a quick getaway be needed. Find this tavern easily by looking out for the figurehead of a ship above the door; a carving of a well-bosomed lady.

Latterly: Now a private residence at 47 Quay Street, Scarborough.

YORK

THE GOLDEN FLEECE
'Where wool may be pulled over thy eyes'
If thy view of merchants be somewhat poor for thee think that they are trying to make thee pay more for their wares than they are truly worth then thee will offer up a wry smile at the name of this inn. The Fleece once belonged to the Merchant Adventurers, that company who have taken their trading wiles across the seas. Their ancient and marvellous hall, built in 1357, lies behind the inn itself. Here the merchants may parley with a pint and chew over the price of wool as they feast at prices that reflect the clientele. Some say that Guy Fawkes, a troublesome Catholic born of this city, be sometimes found here on visits home from meddlesome travels supporting Catholic monarchs abroad.

Latterly: The Golden Fleece, 16 Pavement, York, YO1 9UP, tel: 01904 625171, www.thegoldenfleeceyork.co.uk.

The tall story of a tippling Yorkshire monk

York hath been a popular drinking spot for centuries as the monks of old St Leonard's Hospital would attest. Take heed though of the tippling room tale of one of their novices, Jocundus, for he succumbed to the temptations of drink at a fair. Jocundus' superiors decided that his punishment should be to suffer bricking up alive, it being believed that killing him would teach him the errors of his way. Yet Jocundus be a porky priest and when laying against the bricks of his dungeon, they gave way, the Yorkshire brickie possibly being on the beer himself. Dusting himself down, Jocundus found himself in the next-door abbey of St Mary's where, chancing upon some robes, he became accepted into that order. Having got himself into the habit, the monks of St Mary's liked Jocundus so much they gave him the job of cellarer, putting the tipply rogue in charge of beer and wine. This proved foolish as Jocundus had form when it came to the temptations of the grape and the grain. One day, after being sent to test the wine for a feast, Jocundus failed to return and, being found inebriated, incoherent and some say incontinent, was once more sentenced to be bricked up. Yet Jocundus had lost none of his girth and soon fell through the walls of the chamber again, this time finding himself back in St Leonard's, singing his head off still drunk. The good people of St Leonard's first feared this was Jocundus's ghost, but then they declared a miracle. This was an omen, they decreed. So Jocundus, being deemed something special, was appointed as friar, his tenure lasting many years but losing none of his taste for booze along the way.

❂

❊ SCOTLAND

For those that venture north of the border or are travelling in that wild kingdom, currently presided over by James VI, we have little in the way to offer of fine inns. But there are some lodgings and places selling ale that we have heard of and could provide some use.

The main city be Edinburgh, home to some 15,000 people and famous for its castle, its palace at Holyrood and the city now hath a university too. A writer recently described Edinburgh thus, saying that from the:

> … palace in the east the city rises higher and higher to the west and consists mainly of one broad and very fair street. The rest of the side streets and alleys are poorly built and inhabited by very poor people. And its length from east to west be about a mile while the width of the city from north to south be narrow and cannot be half a mile.

'Tis along this main great thoroughfare that the city of Edinburgh's main inns are to be found. One of the most reassuringly well-supplied be The White Hart, where the cellars date back to 1516. The city be famous for its drinking dens. Half a century ago there were some 288 alewives in the city and there are still many inns and watering holes for thee and thy horse. Thee will find it a good place to do business, with around 500 merchants selling wares of all kinds. Thee may even get a new set of clothes after thy travels for the place be rich in tailoring.

Thee will find that people here are almost all of the Protestant or Calvinist persuasion when it comes to their faith, despite the antics of that Catholic Mary, Queen of Scots, forced to abdicate and flee to England where she was, in the fullness of time, beheaded in 1587.

The century hath seen many flare-ups between the two kingdoms of England and Scotland but none hath been decisive. This may be because of the difficulties of transporting enough beer to complete any conquest.

In 1542 the Duke of Norfolk was due to march on Scotland but wrote to Henry VIII worried about the amount of beer for his soldiers. Even if he rationed it to as little as two pots a day, he bemoaned there would only be enough for a six-day campaign. After much pondering by the English he was forced to retreat.

EDINBURGH

THE SHEEP HEID INN
'Named after a king's gift'
A drinking house hath stood here since at least 1360, 'tis now an inn of some renown. Standing halfway between the royal residences of Craigmillar Castle and Holyrood, 'twas patronised by Mary, Queen of Scots in her time. But its most recent royal visitor was King James VI of Scotland, one of those with a claim on the English throne should our present virgin Queen Elizabeth bear no children, which be, given her years we venture, likely.

The story goes that in 1580 he visited the inn and enjoyed a game of skittles which was one of the distractions for which the place was known. No record be made of whether he was victorious, but the king was certainly said to have enjoyed it so much that he bequeathed an ornate ram's head snuffbox to the inn and 'twas renamed in memory of the occasion. 'Tis fitting since there was also a royal park nearby where sheep were reared for the city's market.

In fact, there be also a local delicacy which may or may not suit thy tastebuds: sheep's head broth, known here as powsowdie. Thee may prefer to stick to a round of skittles.
Latterly: The Sheep Heid Inn, 43–45 The Causeway, Duddingston, Edinburgh, Scotland, EH15 3QA, tel: 0131 661 7974, wwwthesheepheidedinburgh.co.uk.

JEDBURGH

SPREAD EAGLE
'Where a queen fled a fire?'

Jedburgh be no stranger to fire, having been burned to the ground three times in the last century and again, by the English, in 1544. There be a tradition held in Jedburgh that Mary, Queen of Scots once lodged in this inn and while the story may be taken with a pinch of salt, she did certainly visit the town, in the year 1566. The queen arrived in the town, so the story goes, and chose the Spread Eagle as her lodging. But there was a fire here which meant she and her retinue had to flee to another house. This was not the only drama for the queen on her visit. After a long ride to Hermitage Castle she fell ill with a terrible vomiting disease which many put down to the stress of her dispute with her husband, Lord Darnley. Mary was later to die, captive in England. The Spread Eagle hath outlived her and be certain to provide warmth to the traveller – of one sort or another.

Latterly: The Spread Eagle Hotel, 20 High Street, Jedburgh, TD8 6AG, tel: 01835 862870, www.hoteljedburgh.co.uk.

PERTHSHIRE

THE KENMORE
'An honest hostelrie'

On 3 November 1572 Sir Colin Campbell of Breadalbane gave a lease to his servant How Hay and his wife Christian Stanes to establish 'an honest hostelrie' upon the spot where Loch Tay becomes the River Tay. 'Tis an important crossing place and Sir Colin, who also constructed the nearby Balloch Castle wanted to be sure that well-respected travellers in these parts were sufficiently catered for with enough ale and bread as they would require.

In these largely uncharted lands the warm fire and food are a salvation and the place be still a haven for the honest in a land frequented by bandits and ruffians.

Latterly: The Kenmore Hotel, The Square, Kenmore, Aberfeldy, PH15 2NU, tel: 01887 830205, www.kenmorehotel.com.

❧ WALES

Since King Henry VIII's time Wales hath been legally brought under England's control and 'tis somewhat fitting, for the present Tudor dynasty be of Welsh origin. A foreign tongue still be spoken here in many places. Indeed, Bishop William Morgan of Wales translated the Bible into Welsh in 1588 and there be still much ferment against the new Church reforms which locals believe have been foisted upon them. However, those Welsh who have wealth and influence have begun to forsake their Celtic roots and speak much in the English language, so the traveller will find he can oft be understood and even, sometimes, be served.

The countryside be still dotted with great castles. At the small town of Cardiff runs the River Taff under the castle and the sea flows to its walls too, making it a very wet but much protected castle. Piratical activity be much in evidence in Cardiff and hath been hard to stamp out, but it makes for an entertaining evening in the pub where sailors of all types rub shoulders and meet fair maids. Sixteen ships operate out of Cardiff, plying legal trades in leather, butter, wool, grain, iron and coal. To the benefit of the drinkers of Wales, malt be much imported into the port of Cardiff and from there turned into excellent beer.

CAERNARVON

BLACK BOY INN
'By the walls of the great keep'
The Black Boy, which did open in the year 1522, be inside the old walls of the town and just two steps from the castle, so a hasty retreat can be made if invaders be seen.

'Tis a noisy place and not for a quiet drink, for oft people with fiddles and lutes will pick a bawdy tune, which the drinkers like much and be encouraged to imbibe more and oft too much. The people here curse a lot, so 'tis not a place for a fair maid, although the maids here are fair and can be enjoyed at a fair price if they sit on their own. For this inn be at the heart of what be known in some places as the red-lighted district, very handy for the sailors, but mistakes of identity are common, troublesome and may cause discomfort.

In its fabric, the Black Boy could do with some loving care, for the corridors be unkempt and the latrines something to behold whilst holding thy nose. Beds at the inn cost sixpence, but if thy are content to sleep on the floor, the charge be but fourpence.

A nunnery be attached to the Black Boy, so chaste ladies be nearby to remind men that not all ladies are like the ones in the inn, where ladies may be chaste but are more oft caught.

Latterly: The Black Boy Inn, Northgate Street, Caernarfon, Gwynedd, North Wales, LL55 1RW, tel: 01286 673604, www.black-boy-inn.com.

LLANFIHANGEL CRUCORNEY

SKIRRID MOUNTAIN INN
'Hangings in the inn'
Probably the oldest inn in Wales, discussed by chroniclers back 400 years, and a place where justice be dispensed upstairs in a makeshift courtroom. Sheep stealers have learned their fate here, sometimes taking a drink downstairs before the hangman performs his cruel but necessary work.

Indeed nigh on 200 ne'r-do-wells have been strung from the oak beam over the stairwell on the first floor of the inn, which serves as a lesson to those enjoying a beer here, as well as being free entertainment with merriment and cheering as the villains swing.

Naturally the spirits of some of those executed still roam the inn at night, so a strong heart be required of those stopping here.

The last Welsh Prince of Wales, Owain Glyndŵr, may well have drunk here too for 'twas his local when he planned the treasonous revolt against the English king, Henry IV. He stepped out with his men and horses from the cobbled courtyard of the inn, which provided much rest and good wishes. Shakespeare recounts that Owain was a man possessed by magic, but the natives here think of him fondly, a hero never captured by English forces. It may be well not to speak of these old rivalries and rebellions at the inn if thee are English-born.

Latterly: The Skirrid Mountain Inn, Llanvihangel Crucorney, Monmouthshire, NP7 8DH, tel: 01873 890258, www.skirridmountaininn.co.uk.

DENBIGH

BLACK BULL INN

'Good brews near the border'

If the Earl of Leicester, once a favourite of Her Majesty, and latterly Lord of Denbigh, had a local hostelry to which he repaired of an evening, the Bull would be it, though few hath seen him here.

He favours his shire hall or even the castle, which provides protection, for the English and the Welsh have oft battled in the streets outside the Bull. We favour this inn over the Crown Hotel because of the warmth of the welcome extended to all travellers, even if they speak the Queen's English.

The Crown hath pretentious diamond-braced panels adorning its front, and though bejewelled hostelries be nought to mock, the countenance of timber, wattle and daub of the Bull be not camouflaged, but can be seen for what it be. Housing for carts, coaches and associated stabling be plentiful in the rear courtyard.

Accommodation be airy – an attractive staircase being central to the front room and the ale be good for a country not known for the quality of its barley.

Latterly: The Guildhall Tavern Hotel, Denbigh, LL16 3NU, tel: 01745 816533, www.guildhalltavernhotel.co.uk.

Other hostelries of note ...

CONWAY

GROES INN

Famed as the first hostelry to be properly licensed in the province, in the year 1573, and a bastion of good cheer in a town which be best known for its austere castle built as a defence against Welsh rebels in Edward I's time.

Latterly: Groes Inn, Ty'n-y-groes, Conwy, LL32 8TN, tel: 01492 650545, www.groesinn.com.

BEAUMARIS

BULLS HEAD INN

Famed for its castle and as a stopping place on route to Ireland, the inn was originally built in 1472 and makes a comfortable place to stop after the rugged ways of the mountainous terrain of North Wales.

Latterly: Ye Olde Bulls Head Inn, Castle Street, Beaumaris, Anglesey, LL58 8AP, tel: 01248 810329.

KNIGHTON

KNIGHTON INN

Behold the staircase and atrium of this inn, built to impress and that would not be out of place in the house of a fine gentleman.

Latterly: The Knighton Hotel, Broad Street, Knighton, Powys, LD7 1BL, tel: 01547 520530, www.theknighton.com.

LLANFIHANGEL-NANT-MELAN

RED LION INN

Sited in the middle of nowhere, showing that even a good ale can be found among the most barren wilderness, this house hath been here since 1592 to serve the drovers.

Latterly: Red Lion Inn, Llanfihangel-nant-Melan, New Radnor, Powys, LD8 2TN, tel: 01544 350220, www.redlionmidwales. co.uk.

A WHO'S WHO OF *YE OLDE GOOD INN* GUIDE

Anne of Cleves Henry VIII's fourth wife (1515–1557)

Sir Francis Bacon Philosopher and writer (1561–1626)

Anne Boleyn Second wife of Henry VIII (1501–1536)

Andrew Boorde Traveller and physician (1490–1549)

Bishop Edmund Bonner Known as Bloody Bonner for campaign against heretics (1500–1569)

William Camden Historian and topographer (1551–1623)

Catherine of Aragon First wife of Henry VIII (1485–1536)

William Cecil, Lord Burghley Lord High Treasurer and advisor to Queen Elizabeth (1520–1598)

Geoffrey Chaucer Author of the Canterbury Tales (1343–1400)

Thomas Cranmer Archbishop of Canterbury and leader of the Reformation (1489–1556)

Robert Devereux, Earl of Essex Nobleman and favourite of Queen Elizabeth (1565–1601)

Sir Francis Drake Vice-Admiral and privateer (1540–1596)

John Donne Poet (1572–1631)

Robert Dudley, Earl of Leicester Nobleman and favourite of Queen Elizabeth (1532–1588)

Edward VI King of England from 1547–1553 (1537–1553)

Elizabeth Queen of England from 1558–1603 (1533–1603)

Sir Thomas Elyot Diplomat and writer (1490–1546)

Lady Jane Grey Granddaughter of Henry VII and Nine Days Queen (1537–1554)

William Harrison Clergyman and writer (1534–1593)

Henry VII Henry Tudor, became first Tudor King of England from 1485–1509 (1457–1509)

Henry VIII King of England from 1509–1547 (1491–1547)

James VI King of Scotland, became James I (1566–1625)

Ben Jonson Dramatist and poet (1572–1637)

John Leland Antiquary and traveller (1503–1552)

Christopher Marlowe Playwright (1564–1593)

Mary Queen of England, also known as Bloody Mary, 1553–1558 (1516–1558)

Mary, Queen of Scots Scottish queen 1542–1567 (1542–1587)

Sir Thomas More Lord Chancellor (1478–1535)

Thomas Nashe Poet and pamphleteer (1567–1601)

John Norden Cartographer (1547–1625)

Catherine Parr Sixth wife of King Henry VIII (1512–1548)

Sir Walter Raleigh Explorer and courtier (b. 1554)

Richard III Last Yorkist King of England reigned from 1483–1485 (1452–1485)

Christopher Saxton Cartographer (1540–1610)

Jane Seymour Third wife of Henry VIII (1509–1537)

William Shakespeare Actor and playwright (1564–1616)

John Skelton Poet (1460–1529)

John Stow Historian and traveller (1525–1605)

Sir Owen Tudor Welsh nobleman who helped found Tudor dynasty (1400–1461)

Sir Francis Walsingham Secretary to Queen Elizabeth and spymaster (1532–1590)

Thomas Wolsey Lord Chancellor and archbishop (1473–1530)

Sir Thomas Wyatt Rebel leader (1521–1554)

Appendix 2

A TIMELINE OF EVENTS

1485 Battle of Bosworth. Henry Tudor becomes Henry VII

1509 King Henry VIII comes to the throne

1515 Thomas Wolsey becomes a cardinal and Lord Chancellor

1516 Thomas More's *Utopia* published

1529 Cardinal Wolsey sacked for failing to get Henry VIII a divorce from Catherine of Aragon

1533 Henry VIII marries Anne Boleyn. Executed 1536

1534 Henry becomes head of the English church

1535 Sir Thomas More executed

1536–1540 The Dissolution of the Monasteries, overseen by Thomas Cromwell

1547 Death of King Henry VIII. Edward VI becomes king

1549 *Book of Common Prayer* published. Kett's Rebellion in Norfolk

1552 Licensing of Ale Houses Act Passed

1553 Lady Jane Grey rules for just nine days. Later executed. Catholic Mary becomes queen

1554 Wyatt's rebellion

1556 Thomas Cranmer burned for heresy

1558 Accession of Queen Elizabeth

1564 Birth of William Shakespeare and Christopher Marlowe

1569 The Rising of the North

1576 James Burbage opens The Theatre, the first purpose-built theatre to the north of London

1577 Survey of Inns, taverns and alehouses in England and Wales

1580 Francis Drake returns to Plymouth having circumnavigated the globe

1587 Mary, Queen of Scots, executed. The Rose be the first theatre to open on London's Bankside

1588 Spanish Armada defeated

1591 Shakespeare pens his first play *Henry VI Part I*

1594 War breaks out with Ireland

1599 Globe Theatre opens on Bankside. Oliver Cromwell born. *Ye Olde Good Inn Guide* published

BIBLIOGRAPHY

Marc Alexander, *Haunted Inns* (Frederick Muller, 1973)

Judith M. Bennett, *Ale, Beer and Brewsters in England: Women's Work in a Changing World, 1300–1600* (Oxford University Press, 1996)

John Bickerdyke, *Curiosities of Ale and Beer* (Spring Books, 1965)

Gordon Blackwood, *Tudor and Stuart Suffolk* (Carnegie Publishing, 2002)

Brandwood, Davison and Slaughter, *Licensed to Sell. The History and Heritage of the Public House* (English Heritage, 2011)

Pete Brown, *Man Walks Into a Pub: A Sociable History of Beer* (Macmillan, 2003)

Ted Bruning, *Historic Inns of England* (Prion, 2000)

John Burke, *The English Inn* (Batsford, 1981)

Joy Childs, *Tudor Derbyshire* (J.H. Hall & Sons, 1985)

Peter Clark, *The English Alehouse: A Social History 1200–1830* (Longman, 1983)

Mary Hill Cole, *The Portable Queen* (University of Massachusetts Press, 1999)

Martyn Cornell, *Beer: The Story of the Pint* (Headline, 2003)

P.R. Cousins, *Newark Inns and Public Houses* (1977)

A.W. Coysh, *Historic English Inns* (David and Charles, 1972)

Maxwell Craven, *The Illustrated History of Derby's Pubs* (Breedon Books, 2002)

David Cressy, *Dangerous Talk* (Oxford University Press, 2012)

P.H. Ditchfield, *Vanishing England* (Senate Books, 1994)

Roger Dobson, *Southwell Inns and Alehouses* (Nottinghamshire County Council, 2008)

Steven Earnshaw, *The Pub In Literature* (Manchester University Press, 2000)

Ken Ford, *Keepers of the Monarch of Old Inns: The George of Stamford* (Mad Publishing, 2006)

G.E. Fussell and K.R. Fussell, *The English Countryman: his life and work from Tudor Times to Victorian Times* (Orbis Publishing, 1981)

Ed Gibbons, *All Beer and Skittles?* (National Trust, 2001)

Frank Graham, *Old Inns and Taverns of Northumberland* (1966)

John Guy, *Tudor England* (Oxford University Press, 1988)

Frederick W. Hackwood, *Inns, Ales and Drinking Customs of Old England* (Bracken Books, 1985)

William Harrison, *Descriptions of England* (1577)

Peter Haydon, *Beer and Britannia: An Inebriated History of Britain* (Sutton, 2001)

Peter Haydon, *The English Pub* (Hale, 1994)

Bibliography

Florence Higham, *Southwark Story* (Hodder & Stoughton, 1955)

Sir Francis Hill, *Tudor and Stuart Lincolnshire* (Cambridge University Press, 2009)

Ian Spencer Hornsey, *A History of Beer and Brewing* (Royal Society of Chemistry, 2003)

Paul Johnson, *Elizabeth: A Study In Power & Intellect* (Weidenfeld & Nicolson, 1974)

W. Branch Johnson, *Hertfordshire Inns* (Letchworth, 1962)

Richard Keverne, *Tales of Old Inns* (Collins, 1947)

F.G. Kitton, *Old Inns of St Albans* (1899)

Suzannah Lipscomb, *A Visitor's Companion to Tudor England* (Ebury, 2012)

Roger Long, *Historic Inns Along the River Thames* (The History Press, 2006)

Madge Lorwin, *Dining with William Shakespeare* (Atheneum, 1976)

Robert Ludy, *Historic Hotels of the World* (David McKay, 1927)

Henry Parr Maskell, *The Taverns of Old England* (Philip Allan, 1927)

H.A. Monckton, *A History of English Ale and Beer* (Bodley Head, 1966)

H.A. Monckton, *A History of the English Public House* (Bodley Head, 1969)

Ian Mortimer, *The Time Traveller's Guide to Elizabethan England* (Bodley Head, 2012)

Lisa Picard, *Elizabeth's London* (Weidenfeld & Nicolson, 2003)

Compton Reeves, *Pleasures and Pastimes in Medieval England* (OUP, 1998)

Sir Albert Edward Richardson, Harold Donaldson Eberlein, *The English Inn, Past and Present: A Review of its History and Social Life* (Benjamin Bloom, 1925)

Alison R. Ridley & Curtis F. Garfield, *The Story of the Lygon Arms* (Porcupine Enterprises, 1992)

Jasper Ridley, *The Tudor Age* (Constable and Robinson, 1998)

A.L. Rowse, *The England of Elizabeth* (Macmillan, 1950)

Pamela Sambrook, *Country House Brewing in England 1500–1900* (Hambledon Press, 1996)

James Shapiro, *1599: A Year in the Life of William Shakespeare* (Faber & Faber, 2005)

Henry C. Shelley, *Inns and Taverns of Old London* (1909)

Alison Sim, *Pleasures and Pastimes in Tudor England* (The History Press, 2009)

Jeffrey L. Singman, *Elizabethan England* (Greenwood Press, 1995)

Walter W. Skeat, *A Glossary of Tudor and Stuart Words* (1914)

Donald Stuart, *Old Sussex Inns* (Breedon Books, 2005)

Arthur Taylor, *Played at the Pub* (English Heritage, 2009)

Leonard P. Thompson, *Old Inns of Suffolk* (W.E. Harrison & Sons Ltd, 1946)

Richard W. Unger, *Beer in the Middle Ages and the Renaissance* (University of Pennsylvania Press, 2007)

Various, *The Oxford Companion to Beer* (Oxford University Press, 2012)

Sedley Lynch Ware, *The Elizabethan Parish in its Ecclesiastical and Financial Aspects* (Baltimore, 1908)

A.N. Wilson, *The Elizabethans* (Hutchinson, 2011)

John Riddington Young, *Inns and Taverns of Old Norwich* (Wensum Books, 1975)

INDEX